Practice Theory, Work, and Organization

Practice Theory, Work, and Organization

An Introduction

Davide Nicolini

OXFORD
UNIVERSITY PRESS

OXFORD
UNIVERSITY PRESS

Great Clarendon Street, Oxford, OX2 6DP,
United Kingdom

Oxford University Press is a department of the University of Oxford.
It furthers the University's objective of excellence in research, scholarship,
and education by publishing worldwide. Oxford is a registered trade mark of
Oxford University Press in the UK and in certain other countries

British Library Cataloguing in Publication Data

Data available

ISBN 978–0–19–923160–7 (hbk)
ISBN 978–0–19–923159–1 (pbk)

Printed in Great Britain by
MPG Books Group, Bodmin and King's Lynn

Links to third party websites are provided by Oxford in good faith and
for information only. Oxford disclaims any responsibility for the materials
contained in any third party website referenced in this work.

To June and Paolo

▓ TABLE OF CONTENTS

■ LIST OF FIGURES

1 Introduction

What is practice theory? Is there one practice theory or many? Where do practice theories come from? What do they say? Have they really something new to offer organization and work studies?

In this book I will answer these questions by providing an in-depth introduction to contemporary theories of practice, and by discussing their distinctive contribution to the study of work and organization. Rather than introducing *a* practice theory, the book provides a primer and a critical introduction to the scholarly traditions that have collectively contributed to what has been described as the practice turn in social and organization studies (Schatzki, 2001; Miettinen *et al.* 2009). It does so because a unified theory of practice does not exist. Practice theories constitute, in fact, a rather broad family of theoretical approaches connected by a web of historical and conceptual similarities. Put another way, the book builds on the assumption that while practice theories can offer a radically new way of understanding and explaining social and organizational phenomena, they can only be approached as a plurality. Much is to be gained if we appreciate both the similarities and differences among practice theories, and if we make such differences work for us.

The aim of this introduction is to set the scene for the discussion that follows and explain why it is worth engaging with practice theory and the material discussed in the book, and what a reader should expect to find in the rest of the volume.

To start, I would like to address a basic but critical issue: what is to be gained by adopting a practice view of organizational matters? Why learn about practice theory at all?

1.1 What is new? The affordance of practice theories

One possible response to the question 'why bother to learn about practice theories?' is that the practice idiom has become fashionable. The notion of practice has become, in fact, increasingly popular among work and organizational scholars and, in recent years, we have witnessed a dramatic growth in analyses utilizing terms such as practice, praxis, interaction, activity, performativity, and performance. This growing interest mirrors an attention to material practices in both social and human science at large. Starting with the 1970s, practice-oriented approaches have become increasingly influential and applied to the analysis of phenomena as different as science, policy making, language, culture, consumption, and learning.[1]

So what lies at the bottom of this increasing interest? Is it just another fashion? Is it only hot air?

In an influential volume that contributed greatly to the creation of the practice 'bandwagon' (Corradi *et al.* 2010), Schatzki suggested that the interest in practice in social theory builds on the intuition that 'phenomena such as knowledge, meaning, human activity, science power, language, social institutions and human transformation occur within and are aspects or components of the field of practices' (Schatzki 2001, p. 2). The appeal of what has been variably described as practice idiom, practice standpoint, practice lens, and a practice-based approach lies in its capacity to describe important features of the world we inhabit as something that is routinely made and re-made in practice using tools, discourse, and our bodies. From this perspective the social world appears as a vast array or assemblage of performances made durable by being inscribed in human bodies and minds, objects and texts, and knotted together in such a way that the results of one performance become the resource for another. As such, practice theories potentially offer a new vista on all things organizational (and social). The attraction of the practice idiom stems in particular from its capacity to resonate with the contemporary experience that our world is increasingly in flux and interconnected, a world where social entities appear as the result of ongoing work and complex machinations, and in which boundaries around social entities are increasingly difficult to draw. When we enter an office, superstore, or a hospital it is increasingly difficult to think of it as the outcome of the application of a detailed blueprint and plan, or a single system with definite boundaries as in the traditional structural-mechanistic and functional-systemic views of an organization. Things seem to fall into place much better if we think of the fluid scene that unfolds in front of us in terms of multiple practices carried out at the same time. In other words, there seems to be particular purchase in a practice view that consider organizations both as the site and the result of work activities; a view that connotes organizations as bundles of practices, and management as a particular form of activity aimed at ensuring that these social and material activities work more or less in the same direction.

A practice-based sensitivity, however, promises to do more. Authors such as Ortner (1984), Schatzki (2001; 2002), Reckwitz (2002), and Rouse (2007) suggest, in fact, that a practice-based view of the social also offers a remedy for a number of problems left unsolved by other traditions, especially the tendency of describing the world in terms of irreducible dualisms between actor/system, social/material, body/mind, and theory/action. In the view of these authors, the enhanced explanatory power of the practice approach, and its capacity to dissolve (rather than resolve) such enduring dualisms, stems from the fact that adopting such a theoretical stance produces a radical shift in our understanding of social and, in our case, organizational and work matters. Practice-based approaches are radically different on at least five different accounts.

Firstly, all practice theories foreground the importance of activity, performance, and work in the creation and perpetuation of all aspects of social life. Practice approaches are fundamentally processual and tend to see the world as an ongoing routinized and recurrent accomplishment. This applies even to the most durable aspect of social life—what scholars call social structures. Family, authority, institutions, and organizations are all kept in existence through the recurrent performance of material activities, and to a large extent they only exist as long as those activities are performed. Several events at the turn of the millennium provided plenty of evidence of this. Countries recently new to the concepts of democracy and/or the free market found out very quickly that setting up such institutions requires, first and foremost, establishing practices (campaigning, voting, etc.) and making them work together (for example, you cannot have a free market without a combination of contractual practices that makes the workings of that market enforceable). So, staging a free election has to do not only with ideas and principles of free choice and determination but also, for example, with how the practice of voting is carried out and whether such apparently mundane things such as anonymity of the ballot, whether polling stations are open long enough for everyone to vote, and how the votes are counted, are guaranteed.

It is important to emphasize that claiming that the world we live in is the result of practices does not make it less 'solid' or 'relative'. Gendering and other discrimination practices, for example, are all too 'real' and highly consequential for all those involved (Yancey Martin 2003). They are also very resilient and often difficult to change because, *qua* practices, they are taken for granted and often considered as part of the 'natural' order of things. The contribution of a practice approach is to uncover that behind all the apparently durable features of our world there is always the work and effort of someone. It also highlights that the relation between practices and their material conditions—between 'structure and process'—is conceived recursively as two-way traffic. It also suggests that social structures are temporal effects that can always break down, be taken down, or collapse if and when the plug is pulled. Finally, this view makes untenable old ways of theorizing that postulate separate levels of reality and the existence of superstructures and similar paraphernalia. Practice theories are inherently relational and see the world as a seamless assemblage, nexus, or confederation of practices—although not all having the same relevance.

Secondly, and strictly related to the above, practice theories bring to the fore the critical role of the body and material things in all social affairs. Most practice theories conceive practices as routine bodily activities made possible by the active contribution of an array of material resources. Practices with no things and no bodies involved are thus simply inconceivable.

For one thing, the body is not an 'instrument which the agent must use in order to act' (Reckwitz 2002, p. 251), as a practice *is* the routinized activity of the body. The practice of being a competent class student (i.e. disciplined, silent, and, very likely, passive) is inscribed in the habituated bodies of children from their tender age. As any teacher who has had to deal with an 'undisciplined' set of pupils would tell you, conducting a class in these circumstances is impossible. The social order that we call a class is, thus, largely inscribed in the bodies of all the participants, and manifests through particular bodily (and discursive) practices.

Seeing a class as the coming together of the activities of its participants also foregrounds the active role of objects. Objects, in fact, both make practices durable and connect practices with each other across space and time. For one thing, the seats in the classroom (likely to be facing the teacher) and the rest of the objects in the room (board, clock, etc.) actively participate in both producing and perpetuating the activity of conducting a class. Teachers do not have to negotiate roles and the division of labour (who has the right to speak and who is supposed to take notes) with students every time they start a class, as the objects take care of most of this. And they do not have to make too much effort to keep attention focused on them, as the desk orientation does much of the work. Objects thus both participate in the accomplishment of the practice and make this accomplishment durable over time (although note that this does not mean immutable). By the same token, objects also bring into the scene of action the results of other practices, thus establishing connections in space and time. The desk used by the students, the equipment used by the teacher, and even the fact that the room is likely to be clean are also the results of other activities which become the resources for the practice at hand. Similarly, the arrangement of the furniture, books, and other tools carries on to the scene of action many of the refinements on how to conduct (or how not to conduct) a class developed over decades and centuries. This, of course, makes practices, sociality, and all social phenomena, situated occurrences, and contributes to positioning them in a specific set of historical conditions.

Thirdly, practice theories carve a specific space for individual agency and agents. While *homo economicus* is conceived as a (semi) rational decision maker and *homo sociologicus* is depicted as a norm-following, role-performing individual, *homo practicus* is conceived as a carrier of practices, a body/mind who 'carries', but also 'carries out', social practices (Reckwitz 2002, p. 256).

All practice theories thus leave space for initiative, creativity, and individual performance. These are in fact necessary, as performing a practice always requires adapting to new circumstances so that practising is neither mindless repetition nor complete invention. Yet individual performances take place and are intelligible only as part of an ongoing practice and against the 'more or less stable background of other practices' (Rouse 2007, p. 505). The focus is thus not on the action of the individual but on the practice, and the horizon of intelligible action that it makes available to the agents. Social practices thus provide a precise space for agent and agency accepting 'all three sides of the [...] triangle: that society is a system; that the system is powerfully constraining, and yet that the system can be made and unmade through human action and interaction' (Ortner 1984, p. 159).

Fourthly, adopting a practice approach radically transforms our view of knowledge, meaning, and discourse. From a practice perspective, knowledge is conceived largely as a form of mastery that is expressed in the capacity to carry out a social and material activity. Knowledge is thus always a way of knowing shared with others, a set of practical methods acquired through learning, inscribed in objects, embodied, and only partially articulated in discourse. Becoming part of an existing practice thus involves learning how to act, how to speak (and what to say), but also how to feel, what to expect, and what things mean.

Think, for example, of falling in love in a 'romantic way' (Reckwitz 2002) or caring for someone in a hospital. These are both culturally-understandable practices which consist in patterns of routinized bodily conducts carried out using tools and discourse (e.g. flowers and 'sweet nothings', in the case of romantic love). When individuals 'take over' such existing practices, they are enrolled in the specific horizon of intelligibility associated with it, and which implies a certain way of understanding oneself, others, and the events that occur as part of the practice. However, this is not all. Absorbing, or being absorbed in, a practice also implies accepting certain norms of correctness (what is right and wrong) as well as certain ways of wanting and feeling. In the practice of romantic love, you do not contact the family and offer a sum of money—although this is perfectly acceptable in the context of arranged marriage practice. As Reckwitz (2002) writes, 'Every practice implies a mode of intentionality made routine; i.e. wanting certain things and avoiding others... [and] contains certain practice-specific emotionality' (p. 254) even if that means a high control of the emotions as you would expect in the practice of nursing in a hospital. This means that the sense of what is right or wrong, and also wants and emotions 'do not belong to individuals but—in the form of knowledge—to practices' (Reckwitz 2002, p. 254).

Discourse, in this sense, becomes itself a practice: discursive practices are not seen as ways to represent the world as much as ways to intervene and act on it. However, this is not a reason for granting them special priority or studying them in isolation from other activities. While discursive practices carry meaning and intentionality onto the scene of action and give the actors ways of influencing each other and the situation (for example, by introducing new forms of intentionality of new meaning), discourses alone are not enough to explain the world we live in. Discursive practices thus need to be considered side by side with other forms of social and material activity. Practice theory is thus an alternative and a corrective to extreme forms of textualism that reduce organizations and the world to texts, signs, and communication.

Finally, all practice-based approaches foreground the centrality of interest in all human matters and therefore put emphasis on the importance of power, conflict, and politics as constitutive elements of the social reality we experience. Practices, in fact, literally put people (and things) in place, and they give (or deny) people the power to do things and to think of themselves in certain ways. As a result, practices and their temporal and spatial ordering (i.e. several practices combined in a particular way) produce and reproduce differences and inequalities. In so doing they serve certain interests at the expense of others. As Ortner (1984) notes, anything people do bears intentional or unintentional implications for how they fit into the 'system', and its distribution of power and privileges. Practices are thus always necessarily open to contestation and this keeps them continuously in a state of tension and change. This, in turn, contributes to the idea that practices and the world they conjure are highly situated in historical and material conditions and, at least in principle, given different practices, the world could be different. Accordingly, the study of practice has, or should address, the study of all forms of human action from a particular 'political' angle (Ortner 1984, p. 149).

In summary, a practice-based view of social and human phenomena is distinctive in that it:

- Emphasizes that behind all the apparently durable features of our world—from queues to formal organizations—there is some type of productive and reproductive work. In so doing it transforms the way in which we conceive of social order and conceptualize the apparent stability of the social world (the nature of social structures, in sociological jargon, as a socio-material accomplishment).
- Forces us to rethink the role of agents and individuals; e.g. managers, the managed, etc.
- Foregrounds the importance of the body and objects in social affairs.
- Sheds new light on the nature of knowledge and discourse.
- Reaffirms the centrality of interests and power in everything we do.

By the same token, adopting a practice-based approach also constitutes a radical departure from the traditional ways of understanding social and organizational matters. When pursued coherently, this approach produces in fact a new sensitivity, orients towards new objects of inquiry, and eventually generates a new view of organizational matters (Schatzki 2002). For example:

- A practice-based approach suggests that the basic units of analysis for understanding organizational phenomena are practices, not practitioners. Practices thus come first, because it is only once we appreciate the set of practices involved in a scene of action that we can ask what sort of agency and 'actor-ship' is made possible by these specific conditions. Practice theories are thus an alternative to the (many) views which suggest that organizational phenomena stem from the more or less rational action of individual subjects (Cohen 2000). In other words, practice theories require a 'Copernican revolution' in addressing many of the seemingly familiar phenomena in organization and management studies. In so doing, however, they offer an opportunity to reinterpret all imaginable organizational phenomena, suggesting for example that the object of inquiry should be managerial and entrepreneurial activities, not managers and entrepreneurs; strategy making and sale practices, not strategists and sales persons; leadership practices, not leaders. Adopting a practice-based view thus opens a Pandora's Box that holds a potential treasure trove for scholars.

- Practice theories do more than just describe what people do. Practices are, in fact, meaning-making, identity-forming, and order-producing activities (Chia and Holt 2008, Nicolini 2009b). Accordingly, practice-based approaches steer away from the misleading idea that by simply observing the activities of the world in more detail, one gets closer to 'reality' (what is known as naïve empiricism). Practice-based theories use a performative perspective to offer a new vista on the social world. As I discuss below and explain in depth in Chapter 9, practice theories are thus necessarily theory-methods packages that produce a shift in our understanding of social and organizational phenomena. The idea that social science is simply about capturing what people do is, in fact, still very much compatible with the positivist and rationalist project that practice theories try to overcome (Geiger 2009, p. 132).

- Practice-based approaches consider cognition and sense-making as emerging from the practices carried out in an organization (see, for example, Chapter 7). In this sense, a practice-based view is an alternative to cognitive perspectives that try to explain organizational conduct and phenomena as something stemming from the mind or brain of an individual.

- The practice view embraces the idea that organization emerges as the result of sense-making, but eschews the idea that sense-making constitutes an intangible mental process, a form of symbolic exchange, or an abstract processes of coordination based on some type of communicative processes (Weick 1979; Hutchins 1995). Sense-making and knowing are thus foregrounded, but they are located in the material and discursive activity, body, artefacts, habits, and preoccupations that populate the life of organizational members.

- Practice theories suggest that organizations and institutions are made and remade thanks to material and discursive work. In so doing, practice theories support a dynamic view of institutions and offer a set of concepts to further the understanding of promising but still rather vague and often individual notions such as 'institutional work' (Lawrence *et al.* 2009).
- Practice theories accept that discursive practices are central to the construction and reproduction of all organizational and social things, but resist the idea that language and discourse (understood as language in action) alone can explain all the features of organizational life. Practice approaches suggest that we need theories that take into account the heterogeneous nature of the world we live in, which includes an appreciation that objects and materials often bite back at us and resist our attempts to envelope them with our discourses.
- Practice theories depict the world in relational terms as being composed by, and transpiring through, a bundle or network of practices. In so doing they join forces with other relational sociologies and reject the idea that the world comes nicely divided into levels and factors, or that there is a fundamental distinction between micro and macro phenomena (Reckwitz 2002; Latour 2005). Practice theories conceive social investigation as the patient, evidence-based, bottom-up effort of understanding practices and untangling their relationships. They question how such practices are performed, and how connected practices make a difference; they ask why it is that the world that results from the coming together of several practices is the way it is, and how and why it is not different. Practice theories are thus complementary to all variants of realism (both naïve and critical) in that they ask how the apparent features of our daily world that realists and critical realists trade in, are brought into existence in the first place.

1.2 There is no such a thing as a unified practice theory

Summarizing the previous sections, my argument is that the practice idiom offers a new way of understanding social and organizational phenomena that is complementary and often alternative to many of the mainstream and non-traditional approaches to the study of organization. While practice approaches do not accept that the world is populated by individual actors who undertake actions following rules aimed at maintaining the integrity of the system (as in the traditional functionalist sociology),[2] it also steers away from views that understand social affairs as mere symbolic exchanges between humans (as in the symbolic interactionism tradition) or that suggest that the social world is talked into existence through signs and texts and semiotic processes (as in modern forms of textualism). The great promise of the practice lens is that of explaining social phenomena in a processual way without losing touch with the mundane nature of everyday life and the concrete and material nature of the activities with which we are all involved.

The problem, however, is that the set of assumptions and principles outlined above, and that I have generically associated with a practice-based view, or practice-based approach, or practice idiom, does not stem from a single unified theory of practice but emerges instead from the coming together of several distinct scholarly traditions. While these traditions share a series of family resemblances, each of them has its own history, vocabulary, and set of basic assumptions. And while they can be compared to the tributaries of a lake (the 'grand lake' of practice-based approaches) they do not contribute to a 'grand' theory of practice and form; instead, they comprise a complicated network of similarities and dissimilarities. It is in this sense that, as I said above, while all practice theories belong to the same family, 'there is no unified practice approach' (Schatzki 2001, p. 2).

It is for this reason that, in this book, you will not find an introduction to *the* theory of practice or *a* theory of practice, but an introduction to six different ways of theorizing practice. As I explain in more depth in the final chapter, my view is that much is to be gained if we learn to use these approaches in combination, rather than attempting a grand synthesis. In fact, a grand synthesis would run against the spirit of most practice approaches which strive to provide a thicker, not thinner, description of everyday life.

It is also for this same reason that in this introduction I did not start with a definition of what practice is.[3] Practice theories are fundamentally ontological projects in the sense that they attempt to provide a new vocabulary to describe the world and to populate the world with specific 'units of analysis'; that is, practices. How these units are defined, however, is internal to each of the theories, and choosing one of them would thus amount to reducing the richness provided by the different approaches. Compare, for example, the following two definitions of practice from Chapter 5:

'[A practice is a] coherent and complex form of socially established co-operative human activities' (MacIntyre 1981, p. 187).

[Practice is] 'doing, but not just doing in and of itself. It is doing in historical and social context that gives structure and meaning to what people do. In this sense, practice is always social practice' (Wenger 1998, p. 47).

MacIntyre's formulation foregrounds coherence and cooperation. His definition points toward stability, and the focus is particularly on human actions which is not surprising as the author sees practice mainly as a form of cultural tradition. Wenger, on the contrary, focuses on practices as social and historical occurrences. By suggesting that practices have an internal structure, the definition allows for components of the practice to be in contradiction. Wenger also links practices to their historical and social contexts, a condition that, unlike MacIntyre, is likely to make them only partially stable—they will be 'established only as long' as the conditions that support them remain in place.

It can be added that a similar problem occurs when attempting to provide specific examples of what counts as a practice. While, here, differences are less radical, disagreement still exists among authors. Among practice theorists there is, in fact, a certain consensus that practices (in the plural) are historically and geographically recurring localized occurrences. Talking about practices is thus different from simply referring to the opposite of theory or meditation (see Chapter 2 for a discussion). There is also a consensus that practices are molar units; that is, they are complex wholes composed of other 'smaller' elements—for example, bodily motions and simpler actions. Practices are thus configurations of actions which carry a specific meaning: moving a hand forward is thus not a practice but can become a component of the practice of 'greeting by shaking hands'. However, how big or small these units are and what counts as a practice again varies across theories. Examples of practice thus range from mundane doings such as sitting correctly at a table (Bourdieu 1981), and making phone calls (Schegloff 1986), to short patterns of activity such as trading on the stock market (Schatzki 2002), or cooking a meal (Schatzki 2005), to more durable organized corpuses of activity such as Nordic walking (Shove and Pantzar 2005), vegetarianism and acupuncture (Barnes 2001), scientific experiments (Pickering 1995), and science as a whole field itself (Pickering 1992). Choosing one example or another is, however, highly consequential. Naming, defining, and exemplifying practices is already theorizing them.

As I will discuss extensively in Chapter 9, faced with this plurality one has two options. One is to try to reduce the variety by proposing a single unifying theory. As I shall show, in my view this would amount to a sort of betrayal of the ethos of most practice approaches which strive to make the world richer, not poorer, in meaning. The alternative is thus to actively embrace this plurality. This means two things.

First, practice can only be approached through an appreciation of difference. In clearer terms, one has to familiarize oneself with the different traditions that constitute the historical tributaries to the great sea of practice theory. For this reason, the book provides a primer to several different approaches.

Second, an opportunity exists to use some of these approaches in combination. As I will show in Chapter 9, this is possible because all the practice theories surveyed in this book are connected by a complex web of similarities. Accordingly, these theories can be mobilized *together* to enrich our understanding of practice and to provide a practice-based understanding of everything social (and organizational). As I show in Chapter 9, mobilizing them together does not mean trying to unify them. On the contrary, the idea here is to exploit both their similarities and differences, following what I call a toolkit approach. This, however, requires familiarizing oneself not only with their lexicon but also with their assumptions, so that we do not end up using theories that contradict each other.

1.3 **Practice theories and the study of work and organization**

As I hinted above, the theoretical affordances of practice theories make this approach particularly attractive for modern organizational studies, especially after this academic community's radical shift in the 1990s on the object of inquiry. In the last three decades the focus of organization studies has, in fact, shifted from the examination of organizations as entities (organizations as things) to the examination of organizations as theoretical discourses (organizations as phenomena), to the study of organizing as a social process (Clegg, Hardy, and North 1996, p. xxiv). This, in turn, has created a fertile ground for practice theories especially due to their capacity to provide a processual view of organizational matters and to foreground the central role of mundane activities. Indeed, the approach has made significant inroads in organization and work studies in the last three decades.

According to Corradi *et al.* (2010), the starting point of the current bandwagon of practice-based organizational studies can be traced back to the contributions of three specific research streams. These are the study of learning and knowing phenomena as situated practices (Lave and Wenger 1991; Brown and Duguid 1991; Cook and Yanow 1993; Tsoukas 1996; Raelin 1997; Gherardi *et al.* 1998; Gherardi 2000; Orlikowski 2002; Nicolini *et al.* 2003), the study of technology as practice (Orlikowski 1992; Suchman *et al.* 1999; Orlikowski 2000), and the study of strategy as practice (Whittington 1996; Jarzabkowski 2003; Whittington 2006). While factually correct, this genealogy only considers the authors who explicitly embraced the practice 'label'. In this way, however, we exclude from this genealogy other practice-oriented research traditions that do not use the word 'practice' but whose contribution to organization studies often predates the formation of the current practice bandwagon. These include Bourdieu's praxeology (Özbilgin and Tatli 2005), activity theory (Engeström 1987; Blackler 1995; Middleton and Engeström 1998; Engeström, Miettinen, and Punamaki 1999; Engeström 2008; Blackler and Regan 2009), ethno-methodology and workplace studies (Garfinkel 1967; Suchman 1987; Drew and Heritage 1992; Heath and Luff 1996; Luff, Hindmarsh, and Heath 2000; Heath and Button 2002; Llewellyn 2008; Heritage

2009; Llewellyn and Hindmarsh 2010), and some fringes of the Scandinavian neo-institutionalism, and especially authors who are conversant with the sociology of translation and actor-network theory traditions (Czarniawska and Joerges 1996; Czarniawska and Sevon 1996; Lindberg and Czarniawska 2006).

According to Feldman and Orlikowski (2011), the interest in practice over the years gained momentum, and in fact a rapid survey of the literature would confirm that the approach has made inroads in other areas of study such as the study of institutions (Lawrence and Suddaby 2006; Lounsbury 2008; Lounsbury and Crumley 2007; Zietsma and Lawrence 2010), marketing (Echeverri and Skålén 2011; Skålén and Hackley 2011), consumption (Røpke 2009; Shove and Pantzar 2005; Warde, 2005), accounting (Ahrens & Chapman 2007; Lounsbury 2008; Quattrone 2009), projects (Blomquist, Hällgren, Nilsson, and Söderholm, 2010; Hällgren and Söderholm, 2011), strategy (Johnson *et al.* 2007; Golsorkhi, Rouleau, and Seidl, 2010), organizational learning and knowledge (Gherardi 2006; Nicolini 2011), routines (Feldman and Pentland 2003; Pentland and Feldman 2005; Feldman and Orlikowski 2011), technology use (Orlikowski 2000), social innovation (Pantzar and Shove 2010), decision making (Cabantous and Gond 2011; Cabantous, Gond, and Johnson-Cramer 2010), and many others.

1.3.1 RETURNING TO PRACTICE: A WEAK AND STRONG PROGRAMME?

This widespread turn or 're-turn' to practice theory in the field of organization and work studies (Miettinen *et al.* 2009) has been characterized by the presence of what, following Bloor (1976), we can describe as a strong or weak practice-based programme.[4]

The weak programme stems from a valid, but often vague, perception that organization theory has become too abstract and uncoupled from the concrete activities it purports to describe and explain.[5] According to Barley and Kunda (2001), this requires us to 'bring work back in' to the study of organization so that we can provide a solid empirical basis for the understanding of existing and newly emerging organizational phenomena. For example, say the authors, when managers impose new organizational structures or introduce new technologies or promote new ways of organizing, they invariably alter patterns of work. In order to say anything meaningful about the former, we need to pay close attention to the latter. Organization and management studies, therefore, need to return to the study of what people do, and put the material activities of organizational members at centre-stage. This also means 'embracing methods that yield detailed descriptions of work life' (Barley and Kunda 2001, p. 84).

While this call is sensible and commendable,[6] it can be, and indeed has often been interpreted as simply an invitation to pay more attention to what people do. A renewed attention to the details of everyday work, however, may not be enough. For example, following the seminal work of Mintzberg (1973), dozen of scholars recorded and assembled long catalogues of things that managers do. Reading through their painstaking, but often plain, descriptions of roles and tasks, one is left wondering 'so what'? The mere 'a-theoretical' cataloguing of what practitioners do may be an exciting endeavour for academics who are unfamiliar with the specific occupation, but it sheds little light on the meaning of the work that goes into it, what makes it possible, why it is the way it is, and how it contributes to, or interferes with, the production of organizational life. In other words, listing and enumerating practices by taking them at face-value constitutes a weak approach to practice. Such a descriptive and a-theoretical way of addressing practice, which builds on the misleading assumption that practice is self-explanatory, is scarcely capable of providing the affordances described above. It is also likely to be conductive to a form of social science that is scarcely relevant, as once the excitement and surprise of learning about an exotic occupation wears out, we are left with a 'so what' question, as are the practitioners.

The strong programme differs from the weak one in that it goes much further. While the two share an interest in the mundane and often unsung details of organizational life, the strong programme strives to *explain* organizational matters in terms of practices instead of simply registering them. Claiming that actors or organizations deploy certain practices in certain situations or that their competitive advantage lies in that fact that organizations 'have' a set of practices adds relatively little to our understanding unless we also explain the 'dynamics of everyday activity, how are these generated, and how they operate within different contexts and over time' (Feldman and Orlikowski 2011, p. 1241).

To provide an authentically novel and alternative vista of a number of organizational phenomena, we thus need to take a further step and commit, in one form or another, to a practice-based ontology—that is, the belief that many social and organizational phenomena occur within, and are aspects or components of, the field of practices (Schatzki 2001, p. 2). We also need to conduct our analysis on the basis of such premises. Anything less than this would mean being exposed to the risk that the practice approach becomes simply a further exercise of mimetic isonomism; i.e. the rebranding of existing categories to benefit from the bandwagon effect (a risk that is implicit in the weak approach (Erlingsdottir and Lindberg 2005). From a strong perspective, the practice idiom is therefore much more than a theoretical lens that one can adopt in response to the latest academic fashion or can retrofit to the usual way of doing research. Rather, the practice idiom is an ontological choice, a recognition of the primacy of practice in social matters, as well as the adoption of the idea that practices (in one way or another) are fundamental to the production, reproduction, and transformation of social and organizational matters. As a new vocabulary, practice populates the world with new and different phenomena, objects of inquiry, questions, and concerns. It introduces a new ontology and alternative truth values, 'and does not limit changing or elaborating on existing ones' (Rorty, 1989).[7]

From a strong perspective then, the attention on activity and the doing are only a departure point, a sort of ticket that grants entry to a novel world,[8] where everything is made and remade and where, by implication, things could be different (Lynch 1993, p. 18). As soon as one crosses the threshold, however, the ticket is useless and one has to start working to make sense of this new world—or of the world seen from this new angle. Practices need to be studied analytically rather than descriptively (Llewellyn 2008). Advocates of any of the strong programmes thus look with suspicion at the idea that work, activity, and practice can be described using lay categories and without reference to a specific theoretical tradition. Describing what people do is, in fact, a theory-laden operation. Therefore there is no such thing as a neutral description, especially when it comes to answering the critical questions of 'what does this mean?' and 'why does it matter?' By the same token, the strong programme also looks with suspicion at the idea that practice can be studied only through the accounts of practitioners; i.e. on the basis of a set of off-line, after-the-fact interviews. As Suchman (1987) convincingly argued, work tends to disappear with distance as members systematically disregard the type of work they do not see or that they take for granted. Practitioners understand and apply the term 'work' in relation to their professional activities in a very selective manner, and hence tapping into their expertise through their accounts means contemplating a specific practice of selection and deletion. Accordingly, the strong programme requires a commitment to an observational orientation *and* the adoption of methods that allow an appreciation of practice as it happens.

In sum, this book is an invitation to embrace coherently a strong version of the practice approach, on the assumption that such an approach may yield a radically new way of understanding work organizations and organizational phenomena, albeit many of its affordances are still to be explored.

1.4 **The content and structure of the book**

The content and structure of this book follow from the idea that practice is many things to many people, and that reducing such plurality risks weakening the explanatory power of this approach. Accordingly, each of the central chapters of the book examines the theoretical assumptions and conceptual apparatus of six scholarly traditions that contribute collectively to the current interest in practice theory. At the end of each chapter, I present a fully worked example of the theory through its application to the case of telemedicine.

The book opens in Chapter 2 with a brief history of practice theories. Such a recap of the changing fortunes of the idea of practice helps us to understand why authors such as Miettinen *et al.* (2009) talk about a *re*turn to practice and why a focus on practice is still potentially subversive and innovative.

Each of Chapters 3–8 introduces readers to a particular practice theory and orientation. Chapter 3 examines the work of Bourdieu and Giddens. The two authors are the founders of 'social praxeology', an approach that elaborates on the basic idea that social life is a contingent and ever-changing texture of human practices. Although with different nuances, these two authors have the historical merit of suggesting that practices ordered across space and time are the basic domains of study of social science, thus establishing practice theory as one of the leading social theories at the turn of the millennium.

Chapter 4 discusses the idea of practice as a form of tradition reproduced in time through a process of active engagement and participation sustained by a specific community. The gist of the discussion is that while practice theory needs a theory of learning, there is a fine balance to be struck between recognizing that all practices need to be handed down by a group of practitioners, and that the reification of such a collective into a social body that exists independently of the practice.

Chapter 5 examines activity theory, a tradition that originated in the Soviet Union during the early twentieth century and that, over a century, developed a sophisticated and far-reaching practice approach which gave special attention to the role of objects in human activity, and offered a sensitivity to the conflicting, dialectic, and developmental nature of practice that many other practice approaches lack.

Chapter 6 briefly introduces the research programme of ethno-methodology. Although, strictly speaking, ethno-methodology is not a theory of practice, it was set squarely from the beginning as a way to 'treat practical activities, practical circumstances, and practical sociological reasoning as topics of empirical study' (Garfinkel 1967, p.1). In this way, ethno-methodology constitutes one of the most important and promising ways of understanding practice and practical action.

Chapter 7 examines some of the contemporary theories of practice which build on the legacy of Heidegger, Wittgenstein, or a combination of the two. In this chapter I consider the rich and often complex work of Theodore Schatzki. I focus on this author both because over the last two decades, Schatzki has developed one of the strongest and far-reaching versions of practice theories available to date, and because Schatzki's work is directly, and often incorrectly, quoted in the organizational literature.

Chapter 8 surveys, albeit briefly, some of the traditions such as conversation analysis, critical discourse analysis, and mediated discourse analysis that developed the idea of language as a discursive practice and a form of social and situated action. The goal here is not that of providing a comprehensive introduction to these complex theories. More modestly, the goal is to examine how their assumptions translate into particular research questions and methodological orientations regarding the nature of social practices.

Finally, in Chapter 9, I try to bring this multiplicity of theories together and offer some ideas on how we can put this plurality to work. In this chapter, I suggest embracing a form of programmatic eclecticism and a toolkit approach. My main tenet is that to study practice empirically, we are better served by a strategy based on deliberately switching between theoretical lenses. In this chapter I also offer some proposals on how to go about studying practice, including what to do, what to watch for (and to listen to, to smell, to touch, etc.), and how to write about it. The core suggestion is that understanding and representing practice requires a reiteration of two basic movements: zooming in on the accomplishments of practice, and zooming out of their relationships in space and time. The chapter and the book conclude with some reflections on what zooming in and out is not, and on where the practice bandwagon is going.

As this book has been designed as an invitation to practice theories, and has been written for curious minds, advanced novices, or simply eager learners, the chapters have been designed to be self-contained. They can thus be read either in sequence or individually. Chapter 2 is quite philosophically oriented, and those who think that the words 'Heidegger' and 'Wittgenstein' have too many syllables should consider skipping this part. Chapter 9 is the more methodologically oriented, so those who want to find some suggestions on how to study practice should try not to give up too soon.

1.5 **The rolling case study**

There is of course an irony in writing a highly theoretical book about practice. While the issue constitutes one of the central concerns of all practice theorists (how do you translate practice into a text?), and therefore it *is* addressed in several places in the book, in writing this volume, I also took into account Wittgenstein's observations that meaning and theory are best conveyed through paradigmatic exemplars (Wittgenstein 1953).

Accordingly, at the end of Chapters 3–8, the reader will find a grounded illustration of each approach through its application to the case of telemedicine. In these sections I will thus use the theoretical framework and conceptual toolkit discussed in the preceding chapter for analysing and describing aspects of the emerging practice of monitoring patients at a distance.[9] The rolling case study constitutes, in a sense, an exercise in style[10] that aims to clarify the topics discussed in the text, and illustrate the affordances provided by the different theories of practice. My hope is that the exemplars will help to shed some light on both what the different approaches make us see and what they conceal from view.

I use the case of telemedicine because this new emerging practice constitutes a particularly rich empirical setting that is especially appropriate for thinking through some of the issues discussed in the book. Caring for patients from a distance using technological mediation introduces, in fact, far-reaching changes in a number of well-established and often very entrenched practices of both healthcare professionals and patients.

Although the rolling case study has been produced for illustrative purposes, it is based on extensive four-year empirical research conducted by the author in northern Italy.[11] The study included several weeks of participant observation in two specialized medical centres. During this period I observed the practice in the context of the daily ward's routine, I attended a number of meetings, promotional workshops, and training sessions, and I conducted about fifty ethnographical and semi-structured interviews with doctors, nurses, managers, and health officials. Finally, I examined a variety of technical and policy documents, reports, and scientific materials.

In the following paragraphs, I provide some background information on telemedicine and the setting of the practice of telemonitoring.

1.5.1 WHAT IS TELEMEDICINE?

The term 'telemedicine' is commonly employed to indicate the use of communication and information technologies in the context of healthcare activities. Telemedicine is not a totally new phenomenon. The first experiments in 'phone stethoscopy' and long-distance transmission of X-ray images dates back to around the First World War. The use of telemedicine has however increased dramatically in the last two decades due to a combination of increasing demand and pressure on the healthcare systems of Western countries, and the appearance of cheaper, more effective, and more user-friendly technologies.

An increasingly important subset of telemedicine is telecare, a set of services bringing care directly to users. It includes the provision of health and service information (e.g. health advice, and access to self-help groups), safety and security monitoring (e.g. monitoring of critical aspects of 'house-holding' such as whether the gas has been left on), and personal telemonitoring (e.g. the telemonitoring of vital parameters such as breathing and heartbeat, and changes in lifestyle). According to Barlow *et al.* (2006) telemonitoring critically differs from other types of telemedicine (such as teleradiology or teledermatology), in that it is mainly aimed at crisis response and prevention. As such, it is particularly appealing in all those conditions which require long-term care and that, until recently, required long and expensive periods of hospitalization. By bringing the hospital outside of its usual environs, telecare and telemonitoring promise to contribute to an individual's chronic disease management, and to reduce the associated economic, social, and psychological costs.

1.5.2 WHAT IS CHRONIC HEART FAILURE?

The case study discussed here has to do with the emerging practice of monitoring serious chronic heart failure patients. Chronic heart failure is a highly debilitating chronic condition affecting a growing number of patients, mostly aged over 60. In simple terms, heart failure means that the heart doesn't work properly. People cannot carry out their daily activity, they feel out of breath, and experience deep chest and other pains while doing even the most light activity (e.g. combing their hair). Acute crises are not uncommon, especially in more seriously ill patients. When such crises occur, patients need to be rushed to the hospital, put under intensive care, and stabilized with an appropriate cocktail of medicines. This pathology afflicts about 1–3 per cent of the population, but in the over-75 age-group, this rises to 10 per cent (McMurray and Stewart 2003).

Until a few years ago this condition was typically treated through a recurrent pattern of hospitalization, intensive therapy, discharge, deterioration of condition, and subsequent new hospitalization. Hospitals intervened in acute crises and then discharged their patients who were then either left to their destiny or taken up by their general practitioners. This cycle, however, contrasted with the emerging evidence that unless the disease was properly managed, patients' conditions could seriously deteriorate over time. In this context, health practitioners in different parts of the world started to consider the possibility of using information and communication technologies, i.e. telemedicine, for addressing the issue in a novel way. In Italy, this idea took first root in the northern region of Lombardy. One of the first sites to experiment with this new approach was the centre in Garibaldi, a branch of a national medical foundation with several outlets in different cities which specialized in the care of chronic heart conditions.

1.5.3 TELEMONITORING IN GARIBALDI

The centre in Garibaldi,[12] where the telemonitoring activity to be discussed takes place, is one of nine medical centres owned and operated by a large Italian non-profit (charitable) medical foundation. It is a relatively small, highly-specialized hospital with three wards and about sixty beds. Each ward has an annex outpatient clinic. The telemedicine service depends functionally on the cardiology department, the largest at Garibaldi. The department is occupied by about forty healthcare professionals who look after thirty-five beds. The department is nationally renowned for its work on chronic heart failure and other chronic cardiopathies. For this reason, it attracts patients not only from the town of Garibaldi and its immediate surroundings, but also from other parts of Lombardy (the centre of Garibaldi has an established partnership with two of the best-known cardiac surgeries in the country), and other regions of Italy, some quite distant.

In Garibaldi hospital, the practice of telemonitoring remote patients is well organized. It unfolds as a sequence of regular telephone contacts and check-ups from a well-established point in time. The activities are also easily identified. To benefit from the service a patient must be 'enrolled'. Most of the following exchange is through telephone contacts by telemedicine service staff (telemonitoring), or by the patients themselves (tele-assistance). All activities are carefully recorded in a personal medical file. The assistance is carried out by nurses who monitor patient status, make dietary and lifestyle recommendations, correct and adjust the therapeutic regime, and provide other information and instructions to patients and their families. Nurses also coordinate their activities both with hospital cardiologists who refer most of the patients (with the telemedicine service acting as an extension of the hospital's services), and with family doctors who assist the patients staying at home. In most cases, however, the nurses are free to manage the assistance as they see fit.

Serious chronic heart failure is a disease that can only ultimately be cured by a transplant. The waiting time for a heart transplant in Italy at the time of the empirical study was between two and three years. For those who do not have a transplant, there is no cure, and sufferers need to learn how to live with their condition. Telemonitoring is a long-term affair.

1.6 **Words of thanks**

In writing this book I have been the beneficiary of a number of encourage-ments, observations, suggestions, and comments. A short written acknowledg-ment is a small token in return for the time and attention given to me by many generous individuals, but thanking them publicly is the least I can do. I would like to start with a special thanks to Frank Blackler, who encouraged me in the early stages of this project, and in the process provided a positive academic role model. A number of promising scholars have road-tested the chapters of this manuscript and provided invaluable feedback on their suitability as an introduction to practice theory. These individuals include Emmanouil Gkere-dakis, Maja Korica, Jeanne Mengis, Bjørn Erik Mork, Niki Panourgias, Edouard Pignot, Etty Nilsen, and Blair Winsor. Thanks also to Maxine Robertson and Dvora Yanow for providing valuable feedback on the material discussed in Chapter 9. While I am happy to share with these generous individuals whatever merit there is in this book, as is customary to write, the responsibility for ignoring their advice falls entirely upon the author. I would also like to acknowledge the collegial support of my colleagues at IKON, Jacky Swan, Harry Scarbrough, Joe Nandhakumar, and Dawn Coton, who provided the conditions for this project to come to fruition. Finally, special thanks to Adam James for his invaluable editorial support and for helping to make this book as readable as possible. Thanks also to my wife Katie and my daughters Clara and Giulia for putting up with me and my (professional) obsession for practice. Financial support for the research that underpins the rolling case study was provided in part by the Provincia Autonoma of Trento (Italy), Project 6–2001.

■ NOTES

1. As early as 1984 Sherry Ortner was writing about the 'growing interest' in the concept of practice and suggested that this interest had been going on for 'several years' (Ortner 1984, p. 144).
2. See Cohen (2000) for an in-depth discussion. Norms and decisions are, in fact, carried by practices that the individual contributes to perpetuate but does not own. Moreover, following a practice has an inherently tacit dimension, as practical knowledge is inscribed in the body and in artefacts and, as such, is not subject to deliberation. Accordingly, actions can only take place as part of a practice and they cannot constitute the building block of sociality.
3. Or even worse, a dictionary definition. Another reason is that several authors such as Marx, Bourdieu, Heidegger, and also Garfinkel, do not provide a definition of practice.
4. The existence of different levels of engagement with practice theory has been also observed by Feldman and Orlikowski (2011) who distinguish between an empirical, a theoretical, and a philosophical focus on practice in organization theory (p. 1240); and Corradi *et al.* (2010) who differentiate between practice as a 'way of seeing' and 'practice as an empirical object' (p. 268).
5. The presence of these two different programmes is due in part to the bandwagon effect mentioned above. When new innovations start to be perceived as fashionable, members of a community tend to jump on the bandwagon (and are later forced to do so by peer pressures) in order to reap the practical and/or legitimization benefits afforded by the new approach (Erlingsdottir and Lindberg 2005). This, however, does not necessarily require full conversion to the new paradigm. Jumping on the bandwagon can also be achieved by adopting the new label while continuing to do what one was doing before ('isonomism' or putting a new label on an old bottle); or, *vice versa*, by adopting the new approach without changing the existing name ('isopraxism', as in the case of established approaches that join forces with the new fashion in order to reap some its benefits in terms of visibility and influence).

6. Significantly, the above quote continues as follows: 'Particularly crucial are field studies that examine work practices and relations in situ. Students of work have repeatedly shown that work practices are highly situated... in fact people are likely to misreport with whom they interact during the course of the day... For this reason, ethnography, participant observation and other qualitative methods have continued to play a more prominent role in the sociology of work and occupations, and in industrial relations, than they have in organization studies' (Barley and Kunda 2001, p. 85–6). Put more clearly, Barley and Kunda, who are two sophisticated ethnographers, provide support for a strong, not a weak practice approach.

7. To see how this can make a difference we can briefly compare weak and strong ways of examining the practice of strategy making, one of the areas where the practice idiom has been more successful (Johnson *et al.* 2007; Golsorkhi *et al.* 2010). Many of the contributions from the first generation of the so called strategy-as-practice approach would fall within the weak programme. This is because the original concern of these studies was with 'how managers actually "do strategy"' (Whittington 1996, p. 732). In other words early strategy-as-practice studies focused mostly on examining in fine detail the day-to-day internal life of strategy processes by describing, often with a sense of awe and admiration, meetings, workshops, strategy making sessions, and other micro-activities of skilled individuals. The goal of these descriptions was to respond to questions such as 'where and how is the work of strategizing and organizing actually done?' and 'who does this strategizing and organizing work, and with what skills and tools?' (Whittington 2003, p. 119).

   Compare this with the work of authors such as Chia and Holt (2008), Chia and Mackay (2007), and Samra-Fredricks (2005) who on the contrary endorsed a 'strong' approach to strategy-as-practice (over the years authors such as Jarzabkawski and Whittington have moved towards the strong program: see e.g., Whittington, 2006).

   Chia and Mackay's (2007) point of departure is the observation that too often within the (first generation) of strategy-as-practice studies 'there is basic lack of clarity about what practice really is in relation to processes and individual activities' (Chia and MacKay 2007, p. 219). As a result 'activities, practices, and processes are sometimes treated interchangeably and viewed as ultimately epiphenomenal and hence reducible to the actions and intentions of individual agents... The tendency, therefore, is for the basic locus of analysis in strategy-making to remain the individual' (ibid). In other terms, the first generation of strategy-as-practice did not break with the traditional actor-centred approach. To address this shortcoming, Chia and his co-authors embrace a coherent Heideggerian sensitivity (discussed here in Chapter 6) and offer an alternative view of what strategy is. From this perspective, strategizing is reconceptualized as stemming from a basic orientation that we all adopt in our daily commerce with the world and that he calls a 'dwelling' mode. The claim is that strategy emerges non-deliberately through everyday practical coping so that 'strategic outcomes do not presuppose deliberate prior planning or intention [and] secondly strategy is not some transcendent property that a priori unifies independently conceived actions and decisions, but is something immanent—it unfolds through everyday practical coping actions' (Chia and Holt 2008, p. 637). While a detailed discussion of this fascinating idea goes beyond the scope of the present discussion, it is clear that the adoption of a strong practice approach does much more than simply 'opening the black box of the firm and humanizing the field of strategic management' (Pettigrew *et al.* 2002: 12). Adhering to the strong programme provides, instead, a radically new way of thinking about strategy and strategy making which has far-reaching theoretical and practical consequences (see Sandberg and Tsoukas 2011 for a discussion).

While Chia and his colleagues build on the Heideggerian tradition, Samra-Fredericks (2005), who can also be considered as a representative of the strong programme, analyses strategy as practice by adopting a different yet coherent practice approach; i.e. ethnomethodology (discussed here in Chapters 5 and 7). Her focus is on how power is produced and reproduced in strategy-making processes. However, her work is not limited to registering that power is a significant element in the process or to observing that powerful actors have the upper-hand in the process. Instead, she proceeds analytically and provides substantial forensic evidence on how such power effects are constituted in the moment-to-moment discursive interaction among strategy makers. Among other things, her analysis uncovers in painstaking detail how power is reproduced through the collaborative construction of speaking prerogatives (who can say what and when) and how fleeting moments in conversation can have very lasting consequences.

8. The image is taken from Lynch (1993), p. 18. See Chapter 5 for a full discussion in its original context.

9. The rolling case study is made possible by the theoretical and methodological family resemblances between practice theories discussed in Chapter 8. It should not be used as a support for the functionalist idea that theories can be applied *post hoc* to data. The study of telemedicine was, in fact, conducted using multiple sensitivities and methods in the first place.

10. 'Exercises in Style' is of course the title of Raymond Queneau's masterpiece (Queneau 1981). In the book the author re-tells ninety-nine times the same simple story using each time a different style.

11. For further details on the research project and methodology please see Nicolini (2006; 2007; 2009b; 2011).

12. Garibaldi is a pseudonym. There is no such a city in Italy. There is a Porto Garibaldi, but this has nothing to do with the town where the study took place. Thanks to Maja Korica for suggesting using a real name rather than an abbreviation.

2 Praxis and Practice Theory: A Brief Historical Overview

In this chapter I will provide an overview of the history (and some may say pre-history) of practice theories. There are two good reasons for doing so. Firstly, as will become apparent in the rest of the book, many if not all contemporary theories build on the seminal work of Marx, Heidegger, and Wittgenstein. A short overview of their work and how they contribute to the current interest in practice theory is therefore in order. Secondly, this brief historical overview will help understand why authors such as Schatzki (2001) talk about a 'return' of practice. As I will try to show in this chapter, the demotion of practice is a constant characteristic of Western thought and it is for this reason that a focus on practice is still potentially subversive and innovative. I will start my account with a short discussion of the view on practice from two major founders of Western thought: Plato and Aristotle. Although I will only address them in brief, the discussion is important to illustrate what historical baggage a practice view has to lose in order to generate an alternative view of the world. So even if philosophy is not your thing, bear with me.

2.1 The legacy of Greek classical thought and the demotion of practice in the Western tradition

'Philosophy begins with Aristotle not with Socrates or Plato', Foucault once stated provocatively (cited in Flyvbjerg 2001, p. 110). As a founder of discursivity, in fact, Aristotle laid out most of the categories that during the Middle Ages were constituted as the basis of Western thought. What is less well known, however, is that there are at least two 'Aristotles' represented in the modern debate on praxis and theory. One is the villain of many a work in the pragmatist tradition, after the characterization proposed by Dewey (1929). Dewey considered Aristotle the father of metaphysics, the arch-enemy of modern science, and the nemesis of the idea that knowledge results from a process of active inquiry. According to this characterization, by introducing the idea that practice and theory are two distinct and unequal epistemic objects, Aristotle laid the foundation for the historical demise of practice in the Western tradition.

The other, less well-known Aristotle is the author of the *Nichomachean Ethics*, which established praxis as a separate form of knowing with its own logic and legitimacy, and which provided the basis for legitimating both. This second, less-popular (and dogmatic) interpretation of Aristotle, was highly influential on the development of the ideas of a host of modern authors including Heidegger, Foucault, and Bourdieu. My brief history of the notion of practice needs therefore to start with an outline of Aristotle's view on practice and theory, its Platonic origins, and its fate over the course of the centuries.

2.1.1 PLATO'S INTELLECTUALIST LEGACY

Most of the work of the classic Greek thinkers can be understood anthropologically as a quest for certainty. The aspiration was 'to make goodness of good human life safe from *tuche* (chance, luck, the unforeseeable) through the controlling power of reason' (Nussbaum 1986, p. 3. See also Dewey 1929, Ch.1; Detienne and Vernant 1974). Plato's response to this challenge was to search for stability in the hyper-world of pure forms and for a solution to human uncertainty in a life inspired by those principles. According to Plato, to the extent that all humans would use the knowledge of those principles not only to solve problems but also to formulate them, and as long as such an episteme would be based on eternal and non-context-dependent universals, *tuche* could be eradicated for good from human affairs. Every action would in fact be conceived as the application of general, calculable, precise, and truthful principles, while reference to universals, such as to the universal pure idea of 'good', would make it always possible to choose the best course of action. In this way, Plato established an intellectualistic prejudice at the very core of his philosophy and most of the Western tradition. This was the notion that good practice derives from the application of general and eternal principles.

Plato's extreme representational epistemology was meant to be not only an intellectual position, but also the foundation for a virtuous way of conducting one's life. In his later dialogues, and especially in the *Republic*,[1] Plato makes a strong case for contemplation as an epistemic position and asceticism as an existential choice. Plato believed that because needs, passions, and appetites are sources of instability and disorder, they need to be eliminated or repressed in the pursuit of truth and knowledge. As he wrote: 'the best life for human beings is the life of the philosopher, a life devoted to learning and the contemplation of truth' (Nussbaum 1986, p. 138). It is not surprising then to discover that Plato makes several disparaging comments about all practitioners, including applied mathematicians! His accusation was that they were driven by external needs and forces that polluted the type of knowledge to which they should aspire. By placing the source of stability literally out of reach and out of this world, as in the famous metaphor of the cave in Book VII of the *Republic*, Plato therefore creates at the same time a new metaphysics and epistemology, a new ethics, and a new social class of experts, the philosophers, whose job becomes that of contemplating true *episteme* and placing it at the foundation of human conduct. With Plato, philosophers established themselves as both contemplators of truth and legislators of rational conduct, as well as educators and moralists who were the main disseminators of such conduct. In this way, however, Plato effectively cast practice, materiality, and performativity beyond, or more precisely *below,* the scope of theory of knowledge and ethics. These aspects are necessary evils, so to speak, for the survival of humankind, but they should treated as such; necessary evils that ought to be ignored or even removed in the pursuit of true knowledge.

2.1.2 ARISTOTLE ON PRAXIS

Aristotle was for a long time Plato's preferred pupil and taught at his school for many years until the death of his teacher. Having been denied succession in leading Plato's Academy because he was a foreigner (he was born in Thrace), he founded his own school. The Lyceum, or Peripateta, soon became established as one of the most prominent schools of philosophy in ancient Greece. It is no surprise, then, that Aristotle's overall framework bears a significant resemblance to Plato's. Yet, as we shall see in a moment, his view on practice differs from that of his former employer in substantial ways.

We can start by noting that Aristotle articulates a view in which there is a multiplicity of incommensurable forms of knowledge. Sure enough, they are ranked in terms of status and there is never a doubt that for Aristotle epistemic science, the science of first principles, rests on a step above the other forms:

For Plato, too, was right . . . wisdom must plainly be the most finished of the forms of knowledge . . . wisdom must be intuitive reason combined with scientific knowledge— scientific knowledge of the highest objects which has received as it were its proper completion (Aristotle *Nicomachean Ethics* (*NE*), Book I, §4 and VI, §7).

Nevertheless, contrary to Plato's intellectualist views, all forms of knowledge have their own legitimacy, their own criteria of validity, and are valuable in the pursuit of human affairs:

we need not look for precision in all things alike, but in each class of things such precision as accords with the subject-matter, and so much as is appropriate to the inquiry (Aristotle *NE*, Book I, §4).

In many writings, and especially in his *Nicomachean Ethics*, Aristotle distinguishes between three kinds of knowing, three activities of the human mind or dispositions of the intellect: *episteme, phronesis,* and *techne. Episteme,* translated by Ross as 'scientific knowledge', is the apprehension of universal principles and essences arrived at through use of analytic rationality. Nothing new here, then. Unlike Plato, however, Aristotle takes into consideration two more ways of knowing and forms of wisdom: *phronesis,* usually translated as practical wisdom, and *techne,* close to our modern notion of art or skill. The aim of *phronesis* is to produce *praxis* or action informed by knowledgeable value-driven deliberations; the aim of *techne,* instrumental rationality, is *poiesis;* i.e. the creation or production of material or durable artefacts.

The difference between *techne/poiesis* and *phronesis/praxis* is not easily rendered in modern English, for the term *techne* is translated using terms such as 'craft', 'art', and even 'science'. These could all be equally used to describe the outcome *praxis.* Aristotle, however, went to great lengths to distinguish between the two for, as we shall see, they correspond to two different calls of life. To a certain extent one can think of the distinction between *praxis* and *poiesis* as that between the two English verbs 'doing' and 'making' (Lobkowicz 1967, p. 9). We 'do' sports, or business, or music, but we 'make' ships, houses, and statues. *Poiesis* refers then to actions and operations aimed at an end different from the making itself; it has to do with material creation and it is not fulfilled until it has reached its original aim: only it can stop without creating a sense of incompleteness. On the contrary, *praxis* refers to a doing in which the end is nothing else than 'doing things well' (*enpraxia*). Aristotle uses the example of the good flute player, who has achieved her aim regardless of when she stops. Although the example is partly misleading, for Aristotle explicitly defines figurative and material arts as a form of *poiesis,* it helps us to understand that, for the author, life, in all forms, is therefore a form of *praxis,* not of *poiesis.*[2] The term p*raxis,* however, is mostly reserved to describe moral conduct and political activity; that is, the *enpraxia* and fulfilment of the good Athenian citizen:

Practical wisdom is the quality of mind concerned with things just and noble and good for man . . . is concerned with things human and things about which it is possible to deliberate; . . . the work of the man of practical wisdom [is] to deliberate well, but no one deliberates about things invariable, nor about things which have not an end, and that a good that can be brought about by action. Nor is practical wisdom concerned with universals only—it must also recognise the particulars; for it is practical, and practice is concerned with particulars (Aristotle *NE*, Book VI, §8).

Phronesis, the state of mind or intellectual virtue that sustains *praxis,* has therefore to do with ethical action, value-driven deliberation with regards to practical action in the context of human affairs and especially the management of the polis.

By introducing such tripartition in the *Nicomachean Ethics,* Aristotle did two important things that had an enormous impact on the development of Western tradition.

First, he granted *praxis* the status of an independent, legitimate, and worthy form of knowledge, setting an important precedent for the establishment of human and social science as 'a science of the particular and contingent that inhabits the human world and doesn't attempt to rise above it' (Nussbaum 1986, p. 315). As we shall see, this constituted a fundamentally anti-Platonic take that would provide opportunities and ammunition for original thinkers throughout history to break away from the prevailing rationalistic tradition, as in the case of Francis Bacon, Nietzsche, and Heidegger, who all took non-traditional readings of Aristotle's work as their point of departure.

Second, he established the partial incommensurability between practice and theory, and the irreducibility of practical wisdom to theory. Aristotle uses a term that has disappeared from our Western discursivity to describe the mastery of practice: *phronesis*. *Phronesis*, tentatively translated here as 'practical wisdom', refers in fact to a non-inferential and non-deductive form of knowledge. It does not imply the application of universals, but instead, and to the contrary, uses rules as summaries and guides; it must be flexible, ready for surprise and suitable for improvisation. Its criteria of excellence are related to local contingencies and amount, *de facto*, to the abstraction of the deliberations of wise men (Nussbaum 1986, p. 395). *Praxis* cannot even in principle be adequately captured in a system of universal rules—and hence cannot be the subject of *episteme*, because it has to do with mutability, indeterminacy, and particulars. Yet *phronesis* counts as legitimate and teachable knowledge and allows the pursuit of happiness; that is, the fulfillment of the end of humans and the achievement of a 'complete life'—albeit in a form that is different from that granted by the contemplative life of philosophers.

A word of caution must be added at this point, in order not to push to excess this possible sympathetic reading of the ancient master according to a post-critical sensitivity. Aristotle, in fact, also strongly endorsed a distinction between forms of knowledge, sanctioning both ideologically and sociologically the fact that material activity ('real-time practice') and 'real knowledge' lay at opposite ends of a continuum. In so doing, he eradicated materiality and performativity from the horizon of philosophers and positioned them outside the realm of 'knowledge', a place where they remained until the emergence of different forms of materialism in the nineteenth-century. While recognizing its importance for the survival of the human species, Aristotle in fact makes clear that poietic knowledge, that is *techne*, is little more than accumulated experience based on 'past making', transmitted to newcomers and articulated enough to be useful to further making. As such, in spite of his respect for great artists and artistic productions, a life of *techne* is not worth living, is not a call of life that would lead to the fulfillment of human nature and hence to happiness. Aristotle's position can partly be understood against the social background of the Greek *polis*. In the *polis*, all manual labour, from mining to housework, was carried out by slaves who formed half of the population.

This was hardly something that an educated Greek would consider as a call of life leading to happiness. Merchants and retailers were usually foreigners who had to pay a special tax to remain free people. Artisans, some of whom were great artists, were held in high repute but still considered second-class citizens because they were dependent upon their work for income and survival; they couldn't fully participate in the intense and time-consuming political life of the *polis*—perceived by Aristotle and many others as the mark of a 'complete' citizen. Freedom in the *polis* came with a price; that is, the involvement in a number of compulsory, non-remunerated public assignments (juryman, full-time magistrate, member of the Senate and other bodies) carrying severe punishment for those who failed to fulfill their duties. Freedom from material need and political freedom therefore went hand-in-hand for citizens of the *polis*. It is no surprise then that for Aristotle *phronesis* and *praxis* are markedly opposed to instrumental and material knowledge that he associated with a life of mere subsistence

Whatever the reason, however, the fact remains that what was originally for Aristotle a conflict between philosophy and politics as activities and ways of living, later became, in the Western tradition, an opposition between theoretical thought and almost any kind of human activity—productive activity in particular (Lobkowicz 1967, p. 18). It was in fact the latter interpretation of Aristotle which prevailed over the centuries.

2.2 The demotion of practice in the Western tradition

Within a couple of centuries of his death, the political dimension of ethics, and the status and legitimacy that Aristotle had granted to *praxis* were forgotten and replaced with an idea of knowledge and virtue as only the result of contemplative life. This position became part of the Christian tradition and a root of the Western tradition. Those who carry out a life of contemplation are already in contact with the divine while the many others who live a life of practice should expect 'contemplation' as the ultimate reward in the afterlife. So although Christianity valued *vita activa,* a life devoted to charitable acts as a path towards perfection, such a walk of life was still defined in terms of divine perfection as originally suggested by Plato. The reinterpretation of Aristotle in a Platonic or neoplatonic register meant that the notion that theoretical, ethical, and political practical wisdom are radically different was eventually displaced by the notion that *praxis* is simply the practical application of a-practical, purely theoretical insights. This attitude to practice was taken up by the great modernist thinkers of the seventeenth and eighteenth centuries. As noted by Lobkowicz (1967, p. 91), Descartes' notion of science is not much more 'pragmatic' than that of the ancient Greeks. The same applies to other founders of modern science, from Galileo and Newton to Kant; although they treated the Aristotelian method with scorn, the great rationalist thinkers adhered to the basic spirit of the Greeks in that they considered a theoretical discovery as an end in itself which is free of the need for justification by useful results. Moreover, just as in the Platonic and neoplatonic traditions the discovery of a transcendent object of contemplation had for centuries resulted in a degradation of practical wisdom, so in the eighteenth century, the ideal of a natural world completely explicable by eternal laws of geometry and mathematics overshadowed the long-forgotten original spirit of Aristotle.

In conclusion, one could characterize the history of the European intellectual tradition as a process of practical displacement, deferral, and abatement of practice. This process started early and ran like an underground river, connecting traditions of thought and intellectual identities that were in many ways different and often opposed to each other. It was not until Marx, Nietzsche, and the twentieth century that Aristotle's original hierarchy could be rediscovered and inverted, with practice becoming the ontological principle of being in the world.

2.3 The rediscovery of practice: Marx, Heidegger, and Wittgenstein

2.3.1 MARX

Marx represents a fundamental figure in our brief history of the concept of practice. He was, in fact, one of the first authors to seriously challenge the entrenched and institutionalized demotion of practice described in the previous section. One enduring legacy of Marx's work is the successful attempt to challenge centuries of Western rationalist and mentalist tradition, and to legitimate real activity, what 'sensuous' people actually do in their everyday life, as an object of consideration and as an explanatory category in social sciences. As Marx stated in The *German Ideology*:

In direct contrast to German philosophy which descends from heaven to earth, here we ascend from earth to heaven. That is to say, we do not set out from what men say, imagine, conceive, nor from men as narrated, thought of, imagined, conceived, in order to arrive at men in the flesh. We set out from real, active men, and on the basis of their real life-process we demonstrate the development of the ideological reflexes and echoes of this life-process ... men, developing their material production and their material intercourse, alter, along with this their real existence, their thinking and the products of their thinking. Life is not determined by consciousness, but consciousness by life ... Where speculation ends—in real life—there real, positive science begins: the representation of the practical activity, of the practical process of development of men (Marx 1845, Ch. 1a).

The passage is of historical importance because Marx's version of materialism granted access to the citadel of science to a fundamental aspect of human existence, *praxis,* that for centuries had been previously simply ignored.

Marx, of course, was by no means the first materialist. Materialism, the view that all facts (including facts about the human mind, and will, and the course of human history) are causally dependent upon physical processes, or even reducible to them, has a long tradition. Nevertheless, a paradoxical characteristic of almost all pre-Marxian tradition was that most materialists still thought of humans as simply thinking creatures. This tendency to reduce people to their thinking functions remained constant until Marx's time and it became the target of forceful criticism in his famous *Theses on Feuerbach.* Ludwig Feuerbach, a former friend and colleague of Marx, had developed a materialist criticism of religion based on a radical interpretation of Hegel's notion of alienation. In his *Essence of Christianity*, published in 1844, Feuerbach claimed that nothing exists outside nature and man, and that religion is the ultimate form of deception in which mankind reflects and fantasizes its own essence. However, when describing such essence, Feuerbach reverted to an old model in which knowledge was produced only in situations of need and resulted from the brain receiving impressions from the external world.

In the *Theses*, Marx forcefully rejected this form of materialism and argued that while Hegel had abstracted the rational categories he believed were common to all men, Feuerbach had gone in the opposite direction, reverting to a form of passive empiricism in which thinking was reduced to receiving impressions from objects already in the external world. In other words, while Hegel had derived life from thought, Feuerbach had derived thought from the world. In so doing, said Marx, they both made the same mistake, in that they first abstracted thinking from other human activities and then asked how thought so conceived was related to the world (Kitching 1988, p. 26).

For Marx, these positions were both untenable because they failed to recognize that thought and world are always connected through human activity and therefore cannot be separated: on the one hand, man is always an actor and a producer; on the other hand, thinking is only one of the things people do, together with running, fighting, making love, and so on. The object of inquiry for philosophers (and what we would today call social scientists) should therefore be *praxis* intended as what men say, imagine, conceive, and produce *and* think while attempting to carry out these activities.

Marx never provided a definition of *praxis* in his writings, and in spite of the centrality of the notion in his thought, the term is used sparingly and mostly in early works. One reason for this is that from the late 1840s and the shifting of Marx's interest to political economic issues, he started to use the term 'production' to cover all human material practices. However, as Lobkowicz notes, it is possible to gather from early and late works of the German philosopher that by *praxis* he meant a 'relatively homogeneous human activity which can take many forms and can range from bodily labour of the most humble sort to political revolutions' (Lobkowicz 1967, p. 419).

By referring to *praxis* as any activity of men and women which aims to transform the world, and by locating in this characteristic the essence of mankind, Marx created a new set of categories and theoretical sensitivities in the study of human phenomena.

In the first place, Marx introduced the idea that to understand human action one needs to focus on the whole social and historical context of that action. Only by considering the concrete totality of interconnected activities in which socially productive activities are the point of departure can one grasp the meaning of human action. Because productive actions are inherently social, this also means that to grasp meaning and intelligibility, one has to understand the social and historical context in which they take place. As he wrote:

Activity and mind are social in their content as well as in their origins; they are social activity and social mind (*Early Writings*, p. 157).

In this way, Marx introduced a historical *and* social element in the materialist tradition; such a tenet, however, also has the effect of excluding *a priori* any form of strict determinism in human conduct, including the economic determinism imputed by later Marxist scholars. As Marx in fact said, 'circumstances make men (sic) just as much as men make circumstances' (Marx 1845, Ch. 1B § 7); it follows that in order to understand *praxis* fully, one needs to encompass both aspects within the same explanations without according priority to one aspect over the other. As some authors note, this allowed Marx to escape the necessity of taking sides in the subjectivist/objectivist dispute: for Marx, it was impossible to understand actions or ideas apart from their relationship to a system of social practice. It follows that, in Kitching's words, 'questions such as "is [it] the way in which people produce which determines how they think?" or "is [it] the way in which they think which determines how they produce?"' are questions unworthy of an answer because they are senseless. Senseless in that they involve a separation of two 'things' (so that one 'thing' can determine the other 'thing') that are just different forms or expressions of human activity (Kitching 1988, p. 28).

Another significant implication of the centrality of *praxis* is that mind is not conceived as a separate entity and actions are not conceived as the application 'in practice' of mental or transcendental categories. Mind is not only social, as we saw above, but it manifests itself as a property of action in human conduct.

Practice therefore carries meaning 'in practice' without requiring the intervention of the sort of theoretical paraphernalia (universals, categories of pure reason, spirit) which idealists of all times had to introduce to explain anthropological and psychological phenomena:

[the various aspects of the law] assert themselves without entering the consciousness of the participants and can themselves be abstracted from daily practice only through laborious, theoretical investigation (Engels, Supplement to *Das Kapital*, Vol. 3, Introduction, p. 1).

This in turn modifies the status and role of theory (and science), and its relation to *praxis*. In the first place, Marx, in open polemics with his idealist predecessors, clearly stated that one cannot know the world by observing it from an armchair and speculation is not a sufficient basis for developing valid and reliable knowledge. As Marx put it in the *Theses*, the question of truth cannot be solved in theory because this is a practical question: 'man must prove the truth—i.e. the reality, power and the this sidedness of his thinking in practice' (Thesis II). This allows a different, less politically activist-oriented interpretation of the last and highly-contested of the *Theses* in which Marx asserted that 'the philosophers have only interpreted the world in various ways; the point is to change it' (Thesis XI). While cohorts of Marxist scholars have interpreted this mainly as an encouragement to intellectuals to become part of the communist revolutionary movement, one can also interpret it as a broader epistemological proposition; i.e. the need to engage practically as well as cognitively with phenomena in order to understand them. This prescription was rarely adopted within the Marxian tradition, which did not overly focus on the production of empirical data and fieldwork and, apart from some notable exceptions, pursued a style of disengaged and theoretical research that was alarmingly traditional in character.

Second, Marx's notion of the unity of thinking and activity makes it possible to conceive all knowing as a form of practical mastery, and theory as an instrument in the service of such practical wisdom. In *The German Ideology*, Marx refers several times to theories as instruments and weapons; he makes clear that the aim of science is not that of producing theoretical knowledge but more of obtaining practical mastery of the world in order to satisfy the practical needs of mankind. For Marx, however, the ultimate aim of science was not to transcend everyday life, considered as a despicable state by many of his predecessors (for example, only a few years earlier Feuerbach had called everyday *praxis* a 'dirty Judaic manifestation'). As Andrew put it, Marx's vision of the intellectual enterprise was 'not only to relieve the estate of man but also to ennoble man within that estate' (Andrew 1975, p. 308). This, however, also appears to adhere to the Baconian dictum that knowledge is power and in fact, Marx explicitly stated that science does not only disclose what is observed but reveals as well the needs and power of the observer. While rejecting the idea of science as a disinterested reflection, Marx also denounced the power game concealed behind the idea, or rather the ideology of a pure, disinterested, and detached theory. The elevation of the value of theory and contemplation are in fact an expression of the will of intellectuals to preserve their position among the ruling class; as such, the priority of theory is based on material reasons and the hierarchy between the two is the result of a fraud.

Marx's conception of science as a mode of the practical therefore not only introduced a view of the world as a place to be changed as opposed to being contemplated, but also constituted a fundamental departure from the whole Western tradition since Aristotle. It also sanctioned the inherently political nature of human action. Marx inaugurated a tradition that invites us to look at real-time practices in terms of the inequalities and domination that they embody and perpetuate, a way of conceiving action as what people do seen from a particular angle, the political one.

In conclusion, using again Foucault's expression, one can say that Marx established a new domain of discourse, opening up the possibility for a new, and in many ways revolutionary way of thinking *praxis*. Marx introduced a notion of a human being as a corporeal being, mind as a feature of conduct and a feature of action, and human knowledge as the result of an active and mutually determined interaction between a social subject and the object that changed forever the Western horizon of what is thinkable. We may add that this was achieved by subverting, and in many ways turning upside down, the Aristotelian tripartition discussed above. Marx's approach, in effect, recovers the legitimacy of practice for the Western tradition by giving it primacy over *phronesis* and *theoria* and collapsing these two into an instrument in support of the former.

2.3.2 NIETZSCHE, HEIDEGGER, AND THE PRIMACY OF PRACTICE IN THE PHENOMENOLOGICAL TRADITION

Together with Marxism, phenomenology constituted a second fundamental Western intellectual tradition that contributed to the rediscovery and re-evaluation of the role and importance of everyday practice. As will become apparent in the following chapters, many modern practice theories and approaches are rooted either in the Marxist or the phenomenological tradition—or in a combination of the two. The interest of phenomenology in everyday life began even before phenomenology itself. As Edward Andrew has argued extensively, the notion of a primordial unity of theory and practice was already present in the work of Friedrich Nietzsche, commonly recognized as one of the main inspirations for the phenomenological movement (Andrew 1975). Nietzsche posited at the centre of the activity of philosophy a 'human, all-too human subject' that is not only a thinking subject but an initiator of action and a centre of feeling. According to Macquarrie (1972), this whole spectrum of existence, known directly and concretely in the very act of existing, constituted the main concerns of the phenomenological and existential tradition, especially that of Heidegger, whose main concern was to observe and recount a subject who is present in the whole range of her existing.

This position has been propounded more recently by Blattner (2000), who argued that Heidegger's project to rebuild the Western tradition on the ruins of Cartesian metaphysics is firmly rooted in what he calls the 'primacy of practice'. Blattner is the latest of a growing number of scholars who have proposed a similar approach to the German philosopher, following the path of Hubert L. Dreyfus, who remains the foremost exponent of this way of reading Heidegger (Dreyfus 1991, see also Guignon 1983; Okrent 1988).

According to Heidegger's 'everydayness', the basic ontological dimension of our being in the world is, in fact, meaningfully structured by a texture of social and material practices that remain unthought of as such, but that we more or less share in common.

It is worth recalling that the point of departure of Heidegger's reflections is the original unity and relatively unproblematic nature of human existence in the course of worldly activity. Heidegger's (1929) well-known 'hammering' example illuminates clearly in what sense the author believes that in our daily practice we do not experience tools and usable things in isolation (a chair, a screen, a steering wheel) as much as a seamless web of references between objects (a room, an office, a car). Consider a carpenter hammering a nail into a piece of wood. In the carpenter's practical activity, the hammer does not exist as an object with given properties. It is as much a part of his world as the arm with which he wields it. The hammer belongs to the environment and can be unthinkingly used by the carpenter. The carpenter does not need to 'think a hammer' in order to drive in a nail. His or her capacity to act depends upon the familiarity with the act of hammering. His/her use of the practical item 'hammer' is its significance to him/her in the setting 'hammering' and 'carpentry'. When the carpenter is unimpeded in his/her hammering, the hammer with its properties does not exist as an entity: in the usable environment, the understanding of situations is pre-reflexive activity, and the world of objects thus becomes 'simply present' (*Vorhanden*).

The hammer as such acquires a separate 'existence' only when it breaks or is lost: that is, when its unreflective use becomes problematic. For reflexive, investigative, theoretical knowledge to come into play, something previously usable must become unusable. This breakdown only occurs when the carpenter has already understood the hammer in practice. Only when a 'non-usability' situation occurs will the carpenter's activity of 'hammering' take on a problematic form. Heidegger makes it clear that the invisibility of this web of references is a fundamental condition for the possibility of tools to work as such. It is only when the 'usable' resists my project that it emerges from the background as something simply present because, as the German author says, the modes of surprise, inappropriateness, and irrelevance have the effect of revealing the characteristic of the simple presence of objects. A breakdown therefore makes us experience a tool as unusable and hence a simple 'object'; it also reveals for a short period all the web of deferments that connected it with the rest of the 'usables', that everyday practice had always used. In other words, it is only as a consequence of a breakdown that the world announces itself to us as such; that is in the form of something that was already there, something that was already open to us from the beginning and with which we were already intimate but that was not us. For Heidegger, therefore, things always appear to us as imbued with meaning with respect to our life and our aims. His aim was therefore to deepen our understanding of the inner structure of this normality and the different modes in which it revealed itself, as well as to show that an unhampered dealing with the world is both the condition for existence as well as the ultimate source of human delusion.

Dreyfus's (1991) view is that this everydayness is ontologically comparable to a totality of background coping strategies. One's everyday world is meaningfully structured by these practices which can remain untaught and yet which we more or less share in common. Practice therefore implies an individual's social and historical relation to the world, where one's own concrete practices are themselves set up and made meaningful within this wider background system of intelligibility. Mundane everydayness thus becomes the received, yet necessarily indeterminate, cultural manifold within which we are all immersed, and which meaningfully discloses our world by way of our own un-theorized, everyday practical coping strategies. Paraphrasing Heidegger, who limited the use of this expression to language—the usable par excellence—one could say that, for Dreyfus, practice is in a very sense 'the house of being'.

This has some far-reaching consequences in that our primary relation to the world is not by way of meaningful representations but rather through practical activity and its common understanding. According to Dreyfus, 'Heidegger shows that this subject/object epistemology presupposes a background of everyday practices into which we are socialised but that we do not represent in our minds' (Dreyfus 1991, p. 3). Practice is therefore 'prior' to representation. Everydayness is always already a holistic affair and is experience as gestalt; i.e. as a meaningful whole. This meaningful context, the totality of one's practices or coping strategies, is a background totality that in some way escapes representation. For Dreyfus, then, Heidegger opened first the possibility that 'there are only skills and practices' against the notion that we make sense of the world by way of a system of beliefs (1991, p. 22). Furthermore, such an indeterminate context of skills and practices is thoroughly historical, one's own coping strategies are rooted in their common usage and there can be no absolute break with tradition, a condition that reinforces the inherent non-representability of 'significance'.

Besides positing practice as the basis for explaining intelligibility and rationality, in *Being and Time* Heidegger offers some other fundamental insights into the nature of practice.

In the first place, one may note that Heidegger's notion of practice is fundamentally super-individual, although not properly 'social'. Being in the world, as we said before, is always a being with others: *Dasein* (the condition of being in the world) is by definition and originally *mit-Dasein*: we always and already attend worldly matters together with (*mit*) other beings. This implies that we find ourselves within a given, collectively sustained horizon of intelligibility and action that we can bring to awareness and hence transcend, but never exit.

A second important point is that, unlike many of his predecessors, Heidegger does not consider being in the world from a solely 'cold' mental perspective, and in fact, emphasizes that being in the world is always characterized by an 'affective tone'. In their average condition, humans are always operating within an horizon of projection and concerns [*Besorgen*]; that is, they are absorbed and caught up with things to do and achieve; it is within this active 'existential condition' that they encounter the world of objects and other beings and it is this existential condition that constitutes the background of every mode of being. Accordingly, other beings and things are not only understood in a conceptual sense, they are also always experienced emotionally. Emotions, therefore, are not mere ornaments of pure reason; they are both constitutive of and instrumental in our potential to transcend our averageness. It follows that being in the world, and participating in the caring practices that constitute the texture of our everydayness, is not the being of a disinterested pure subject. We cannot be disinterested spectators of things and meanings because, as Vattimo so beautifully puts it, our life projects and our caring practices are always and ultimately 'biased' (Vattimo 1971).

Third, Heidegger brings to the fore the centrality of the temporal dimension of practices. Against the traditional notion of time as a sequence of 'nows' or as the perception of something outside of us, Heidegger, in fact, counterposes an elaborate theory of time as a definitional and primitive way of being in the world. Just as *Dasein* does not fall into the world by accident, but always 'has' the world in its essential structure, *Dasein* has its time. The fact that *Dasein* exists in time is only part of its mode of being, since *Dasein's* capability to reckon with time presupposes a more primordial relation to time. An entity within time, e.g. a stone, may also be in time, but it never exists temporally the way *Dasein* does. The concept of within-time-ness thus complements that of caring and expresses how the world-time is encountered primarily and usually in everydayness: as the temporal attribute of worldly beings which makes them accessible as 'being in time'. Hence, time is not an objective trait of the world or a subjective projection of consciousness onto the world as much as it is a primary and original dimension of being that the encounter with death reveals to have already and always been there. That is to say, the traditional concept of time itself presupposes temporality. It belongs to, and springs from, the temporal being of *Dasein*.

Finally, it must be added that starting with *Being and Time* and throughout his career Heidegger moved towards granting a primacy of one type of practice—discursive—over all others. Although the author does not use the term 'discursive' (which has its origin in the Wittgensteinian tradition discussed below), in *Being and Time* Heidegger discusses language in the context of understanding and instrumentality. It is through signs and discursive practices that we dispose of the world and therefore we are in the world. Being in a world in a comprehensive and competent way entails being in a world in which we are familiar with a totality of meanings; ready-to-handedness, in other words, is not simply knowing how to use things as much as living in a world that makes practical sense. Later in his career Heidegger affirmed that language is the 'house of being', arguing that although we have language at our disposal in a different way we are also *at the disposal* of our language. Language and language practices are therefore a critical aspect of everydayness, and only by questioning our language practices can we open a clearing through which we can experience potentially different ways of experiencing and acting in the world.

Heidegger was extremely influential on most of the contemporary authors that contributed to what Schatzki (2001) calls the 'practice turn' in contemporary theory to be discussed in the next sections, from Michel Foucault (who once said that his entire philosophical development was determined by his reading of Heidegger: see Dreyfus and Rabinow 1993), to Pierre Bourdieu, Schatzki, and many others.

Although Heidegger did not develop a coherent theory of practice, by reversing the Cartesian tradition and making the individual subject dependent on a web of social practices, he made it possible for others to develop one. As we shall see, however, many contemporary practice theorists combine the insights derived from Heidegger with those drawn from the work of another great founder of discursivity: Ludwig Wittgenstein.

2.3.3 WITTGENSTEIN: INTELLIGIBILITY AS PRACTICE

Wittgenstein has left us with some very significant reflections on the notion of practice which have informed the work of some of the most interesting voices in contemporary practice thinking.

Wittgenstein's belief in the primacy of practice is strictly related to the development of his far-reaching view on language and meaning, which is based on the notion of human agents as active and engaged beings who use language as a fundamental resource to get by in their everyday activities.

One of the most lapidary expressions of this position is to be found in an oft-quoted late fragment in which the author builds on a statement from Goethe's *Faust*:

> The origin and the primitive form of the language game is a reaction. Only from this can more complicated forms develop. Language—I want to say—is a refinement, 'Im Anfang war die Tat' [in the beginning was the deed]' (Wittgenstein 1980, p. 31).

The fundamental condition of human beings is one of reactions to our surroundings and other beings within the context of living activities. These actions and reactions constitute the necessary background in relation to which all of what we do makes sense, a background that is always there even though, in most cases, it is pre-reflective and unacknowledged. According to Shotter (1997, p. 225) this has three important consequences.

First, for Wittgenstein to make sense of why we act, we have to look around us, not within us. The meaning of an act, just as much as the meaning of words, is in fact established in the practical context in which it appears. Wittgenstein, for example, notes that interpreting a sign is something that does not necessarily require a conscious, intellectual activity:

> there is a way of grasping a rule which is not an *interpretation*; but which is exhibited in what we call 'obeying a rule' and going against it' in actual cases (Wittgenstein 1953, No. 201).

Intellectual representational interpretation and the capacity to grasp meaning are clearly uncoupled here, and there is scope for affirming that it is practice that determines the meaning over and beyond the form of disengaged interpretation the author seems to have in mind.

Second, for Wittgenstein, the texture of practices that constitutes the unarticulated background of our sense-making is not a static repository as much as a living part of our dealing with the world to which we turn constantly in order to proceed in our daily activities (Shotter and Katz 1996). Above all, such background is not to be perceived in terms of an ineffable 'culture' as much as it is in terms of effective practices. Wittgenstein makes this aspect quite clear in his extensive discussion of rules and rule following.

Rules figure significantly in Wittgenstein's work. As Johannessen (1996) has sensibly noted, such an interest may seem alarmingly traditional. Yet in Wittgenstein's hands, rules become one of the clearer points of departure from the rationalist and representationalist tradition. In fact, in emphasizing rules, Wittgenstein appears to have three main aims: first, to make us see the 'outward-ness' of all our concepts; second, to secure the possibility of mistakes and misuses. The two together allow the author to discard the notion of a private idiom and support the notion of language as a fundamentally collective process: the user of a private idiom should decide each time whether a term is used in the same way as before, and could never know for sure if she is right or wrong. Each instance would be unrelated to the previous ones, and there would be no order in time, and hence no language. Accordingly, the decision to follow or not to follow a rule rests on, and testifies to, the inherent social dimension of language and action discussed above (Johannessen 1996, pp. 286–288). According to Wittgenstein, attempting to follow a rule solely on the basis of a set of explanations (e.g. how to follow a street signal) would raise the possibility of misunderstanding: should I look at the shape, at the text, or at the position of the sign on the road? No matter how detailed the explanation, there would always be further opportunities for misunderstandings that would lead to an infinite regress. However, this runs against our experience and against the fact that we can and do learn how to follow road signs. This is because the understanding of how to follow a rule is always against the background of what is taken-for-granted:

Obeying a rule is a practice...When I obey a rule I do not choose. I obey the rule blindly (Wittgenstein 1953, Nos. 217 and 219).

Through the notion of practice, then, Wittgenstein draws our attention to the untenability of the rationalist programme of 'deciding before acting', and emphasizes the unarticulated nature of the basis of our understanding. As Johannessen (1981, 1996) points out, the concept of practice establishes a bridge between rule following and regular ways of action, and hence can be looked upon as the primary thing. At the same time, however, such practice cannot be fully articulated for it constitutes the 'inherited background against which I distinguish between true and false' (Wittgenstein 1969, No. 95). Nor can this practice be the object of formal instruction: it can only be grasped through *hints, tips,* and *examples* and at the end 'it must speak for itself" (ibid.). There is a limit to our language, but not to our communication. That some of this knowledge is pre-reflective simply means that part of our knowing is expressed and embodied in the form of a practical and unreflective grasp of the surrounding world:

Much of our intelligent action in the world, sensitive as it usually is to our situation and goals, is carried on unformulated. It flows from an understanding that is largely unarticulated...It is always there, whereas we sometimes frame representations and sometimes do not...and the representations we do make are only comprehensible against the background provided by this unarticulated understanding (Taylor 1995, p. 170).

Third and finally, for Wittgenstein practices are also constitutive of the criteria of fitness of our concepts and provide us with solid criteria of truth. As we have seen in the case of rules, we can always find out in practice whether our interpretation of the rule is right or wrong. The fact that rules and meaning are grounded in social practices (or customs or institutions as Wittgenstein on occasion calls them) makes them all the more objective because they are subject to public scrutiny. Accordingly, the capacity to go on with our activity is a sure test of fitness of our understanding: 'understanding is like knowing how to go on' (Wittgenstein 1981, No. 875).

In summary, Wittgenstein develops his non-representational and non-rationalist perspective on meaning and language by developing the notion of practice and practical understanding. For him, meaning (and mind) cannot be properly conceived of as properties of individual consciousness, and instead should be conceived relationally as the result of the practical activity of sensuous and engaged agents. Language and world are interwoven through a huge manifold of interrelated practices (Johannessen 1981; Schatzki 1996). In this way, Wittgenstein's work provides some positive elements for the development of what we may call a Wittgenstenian perspective on practice (see Chapter 7). According to Johannessen (1981, 1996), such a perspective attracts our attention to the fact that:

- Practices are a given in human life; they are the 'regular ways of acting' that articulate the characteristics of our forms of life.
- Practices have a day-to-day performance dimension as well as a long-term aspect. They imply an element of training and exercise and, similar to traditions and customs, they are something to which people find themselves conforming. They are therefore just carried out and generally require no reasons to justify them. In other words, at some point, we 'follow rules blindly' and 'practice has to speak for itself'.
- Practices in their active and sensuous dimension play a central role in constituting signs as meaningful vehicles of human communication and hence,
- Practices constitute the bedrock of sociability.
- Practices indicate the fundamental contextual, albeit not arbitrary, character of sense-making. One and the same sentence can, in different contexts, express a quite different thing, although we cannot freely choose its meaning.

Practices are indicative of the inter-subjective and social character of human language as well as of the essentially practical character of basic forms of human knowledge. Wittgenstein's attention is mainly focused on linguistic practices, but he never denied that the same argument may hold for other forms of knowledge.

2.3.4 THE RETURN OF PRACTICE IN CONTEMPORARY SOCIAL THOUGHT

Toward the end of the 1970s the three traditions briefly surveyed above, the Marxist tradition, the Heideggerian tradition, and the legacy of the work of

Wittgenstein, conjured up a clearing in social theory that finally allowed practice to be rescued from its historical demotion and return powerfully to the centre of discussion. In the seminal words of Sherry Ortner, written at the beginning of the 1980s:

for the last several years there has been growing interest in analysis focused through one or another of a bundle of interrelated terms: practice, praxis, action, interaction, activity, experience, performance. A second, and closely related, bundle of terms focuses on the doer of all that doing: agent, actor, person, self, individual, subject (1984, p. 149).

It would be a mistake, of course, to limit responsibility for this major turn of social theory to the three above-mentioned traditions. In fact, particularly in the USA, this emerging sensitivity was built upon the strong traditions of pragmatism and symbolic interactionsim that had kept alive the regard for action and interaction during the period in which European thinkers had been seduced by all forms of functionalism and structuralism. As Hiley and colleagues aptly put it, ' ... philosophy's interpretive turn is ... a practical turn, one that insists on the philosophical centrality of practice ... In the Continental tradition, this practico-interpretive turn is identified as philosophical hermeneutics, and in Anglo-American philosophy it sees itself as a renewal of pragmatism' (Hiley *et al.* 1991 p. 11). However, as noted by several authors (see e.g. Ortner 1984; Giddens 1984; Reckwitz 2002), the symbolic interactionist tradition, in its attempt to oppose the dominant Parsonian functionalist approach, its obsession with the influence of 'the system', and its interpretation of action as the enactment of rules, often ended up making the opposite mistake; that is, underestimating the importance and influence that institutional order has on what people do and don't do, and how they do it. The story of course, could be told differently. One may say that the so-called 'practice turn' has not been notable within North American social thought simply because an attention to practice and doing has always been very much present. This is thanks to the legacy of the pragmatist tradition among philosophers and social scientists, especially through the work of the so-called Chicago School of R. Park, W. I. Thomas, H. Blumer, and A. Strauss. In this sense, my work should probably be recast as an attempt to make a Continental history of the concept of practice. Be that as it may, one distinctive aspect of the born-again (Continental) practice-oriented sensitivity is that authors within this community of discourse have taken the issue of the system very seriously. However, instead of taking the system as a given to be explained, (*the* major epistemological fallacy of all functionalisms) it expresses an urgent need to understand from where such systems and institutions originate—how these enduring features of our daily 'being in the world' are produced, kept in place, and reproduced.

According to Ortner (1984) the return of practice to sociology, anthropology, literary theory, and other fields of social science, meant that the focus of debate turned toward a set of new issues or traditional issues seen in a new light, namely:

- *The relationship(s) between human action and a different phenomenon called 'the system'.* The new practice-oriented sensitivity meant that this traditional issue is treated in a novel way in the sense that the relationships and the determination can go either way; that is, the system has an impact on practices *and* practices have an impact on the system. In fact, as we shall see in a moment when discussing the work of Giddens, for many authors the two are inextricably linked and can be understood as two ways of looking at the same phenomenon. Seeing the system as instantiated by practices implies, moreover, that it cannot be broken into units or levels. The system is in fact a 'relatively seamless whole' (Ortner 1984, p. 148) in which, however, not all dimensions and practices have the same significance: 'at the core of the system are the specific realities of asymmetry, inequality and domination' (ibid.) Therefore, unlike, for example, in the symbolic interactionist tradition, practices always have political implications so that the study of practice is after all the study of all forms of human action, but from a particular political-angle (ibid.).
- *What people actually do.* Our attention is drawn towards understanding how and under what conditions action is actually carried out. The object of inquiry becomes the capacity of humans to perform actions in a competent way, the temporal organization of such action, and the resources that make this possible. Nowhere is this more visible that in the work of Harold Garfinkel (1967) who took as the main topic for his investigations the study of practical reason and practical reasoning and the accomplishment of practical tasks in specific and 'real' situations, court rooms, police stations, and social science institutions.
- *The role of the agent in the process of production and reproduction.* One of the main attractions of the emerging practice approach was the possibility to make room for both an informed and intelligible agent and an organized context for action that constitutes a field of possibilities and impossibilities for the doing of that agent. Against the excesses of methodological individualism and the (premature) 'death of the individual' announced by French structuralists, practice theory opens the possibility of making sense of individuals as the main 'carriers' of the system. As Giddens put it: 'the pressing task facing social theory today is not to further the conceptual elimination of the subject, but on the contrary to promote a recovery of the subject without lapsing into subjectivism. Such recovery, I wish to argue, involves a grasp of what cannot be said (or thought) as practice' (1979, p. 44). Practice theory therefore tended to dissolve the distinction between

micro and macro, and to institute continuities that help explain both how the 'system' can be reproduced in practice and, at the same time, how practice can become the locus of variation, innovation, and change.

The practice turn in social theory, as Schatzki (2001) called this phenomenon when writing almost two decades after Sherry Ortner, influenced all strands of social science in at least three main ways: altering the perception of what constituted 'central problems in social theory', generating new areas of interest, and, finally, legitimizing marginal research interests and communities. Among others, two authors in particular came to represent this practice turn in contemporary theory: Anthony Giddens and Pierre Bourdieu. Together they constitute the main representatives of what has become known as modern praxeology, to which I now turn.

▨ NOTES

1. 'In the Republic Plato argues that the best life for human beings is the life of the philosopher, a life devoted to learning and the contemplation of truth. The Republic also argues that the best life is a life "ruled" by reason, in which reason evaluates, ranks, and orders alternative pursuits (Nussbaum 1986, p. 138).
2. One notes that a poietic or praxis approach correspond to two deeply different paradigmatic perspectives on the organization phenomenon, one focused on organizations as entities set up to generating some output, as e.g. in the open systems tradition, the other one interested to explore organizations as entities that once established aim at self-perpetuation by any means, of which producing an output is just one. For an in-depth and comprehensive discussion see Eikeland (2008).

3 Praxeology and the Work of Giddens and Bourdieu

There is probably no more fitting place for starting our investigation into the concept of practice in contemporary social and organisational theory than the work of Anthony Giddens and Pierre Bourdieu. These two leading figures of contemporary social theory have developed a programme of research, sometimes referred to as 'social praxeology',[1] which is aimed at elaborating on the basic idea that social life is a contingent and ever-changing texture of human practices. As I shall show in the following sections, both authors agree, although with different nuances, that most of the ordered features of our daily experiences, including seemingly persistent phenomena such as institutions, power relations, social boundaries, and constraints, are to be understood as effects of the structures and relations among practices. The result therefore is that practices ordered across space and time and the effects that derive from them are the basic domain of study of social science.[2]

3.1 Giddens: practice as the basic domain of study of the social sciences

Giddens' fundamental preoccupation was to develop a social theory that makes room for a subject without lapsing into subjectivism. He attempted to achieve this by combining within a single theoretical framework two traditionally opposed sensitivities: the attention for the intentional and meaningful conduct of human actors, and a consideration of the constraints that limit the possibility of action (and that actors perceive as external to themselves).

Giddens situates the antecedents of his approach squarely in the work of Marx. In the preface of his 1984 *The Constitution of Society*, probably the clearest exposition of his structurationist theory of the social,[3] Giddens describes the book as an extended reflection upon Marx's celebrated and oft-quoted dictum that human beings make history but not in circumstances of their own choosing.[4] While acknowledging that this statement helps counterbalance the traditional penchant of Marxist authors for a socially and economically over-determined view of human conduct, Giddens readily observes that this position leaves completely unresolved the issue of the relationship between structure, agency, and the social, a problem that he sets out to resolve.

Giddens' strategy for overcoming this and the other traditional antinomies produced by the opposition between the subjectivist and objectivist sensitivities (e.g. structure versus subject, micro versus macro, change versus persistence) was to develop a theory of structuration; that is, a theory of recursive production and reproduction of society as *praxis* in which the question of 'what comes first' simply becomes meaningless and dissolves.

The concept of structuration expresses the mutual dependence of structure and agency in a generative sense. Structure and agency are not to be thought of only as mutually constraining but also as mutually generative. Giddens call this the principle of the 'duality of structure'. In his words: ' . . . by the duality of structure I mean that the structural properties of social systems are both the medium and the outcome of the practices that constitute those systems . . . structure is both enabling and constraining' (ibid, pp. 70–1).

One can illustrate Giddens' argument using the example of language and the structuralist distinction between *langue* (language or tongue) and *parole* (speech). While *parole*, the speakers' actual usage, is governed by the underlying structures and rules that form *langue*, these rules become operative and persist in time only by virtue of being applied in real-time speech (*parole*). Without *parole*, i.e. without the practice of using a language, *langue* would not exist. Furthermore, it is always possible that usage will alter the rules of language so that *langue* is constantly changing as a result of shifts of usage. Similarly, it is through the conduct of knowledgeable human agents that structures are produced, reproduced, and transformed.[5]

Structure is therefore both the medium and the outcome of the reproduction of practice: it enters simultaneously into the constitution of the agent and social practice, and exists in the generating moment of this constitution. However, structures only manifest themselves as rules and resources; that is, as a material time-space presence, and memory traces orienting our conduct. In this sense society and social practices do not have structures but rather exhibit structural properties: structure is what gives form and shape to social life, but it is not in itself that form and shape. It follows that the study of structure is always the study of structuration.

Practices acquire thus a central role both epistemically and architecturally in Giddens social theory. They constitute the crucial mediating moment of both reproduction and change of social structure. In a poignant way, in fact, practices keep Giddens' immense wheel in motion: practices, and not roles as in Parsons' functionalism, have to be regarded as the point of articulation between actors and structure:

Human social activities, like some self-reproducing items in nature, are recursive . . . they are not brought into being by social actors but continually recreated by them via the very means whereby they express themselves *as* actors. In and through their activities agents reproduce the conditions that make these activities possible (Giddens 1984, p. 2).

The difference between the structural property of practices, social structures, and institutions becomes thus one of degree, not of type: 'The most deeply embedded structural properties, implicated in the reproduction of social totalities, I call structural principles. The practices which have the greatest time-space extension within such totalities can be referred to as institutions' (1984, p. 17). The distinction is analytical, not of substance: for Giddens there is no real ontological discontinuity between social practices and social structures.

3.1.1 GIDDENS' VIEW OF PRACTICE

In spite of granting practices a central role in his comprehensive theoretical programme, Giddens never provides an analytical examination of this important concept. When he addresses the specific issue, he defines practices in their most general sense as regularized types of acts (1976, p. 75). He thus seems to understand practice as the activity of doing itself and the various attitudes and features of acting and knowing in a meaningful world. Although, as we shall later see, he does not discount the idea that acts and activities constitute constellations, his interest is mainly in the relationship between the overarching structuration processes at societal level, and the situated conduct of individual actors.

For Giddens, practices as regularized types of activity have three main characteristics.

First, they are produced by knowledgeable actors who draw on rules (codes and norms) and resources (material and symbolic). Rules are generalizable procedures of action implicated in daily matters and need not be explicitly or discursively formulated. They can be procedural (how the practice is performed), or moral (what are the appropriate and permissible forms of enactment). As in Wittgenstein and in the ethno-methodological movement (see Chapter 6 below), for Giddens, rules describe the regularities and generalized procedures used in the production of social practices which are to be expected from those involved in them; rules are thus neither instructions nor prohibitions and they should not be confused with their codified formulations, which Giddens considers necessarily already an interpretation (making social rules accessible through discourse requires necessarily that we interpret them). Resources are the main medium through which power manifests itself and is exercised. Paying tribute to his Weberian legacy, Giddens interprets power as the capacity of mobilizing people and things in the effort of producing some effect in the world: power is the capacity to make a difference. Resources include capabilities, such as organizing activities, structuring space and time, coordinating actors, and influencing the way in which people perceive themselves and their conduct (authoritative resources); they also include material levers such as control of natural resources, means of production, and wealth (allocative resources).

Rules and resources organize practice and govern individual actions by making certain kinds of conduct possible while precluding others, while not dictating to actors what to do. In fact, for Giddens, there is plenty of space for agents to act strategically by pursuing their desires and interests while man-oeuvring through the complexities and alternatives provided by the system. As Giddens repeats over and over, a critical principle of his construction is that actors could always have acted otherwise (1979, 1984). The idea that actors are knowledgeable and reflexive agents is fundamental to structuration theory.

The renewal of practices comes about through the actions and interactions that compose them: it is by participating in these practices that agents per-petuate both their organizing structures and the conditions of their agency. The accomplishment of these practices, however, requires the active and intelligent contribution of human beings. The production and reproduction of the system therefore depends on active and reflexive agents who employ a large, if tacit, stock of mutual practical knowledge, who have aims and reasons for acting in a certain way, who constantly monitor the uninterrupted flux of their social living, and are capable of articulating why they act in such a way. Although human actors usually proceed unhampered in their daily business they are by no means structural dupes. Agents all the time actively draw on structural resources for their conduct, and although their action is always situated in space and in time (in history, so to speak), they effectively become the carriers of structure in the sense of reproducing social practices that have a recognizable and recognized continuity in time and space. Giddens' pressing task is that of reversing the conceptual elimination of the subject and promot-ing its recovery without lapsing into subjectivism.

Second, practices are always and necessarily temporally, spatially, and paradigmatically situated (1979, p. 53). Analysing the structuration of social systems therefore means attending to the accomplishment of real-time prac-tices (although Giddens never tells us in detail to what we should attend). That such an accomplishment is paradigmatically situated means that all practices are generated within the possibilities and constraints brought to bear by the combined influence of all three main structuring characteristics of social action (structures of signification, domination, and legitimation). In Marxist parlance, practices are always historically connoted. The resources by which agents tap into how they conduct their daily affairs govern practice and reproduce structure by introducing certain ways of giving meaning to the world, certain objective and subjective distributions of opportunities and possibilities deriving from how the resources are allocated, and by constituting a specific normative set of expectations and restrictions. In this sense, the recursive production of the social also thrives on the routinized nature of practices and on the distinction between practical and discursive consciousness. Giddens calls routines those actions that are 'saturated with taken for grantedness' and hence they require a very low regime of reflexive monitoring (the capacity of actor to account for the reason of their conduct). Routine activity is governed mainly by practical consciousness embodied in what actors know about how to continue functioning in the multiplicity of contexts of social life (Giddens 1983). Routines provide both cognitive economy and anxiety reduction and control. In routine social life, the rationalization of action becomes mainly reliant on compliance with mutual knowledge and conventions, hence providing reassurance relatively to social acceptance and integration (reduction of anxiety).[6] While, as we have seen above, actors are always capable of reflexively monitoring their conduct, the verbalization of their conduct only happens in particular circumstances such as breakdowns and conflict. Although he sees human agents as essentially knowledgeable about their actions, Giddens gives a prominent role to tacit knowledge and routines in his theoretical architecture. He thus stays clear of not only the functionalist image of actors as structural and cultural dupes, but also of the equally unrealistic view of agents as voluntary beings and compulsive rational decision makers.

Last, but certainly not least, all practices are interdependent and persist in some kind of relationship of reciprocity: while practices are always inherently unique and situated, they are also connected to social life both locally and, potentially, globally. Practices thus form constellations and (social) systems which exist in space and time and thus differ from structures which only exist virtually through the process of structuration. Social systems, however, amount to nothing more than a manifold of interconnected practices and their enduring cycles of reproduction. Giddens neither elaborates in detail on this aspect nor on the reciprocity between practices, summarily explaining the relationship in terms of abstract causal loops and reflective processes of self-regulation (see e.g. Giddens 1979, pp. 76–9). What is clear, however, is that the interdependency between actors or collectivities across extended time-space is reproduced—or not reproduced—with other structural aspects. The interconnection among practices thus becomes the source of both stability *and* change, so that practices are at the same time the locus of ordering and reproduction *and* the locus of disordering and mis-production. Conceiving human beings as knowledgeable actors who draw on rules and resources for the carrying out of their activity and achievement of their aims implies that a necessary feature of action is its partial indeterminacy. That is to say, at any point in time the agent could have acted otherwise, either positively in terms of intervening in a course of events or negatively in terms of restraint or forbearance. In one sense, then, actions and practices are always situated in history and context and they only make sense in relation to such location. In another sense, actions can have unintended consequences in practice. The knowledge-ability of human actors is in fact always bounded, on the one hand, by the unconscious and, on the other, by unacknowledged conditions. The consequence is that the carrying out of a practice can result in a disordering effect instead of the expected orderly reproduction, with a consequent mutational event and a related mis-reproduction of structure. Accordingly, one may say that 'change, or its potentiality' is inherent in all moments of social reproduction and that '... any and every change in a social system logically implicates the totality and thus implies structural modifications, however minor or trivial this may be' (1979, p. 114).

For Giddens, then, changes have their origin in this micro level and reverberate at system level through a process of progressive accrual. At the practice level, misreplication results in variation that accumulates in time and space to produce some form of structural contradiction. That is to say, practices that depend on each other end up following principles that are not aligned or that contravene each other (1979, p. 141). This generates oppositions or disjunctures of structural principles that result in conflict which, under certain circumstances, can provoke dramatic and revolutionary changes and the search for a new regime of recursive reproduction.[7]

In summary, for Giddens, practices and their association extend themselves by continuously renewing the conditions that determine them,[8] whereas their recurrent accomplishment implies both reproduction and change. Because of their centrality in the constitution not only of sociality but of all recognizable social phenomena, practices constitute the fundamental object of interest of social theory. In fact, for Giddens, practices acquire almost a foundational ontological status: social practices are all that there is to study and, in many ways, all that there is (at least as concerns our daily experience of, and in, the world).

3.1.2 GIDDENS AT WORK

Although Giddens remains one of the most influential figures in contemporary social theory, take-up of his theories in work and organization studies was extremely limited. This was due to a mix of historical, practical, and theoretical reasons.

Historically speaking, Giddens' work coincided with a burgeoning interest in postmodernism in the study of organizations and elsewhere. *The Constitution of Society* appeared in the same year as Derrida's *Postmodern Condition* which was calling for the end of grand narratives of the sort Giddens was energetically developing. Right or wrong, to many of the non-positivistic-oriented organizational scholars who would constitute his natural public, Giddens appeared as the last of the modern authors.[9] To these authors excited by the possibilities opened up by postmodern analysis, Giddens appeared too busy developing a theory of society and individuals which put everything in the right place, portrayed people as reflexive and rational, and allowed almost no room for pathos, emotions, disorder, conflict, and violence. Moreover, Giddens' structurationism failed to inspire a community that had been held to ransom for decades by the boxes, arrows, and loops of system theory. In spite of its innovative, strong, processual character, Giddens' system theory looked suspiciously like more of the same. Finally, critical authors were somewhat unhappy with Giddens' flat and a-conflictual view of the social, and were weary of the potentially deeply conservative implications of structurationism. Authors argued that Giddens' view contained the seeds of an unacceptable justification (all social positions, even the most terrible, are somewhat acceptable as they enable as much as they constrain) and that not all aspects of structure are equally amenable to agency. The historical reality pointed instead towards a 'differentiated (and thus limited) topography for the exercise of agency' rather than 'an endlessly recursive plain'.[10]

This marketing failure, so to speak, was compounded by what we could call the practical limitations of Giddens' work. For one thing, Giddens had little to say about formal organizations as his line of reasoning aimed at connecting more or less directly individual agents and the system. As such he left organizational scholars no path to follow. At the same time, Giddens' analysis was always carried out at a general and highly theoretical level. Unlike Bourdieu and most other contemporary practice theorists, Giddens not only did not put his theory to the test of empirical research, he also failed to provide any exemplification of his approach, and explicitly refrained and even resisted putting his theory into a methodological package for pursuing empirical inquiry.[11] In fact, Giddens frequently stated that structuration was not intended as a concrete research programme (Giddens 1983, p. 77; 1991, p. 310), and that his principles were not intended to supply concepts useful for the actual prosecution of research. It is true that on more than one occasion he spelled out the idea that structurationism provides a set of sensitising principles that should guide empirical research. For example, in the *Constitution of Society* (pp. 281–4) he articulated ten such principles, reduced later to just three: contextual sensitivity, the complexity of human intentionality, and the subtlety of social constraint (Giddens 1991, p. 311). However, even when spelled out, these principles were insufficient for sustaining any kind of empirical inquiry. The onus of developing them into a workable theory-method package was left to others. Not surprisingly, then, structuration made only a limited inroad among organizational scholars, and this was mainly among members of two communities of interest which could benefit most from translating Giddens' work with minimum effort.

The first of these two communities was that of Information System (IS) scholars.[12] Many IS scholars were attracted by Giddens' argument that even the more apparently material allocative resources which might seem to have a 'real existence' (such as land) only become resources 'when incorporated within processes of structuration' (Giddens 1984, p. 33). In this way, Giddens offered a third way between the traditional determinist view of how information technologies influence organizational life and the mounting wave of extreme cultural constructivism, which was getting dangerously close to a 'technologies are in the eyes of the beholder' position. Accordingly, several authors such as DeSanctis and Poole (1994), Barley (1986), and especially Orlikowski (1992) set out to develop Giddens' idea that '[t]echnology does nothing, except as implicated in the actions of human beings' (Giddens and Pierson 1998, p. 82).

Interestingly enough, however, these authors also soon encountered some of the limits of Giddens' approach, which, as expected, became clear only when his framework was put into practice. For one thing, IS scholars quickly encountered Giddens' unsatisfactory treatment of materiality. In order to avoid falling into some form of old-style determinism, Giddens took a formidable position in excluding the idea that artefacts and materials could act as structural resources—their structural property was always to be mediated by rules and memory traces. This idea of 'technology in the mind', however, did not address the issue that the interpretive flexibility of the material word is limited and that, at some point or other, materials start to bite back in more ways than one. It also didn't help to understand the apparent capacity of material configurations to translate structure from one place to another: for Giddens this could not be attributed to inherent properties of the material resources but only to the fact that actors in the different organizations draw on broader social structures. While claiming to be a well-balanced theory, structuration was thus revealed to be skewed on the side of the knowledgeable human agents. As one critic put it, far from overcoming the dualism of agency and structure, Giddens 'was stuck firmly at the pole of agency' (Callinicos 1985, p. 144).

At the same time, authors such as Orlikowski (1992) discovered that while, in Giddens' abstract and almost metaphorical world, structuration as an instantaneous process seems to work satisfactorily, in the world of empirical research and once the duality of structure was asserted, recomposing the pieces was almost impossible. In this way, one ended up either giving prominence to the structural aspects (as in the case of Orlikowski and most IS scholars who had understandable professional reasons for doing so) or reasserting the primacy of the human actor generating an anthropomorphic view of society in which subjects reign supreme, as Habermas put it.[13] In both cases, it was clear that the 'duality approach' didn't pay off; constituting a dualism for the purpose of trying to recompose it was like locking the stable door after the horse bolted. This is evident, for example, in the direction of Orlikowski's work. In spite of being considered one of the more prominent scholars of structurationism in IS and in work and organization studies at large, the author eventually dropped Giddens structurationist theory as her major reference, embracing instead a 'technologies-in-practice' approach.[14] Rather than starting with the technology and examining how actors appropriate its embodied structures, or starting with actors and their rules and resources, this view starts with human practice, thus avoiding the duality altogether. The aim is then to examine how the practice enacts emergent structures through recurrent interaction with the technology at hand. By viewing technologies-in-practice as both shaped by, and shaping the use of, material artefacts, attention can be thus granted to the material property of technology at hand.

While Giddens' residual humanism constituted a problem for IS scholars, it had an almost opposite effect on strategic management researchers. To these scholars, structurationism was appealing precisely because of its flat subjectivism. The theory was, in fact, capable of reintroducing attention to the structural aspects of organizational life, thus rebalancing the traditional voluntaristic and determinist flavour of strategic management studies; it could do this without pulling the rug from under its feet—strategic management is necessarily predicated on intentional individual agency. Building on Giddens' insistence on the capacity of agents to mobilize resources and normative institutions, and to transform the structural properties of social systems, these scholars set out to elaborate what they described as a more realistic view of managerial agency without renouncing the idea that organizations are capable of being governed purposively and reflexively through time.[15] While an in-depth analysis about whether, and to what extent, this was a successful attempt goes beyond the scope of this work, the endorsement of Giddens by this community is significant in at least two ways. First, it tells us something about structurationism itself and its underlying philosophical commitment to methodological individualism and to an over-intellectualized view of agency. Structurationism still treats (or at least makes room for treating) practices as purposeful activities of individuals guided by rules and strategic decisions.[16] While Giddens, significantly, breaks away from functionalism and develops an innovative processual view of the social as an ongoing accomplishment, at the ontological level there is still significant residual overlapping.

Second, and distinctly related, it shows that the endorsement of a discourse of practice does not constitute in itself a break away from traditional assumptions. When practices remain ontologically subordinate to actors and are thus construed as 'activities of' organizational agents, it is not a move far from the traditional ways of thinking from which theories such as Giddens' were trying to distance themselves. It is only when the basic locus of analysis switches from the individual to the social practice itself that a significant rupture is produced.

That is, if you want to understand the social, you have to go and look at what people do, what they talk about, and what they handle while talking.

3.2 **Bourdieu's praxeology: an overview**

While both Giddens and Bourdieu put praxis at the core of social phenomena, it is to the latter that one has to turn to find not only a practice-based approach to social thinking, but also a fully developed theory of praxis. The primary aim of sociology, for Bourdieu, was to construct a general theory of practice capable of capturing the many levels of daily life while at the same time developing an approach authentic to the *'sens pratique'*[17] of the actions that characterize such practices. As a practising ethnographer, Bourdieu always believed in the fundamental importance of starting the study of human conducts from the appreciation and representation of real-time practices. However, one of his key theoretical points was that representing practice is not enough: practice needs to be explained, and this is what makes sociologists different from anthropologists and other social scientists. While the object of the work of the latter is what practices are and how they behave, the former need to address the issue of why practices are the way they are and why they are not different. To this end, he developed over the years a theory of both practice and 'practice-based theorizing' that has fundamental implications for any attempts to extend practice thinking to new domains such as organization studies.

Bourdieu, like Marx, never formulated a definition of practice. Nevertheless, it is clear from his writings that he embraces a broad notion of it. Practice, or better, practices are for Bourdieu a particular, theory-laden way to refer to what people do in everyday life. In Bourdieu's work, the reference to practice serves two strictly related purposes: it situates the sociological eye, that is, the imaginary source of sociological accounts, within real activity; and it helps to position his approach vis-à-vis other existing traditions of social thought. The persistent reference to practice in his opus is thus used to signal both the innovative content of his way of doing sociology and the theoretical coordinates of his theoretical stance. In fact, in most of his works on practice Bourdieu develops his argument in opposition to two conceptions of social theorizing that he describes as 'objectivism' and 'subjectivism'.

Objectivism is identifiable with Comte's 'social physics' and Levi-Strauss's structuralism. The first is challenged because it fails to recognize the active dimension of interpretation and decision making in everyday life. The second, recognized as more sophisticated, nonetheless fails because it is incapable of providing a convincing account of why the world appears both as a given field of objective meaning and as an arena of negotiation and strategic action. For Bourdieu, the roots of this failure lay in Saussure's original division between language and its realization in speech that is found in practice and history, and the inability to understand the relationship between the two 'other than between the model and its execution... which amounts to placing the linguist, the possessor of the model, in the position of a Leibnizian God possessing *in actu* the objective meaning of practices' (1990, p. 33). Objectivism, therefore, condemns itself to all the problems associated with the intellectualism inherent in its epistemology; that is, to the consequences of 'substituting the observer's relation to practice for the practical relation to practice'; i.e. generating explanatory models and then attributing them with causal power. Objectivism is condemned either to ignore the whole question of the principle underlying the production of the regularities which it then contents itself with recording, or to reifying abstractions by the fallacy of treating the objects constructed by science, whether 'culture', 'structures', or 'modes of production', as realities endowed with social efficacy 'capable of acting as agents responsible for historical actions or as a power capable of constraining practices' (Bourdieu 1977, p. 27).

To save appearances, says Bourdieu, structuralism adopts the strategy of invoking the intervention of unconscious forces or, more often, it plays 'on the polysemous nature of the world rule' (ibid.). So *rule* is sometimes used in the sense of (i) explicit juridical-like norm, other times in the sense of (ii) theoretical model to describe empirical observations, and, finally (iii) in the sense of a scheme immanent in practice.

But neither of the three would do for Bourdieu. Understanding rules as (i), as in the case of Levi-Strauss's discussion of the incest taboo and Parson's theory of action, leads to a type of rule-based explanation of social action that ignores the messy and strategic nature of practices and the fact that rules are bent and often broken in practice (Crossley 2001, p. 82). Taken in the sense (ii), rules are useful heuristic tools but they cannot be used as an explanatory principle save turning them into a *vis dormitiva* and so generating circular explanations. Finally, the third sense incurs all the problems of what it means to follow a rule in practice brought to the fore by Wittgenstein and discussed in Chapter 2.

Subjectivism, the other extreme of Bourdieu's Scylla and Charybdis theoretical scenario, is more difficult to define in terms of authors although the criticism levelled toward this position is quite clear.[18] Bourdieu criticizes subjectivism as well as theories of rational action for situating action in an imaginary universe of 'interchangeable possibles, entirely dependent on the decrees of the consciousness that creates it, and therefore entirely devoid of objectivism' (Bourdieu 1990, p. 42). Because they only see the 'objective' as a form of 'social inertia', subjectivists end up committing the opposite mistake of universalizing the experience that the subject of theoretical discourse has of himself as a subject (ibid. p. 46). Thinking of practice in terms of decisions of the will leads however to all sorts of antinomies, the most evident being that in order to account for the actor's rational and economic behaviour in the absence of external and economic conditionings, one has to rely on reason as the foundation of action, therefore generating a circular explanation in which rationality is both the *explanans* and *explanandum*.

The challenge that Bourdieu sets for himself is therefore to put forward a theory of practice which is capable of both avoiding the two opposites, and overcoming the dichotomy. To achieve this, Bourdieu introduces the notion of habitus which, in many ways, constitutes the theoretical pivot and keystone of his vast and intricate social architecture.

3.2.1 ON HABITUS

Bourdieu's idea of habitus, derives from, and revives, the tradition of the 'anthropology of possibilities', that from Aristotle through to St Thomas, informs much of the modern phenomenological movement. Habitus is in fact a powerful intermediate concept with a long and noble lineage capable of connecting recursively the individual/subjective and institutional/objective dimension.[19] The concept is central to Bourdieu's theoretical construction and is used to keep together (i) the not uncommon idea that, through experience, aspects of the social world become internalized and determine the subsequent behaviour of individuals and groups; (ii) an account of how this internalized 'something' generates the lived richness and practices of meaningful actions, without turning actors into dupes; (iii) an account of how the overall setting perpetuates itself through practices. Habitus is thus the theoretical device (some say the *deus ex machina*)[20] that can account for the regularity, coherence, and order in human conduct without ignoring its negotiated strategic nature.

In Bourdieu's texts, habitus is variably defined as a set of mental dispositions, bodily schemas, and know-how operating at a pre-conscious level, that once activated by events (fields) generates practices.

[Habitus is a] systems of durable, transposable dispositions, structured structures predisposed to function as structuring structures, that is, as principles which generate and organize practices and representations that can be objectively adapted to their outcomes without presupposing a conscious aiming at ends or by an express mastery of the operations necessary in order to attain them (Bourdieu 1990, p. 53).

Habitus is, therefore, first and foremost a form of knowing in practice akin to the 'feel for the game' experienced in sport. This feel for, or sense of, the game is not only the spring of practical actions in the field and during the match, it is also what gives practical sense to the rules before and during the game, as in the football 'offside' rule. This helps the game to be reproduced during the match and makes the sport, and sport in general, exist in time.

Not a belief or the arbitrary adherence to rules and dogma, habitus is better conceived as a way of knowing inscribed in bodies, acquired mostly during upbringing and less often during secondary socialization as, for example, the practising of a game or an art through familiarization, silent observation, or 'let's pretend' games. The acquisition of habitus takes place as a by-product of participation in daily activities largely without raising it to the level of discourse. In this sense, it is clear that for Bourdieu habitus is not a way of understanding the world as much as a way of being in the world. It implies a relation of commitment and belonging to a field, a total investment that is so strong that it becomes invisible to the initiator. Explaining to the referee that the goal line is only a social construction and therefore the goal should be disallowed simply won't do! In Bourdieu's words, 'what is "learned by body", is not something that one has, like knowledge that can be brandished, but something that one is' (Bourdieu 1990, p. 73). In this sense, Bourdieu's habitus displays significant similarities with the work of other authors who have explored the central role of bodily or tacit knowledge in generating everyday practices, namely Merleau-Ponty's view of practical knowledge as corporeal schema and habit[21] and Polanyi's notion of personal tacit knowledge.

A few decades before Bourdieu, Merleau-Ponty, writing within the tradition of phenomenological psychology, developed a theory of embodied knowledge inscribed in corporeal schemas. Corporal schemas operate below the level of reflexivity and are, in fact, inaccessible to discourse. They are always activated in relation to practical interests; they situate agents perceptually and linguistically with respect to their material and social environments and can be expanded through the use of 'extensions'. Just as I do not have to think first and speak after, when I drive I do not think about the car, I am at one with the car. The car is an extension of my own corporeal schema. Corporeal schemas operate tacitly until something goes wrong and the breakdown reveals its elements. Schemata moreover do not apply only to individual actions but to social situations as well. Agents are knowledgeable of social situations and their bodily-centred practical intelligibility is critical to the accomplishment of social interaction. Habits (the similarity in terminology with Bourdieu's habitus is all but fortuitous) build on corporeal schemas and involve their modification and enlargement. For Merleau-Ponty, habits allow the sedimentation of past activity into corporeal schemata, so enabling new ways of understanding and acting. The past therefore remains alive as habits embodied in corporeal schemata shape emotions, perceptions, conceptions, and actions. This sedimented past provides a range of capacities for action that become realized only within the action they make possible:

Habit is neither a form of knowledge nor an involuntary action...It is knowledge in the hand, which is forthcoming only when bodily effort, is made, and cannot be formulated in detachment of that effort. The subject knows where the letters are on the typewriter as we know where one of our limbs are, through knowledge bred of familiarity which doesn't give us a position in objective space (Merleau-Ponty 1962, p. 144).

Polanyi's notion of tacit knowledge also exhibits a notable family resemblance with Bourdieu's habitus. Polanyi's main target was the then prevailing neopositivist idea that scientific knowledge resulted from the application of an impersonal and universal method. In opposition to this view, the author set out to develop an alternative version of the work of scientists as well as other types of experts in which the kernel of their competence (and freedom) was shielded from the dictatorship of a method and resided instead at a deep personal and unattainable level. In order to support his view, Polanyi made a strong case for expert-knowing as a way of acting on something which is not rule based, which does not exclude the body by eulogizing the mind, and which remains mostly unsayable, that is, personal (Polanyi 1958). In order to attract attention to this at-the-time neglected knowledge, Polanyi drew a distinction between explicit and tacit knowledge: the former is formalized in scientific terms; the latter is constituted by the *awareness of knowing* how to do something without being able to provide an adequate analytical description of it and, therefore, without being able to translate it into formal, universal, and general knowledge. This is what Polanyi (1962) meant when he said that we know much more than we know we know—an expression used also by Bourdieu (1990, p. 69).

In order to convey what he means by 'tacit knowledge' in the practice of skills Polanyi draws a distinction between two types of awareness: focal awareness and subsidiary awareness. He says, 'when we use a hammer to drive in a nail, we attend to both nail and hammer, *but in a different way*. We *watch* the effect of our strokes on the nail and try to wield the hammer so as to hit the nail most effectively. When we bring down the hammer we do not feel that its handle has struck our palm but that its head has struck the nail' (Polanyi 1958, p. 55). The focal awareness is on driving in the nail, the subsidiary awareness is on the feeling on the palm of the hand, and we pay close attention to these feelings not because they are the objects of our attention, but because they are the instruments of our attention. Similarly, when we learn to use a language, or a probe, or a tool, and thus make ourselves aware of these things, as we are of our body, 'we *interiorize* these things and *make ourselves dwell in them*' (ibid.). That such a form of tacit knowing is inherently personal and aesthetic in nature, and therefore impossible to formalize into discursivity, emerges if one thinks of the simple skill of riding a bike. Polanyi asks: does an analytical description of how to keep one's balance on a bicycle suffice as instruction to someone wanting to learn how to ride a bicycle? And he answers, 'Rules of art can be useful, but they do not determine the practice of an art; they are maxims, which can serve as a guide to an art only if they can be integrated into the practical knowledge of the art. They cannot replace this knowledge' (Polanyi 1958, p. 50).

Even from this sketchy rendition, one can appreciate the extensive similarities in the way the three authors conceive knowing in practice. For all three, the body is deeply involved in the production of competent performance; knowledge is first and foremost acquired in practice and rendered explicit in response to practical necessities without the necessary intervention of consciousness. However, what Bourdieu adds to Merleau-Ponty's, Polanyi's, and to other phenomenological theories of corporeal and tacit knowledge is a strong social and material dimension. Habitus, in fact, is not limited to 'carrying' know-how and to enabling actors to perform competently; it also brings to fruition the objective reality that generated it. Like Merleau-Ponty's habit, Bourdieu's habitus is 'embodied history, internalized as a second nature and so forgotten as history ... the active presence of the whole past of which it is the active presence' (Bourdieu 1990, p. 56). Unlike the constructs put forward by phenomenologists, habitus reflects the structure constitutive of a particular type of social environment such as the material condition of existence characteristic of a class or social group. The habitus thus connects individual conduct to a specific milieu, making even the most (apparently) individual activity inherently social. While producing practices, it also reproduces the 'regularities' immanent in the objective conditions of the production of their generative principle, including the relations of domination and exploitation characteristic of those conditions. This is where Bourdieu sees himself as profoundly different from symbolic interactionism and ethno-methodology. Like them, he is interested in ethno methods, the taken-for-granted ways of doing things actors employ to perform their taken-for-granted worlds; unlike them, he insists that ethno methods differ because each reflects a certain social position and sustains the relation of power between or upon that and other positions (Crossley 2001, p. 85). This is possible because, as a system of generative schemes, habitus allows the free production of thoughts, perceptions, and actions inherent in the particular condition of the production, while at the same time delimiting what is conceivable or acceptable in that particular situation. By erasing other, less probable possibilities as unthinkable or 'undoable', it presents a meaningful world in which expectations almost always correspond to objective structures of experience. By the same token, however, habitus also keeps people in their places, no matter how desperate these places. It does so by giving the impression that the world 'couldn't be otherwise', and that inequalities are a matter of course, or a natural occurrence, or a divine prescription, depending on the circumstances. In this way habitus generates local common-sense worlds rendered objective by the consensus on the meaning of practices; by harmonizing and reinforcing experiences, habitus creates homogeneity in social groups that causes practices to be intelligible and foreseeable—and hence taken for granted. For example, middle-class western metropolitan dwellers consider it taken for granted that, despite significant economic and personal sacrifices, sending their children to school for a protracted period and obtaining the best possible education for them is the obvious thing to do. Schooling is part of their habitus. Accordingly, each of them attempts to get the best school for their offspring, displaying both an uncanny homogeneity of behaviour and so largely reproducing the pattern of inequalities between those who get an education and those who don't.

3.2.2 HOW HABITUS PRODUCES PRACTICE

From the above, it follows that while habitus is critical in generating practice, it never does this alone. Although the concept of habitus remains stricken by inconsistencies and ambiguities (Lau 2004), one thing that unequivocally emerges from Bourdieu's work is that it always and necessarily generates practice in conjunction with two other forces—'social capital' and 'field'. These locate practice within a topology of power positions and govern it from the 'outside', so to speak, while habitus mainly operates from the 'inside'. Practice is thus performed at the encounter between these three elements and it is only by scrutinizing their interaction that we can produce sociological explanations of the actual practising. Bourdieu summarizes this idea using the following formula:[22]

$$(Habitus \times Capital) + Field = Practice^{23}$$

Capital is in broad terms anything that can be exchanged, determining as a consequence a variation in legitimacy and power. Capital therefore includes material possessions (which can have symbolic value), non-material sources of value such as prestige, status, and authority (referred to as symbolic capital), and anything 'rare and worthy of being sought after in particular social formations' (Bourdieu 1977, p. 178). Different forms of capital can be converted although symbolic capital is the most powerful form of conversion. Symbolic capital is in fact the main basis of domination in that it carries with it the power of legitimation. This form of power thus bestows the capacity to attribute names, defines what counts as common sense, and institutes official versions of the social world. In this way, this form of capital renders the whole process of reproduction invisible and therefore seemingly inevitable. Symbolic capital thus sustains domination and inequality through a subtle but very powerful form of symbolic violence.[24]

The idea of capital is critical in Bourdieu's theory of practice in that it allows him to conceptualize the ends of an action from a non-phenomenological basis.[25] For Bourdieu, conduct is always oriented toward the pursuit of some interest defined generally as whatever matters—which in practise translates almost inevitably into accumulating power and capital. Although such pursuit is mostly non-reflective, being governed by habitus, it makes room for man-oeuvre, discretion, cunning; that is, for agency. In this sense Bourdieu's habitus is profoundly different from habit: habitus makes room for performa-tivity and requires agency, although such agency is fundamentally different from that conceived by methodological individualism.

Fields (*champs*) are partially autonomous spaces characterized by 'fields of forces' determined by the distribution of social capital and objective relations between social positions. They correspond roughly to the various spheres of life such as art, religion, economy, and politics. Modern societies are differen-tiated into different fields, some of which coincide with institutions, a good example being the system of higher education in France, while other transcend them, as in the case of the scientific world. Although fields are not completely autonomous, they generate local markets of capital, specific goals, peculiar distinctions, and norms that may look strange to outsiders or those who do not believe in the game but that look like an external and given reality to insiders. Fields are thus structured spaces of both social and power positions in which the distribution, and legitimacy, of capital is constantly disputed.

As mentioned above, field and habitus are locked in a circular relationship: involvement in a field shapes the habitus that, once activated, reproduces the field. On the other hand, habitus only operates in relation with the state of the field and on the basis of the possibilities of action granted by the capital associated with the position. Two important consequences derive from this.

First, strictly speaking, habitus is always a group or class phenomenon; habitus both expresses the common condition of existence, and harmonizes the practices of the members without 'intentional calculation or conscious reference to a norm' (Bourdieu 1977, p. 80), allowing mutual adjustment even in the absence of any direct interaction or explicit coordination. As Bourdieu puts it:

The practice of the members of the same group or, in a differentiated society, the same class, is always more and better harmonized than the agents know or wish because, as Leibniz says, following only (his) own laws, each nonetheless agrees with each other. The habitus . . . inscribed in bodies by identical histories . . . is the precondition not only for the co-ordination of practices but also for practices of co-ordination (Bourdieu 1980, p. 59).

Second, agents' practice is shaped both by their habitus and by their under-standing of the field-specific game as it unfolds in time. It is in this sense that habitus is only a set of dispositions that need to be realized to become practice. There is no determinism in the operating of habitus: agents' practices are improvised according to local, practical, and social conjunctures; agents are continuously engaged in the activity of micro-strategizing permitted by the 'sense of the game' granted them by their habitus and within the boundaries of appropriateness that the latter use. Generating a practice for the agent is a matter of regulated improvisation, where the 'regulation' results from his or her perception of the conditions of the field generated by the habitus, in the form of the sense of the game, what game it is, what game s/he can play or should play, and whether s/he can afford to play it. In this way the habitus both articulates the game and gives sense to the next move in the game, and opens up a repertoire of moves that make sense while, in the process, reactivating the sense of institutions and their norms. For Bourdieu both practical meaning and interests depend on practice. Interest or *illusio*, as Bourdieu liked to call it in emphasizing its esoteric nature, is both field- and game-specific: symbolic capital is the specific *illusio* played and pursued in the intellectual field, although for those inside it is anything but illusory. Note also that because practices are always generated in response to practical circumstances, habitus never produces the same practice twice and, in fact, each individual develops a personal 'trajectory'.

However, according to Bourdieu, because of the homogenizing mechanism performed by habitus, trajectories of members of the same group or class rarely deviate too much from each other, and constitute local variations on a common theme—they retain what Wittgenstein suitably defined 'family resemblance'. Practices are thus conceived of as 'clustered around social games played in different social fields, in which agents act with a feel for the game, a sense of placement in pursuing of interest' (Lau 2004, p. 378). Practice is thus always a strategic but non-reflective (which doesn't mean thoughtless) conduct generated by habitus in pursuit of *illusio* in specific field games.

3.2.3 THEORIZING PRACTICE

This somewhat lengthy exposition of Bourdieu's theory was necessary not only because it constitutes one of the more extended theories of practice available, but also because it provides the necessary background to comprehend one of Bourdieu's main concerns; that is, how to study and represent practice. As I have pointed out above, Bourdieu uses the term 'practice' to signal his intention to embrace a sociology that takes as its main epistemic object what people do when they are in 'practical relation to the world, the preoccupied, active presence in the world through which the world imposes its presence, with its urgencies, its things to be done and said, things made to be said which directly governs words and deeds without ever unfolding as a spectacle' (Bourdieu 1990, p. 53). The issue is then: how do you do it? What does a theory of practice look like in practice? In other words, how do you go about studying practice?

From the above discussion, we know that Bourdieu has a clear idea of what *not* to do. A first mistake to avoid is to fall back into the intellectualist positions; that is, substituting the academic view of the world for that of the practitioner. In fact, according to the habitus model, practice is always generated by agents who are intimately involved with daily endeavours, whose main preoccupation is to proceed unhampered with their daily matters. Because habitus is part of their way of being, the agents simply respond to events according to what makes sense, in view of what they can afford to do, and what they perceive, or foresee, will do them good. This perspective is profoundly different from that of scholars and academics, who, on the contrary, and thanks to the social position granted them by their occupation, can afford to constitute practical activity as an object of observation and analysis, something that ought to be represented, not lived. Attempting to theorize about the generative principles of practice by constructing laws and formulating rules is therefore imposing a logic of practice and its temporal dimension (that of the Academy) over another (that of the practitioner) and therefore forcibly changing the nature of the object under scrutiny. The practice of Western anthropological structuralist-oriented academic work, for example, requires that the scientists produce timeless accounts that display in some form and through some artifice aspects of the life of others. In this way, it extracts an *opus operatum*, i.e. the relations of kinship, the structure of gift giving, from a living *modus operandi*, i.e. real people getting or not getting married, real people exchanging or not exchanging gifts. This move neutralizes *de facto* the temporal, emotional, and improvisational dimension that is integral to the *sens pratique* in practice, causing the scholar to miss the point of the real practice altogether.

Bourdieu uses a vivid example to illustrate this. Consider theories of gift giving such as Levi Strauss' mathematical model of mutual obligations of gift exchange (Levi- Strauss 1950). Models of this kind, whose content we do not need to investigate in detail here, take a totalizing glance and explain what in real life is an irreversible sequence (one which responds not to legalist rules but to a sense dictated by circumstances), with a set of reversible mechanism and/ or a series of mathematical formulas. This elides the fact, however, that in all societies the practice of reciprocating gifts is regulated by a subtle sense of timing and appropriateness that no formal logic can capture. Gift exchange is, in fact, a subtle game of giving and *not* giving, of timing and delaying that only when handled with style prevents turning gift giving or reciprocating into misunderstanding or insult. In many settings, for example, returning the very same gift is not acceptable; reciprocating a gift too soon or too late can generate embarrassment or resentment; reciprocating a small gift with one that is too big for the occasion is not appropriate, etc. Timing in particular is critical: reciprocating a favour with a gift too soon is bound to look like a payment, therefore negating the disinterested nature of the original act and creating embarrassment; conversely, delaying the reciprocation too much is bound to be understood as ungratefulness. Depending on the social positions of agents, moreover, things may change. Gifts to a public official at the wrong moment become bribes, while exceeding or lacking in the value of the gift in relation to the status of the donor and receiver can easily be misunderstood as a statement of disrespect. From the perspective of the engaged agent, these decisions do not present themselves as part of a logical grammar: habitus simply tells agents (makes them feel) what it is that makes sense to do, what is doable; agents do what they feel like doing or decide the right thing to do while being aware of the consequences, or not, of their actions. To break away from the perspective of the person whose urgency is not to offend his neighbour, as any academic observer, participant or non-participant, would necessarily do, means that much of the *sens pratique* of gift giving and its fundamental existence in the here and now gets lost. The practice of gift giving, like any other practice, exists only in the temporal dimension of the urgency of engagement and cannot survive in the reversible universe of rules and formal logic. 'To substitute strategy for the rule is to reintroduce time, with its rhythm, its orientation, its irreversibility', says Bourdieu (1977, p. 9) therefore clarifying that time is a necessary ingredient of practice and a powerful antidote to any universalizing attempt. The practice of gift giving, and the sense of gratefulness that constitutes its main guiding 'logic', are based on playing with ambiguities, indeterminacies, situated clues, and feelings that academic logic accounts, produced from the vantage point of a time-less spectator, just cannot grasp. As Bourdieu puts it, 'practice has a logic which is not that of the logician' (1990, p. 86) and 'science has a time which is not that of practice' (1977, p. 9).

It is important to note that for Bourdieu it is not who attempts the theorization that matters, as the problem is in the differences between the two practices and 'games' and their related habitus. Accordingly, agents are not in a better position than academics when it comes to translating into explicit discursivity the inherent logic of their own practice. Because practical knowledge does not contain knowledge of its own principles, when asked to translate the principles of their practice back into a communicable form, agents revert to representational modes alien to that of their practice and their accounts usually prove to be poor and unsatisfactory. Agents need to struggle just as much as—or perhaps more than—observers to perceive what governs their practice and to bring them to the order of discourse; observers have, at least, the advantage of being able to see the action from the outside, as an object, and this is a privileged condition from which practitioners cannot benefit. In summary, because academic interrogation inclines agents to take up a point of view that is no longer that of action, as soon as they reflect on practice adopting a quasi-theoretical posture, they lose any chance of expressing the truth of their practice, and especially the truth of the practical relation to the practice (Bourdieu 1990, pp. 90–1).[26]

Reaction to the subtle legal formalism that any form of 'objectivism' is bound to introduce in the study of practice must not, however, make one commit the opposite mistake of making the habitus alone the exclusive principle of all practice, the second way not to study practice according to Bourdieu. The attempt to stay authentic to the world of practice as perceived by the agent cannot reduce the task of social science to the identification of constructs of the second degree, as in Schutz, or the simple collection of the accounts agent use to give meaning to their words as in Garfinkel' (Bourdieu 1977, p. 21). According to the French scholar, this is bad and 'complicitous' social science: a social science which fails to pose the fundamental question of the relation between social structures, the practices that accompany them, and the mechanisms that help to reproduce those structures and the inequalities that go with them. In brief, providing a description of the world of practices as self-evident is not good enough.

An interesting question however arises from this account: having spelled out challenging and strict criteria for a theory of practice, does Bourdieu live up to it? Is his habitus-based theory of practice capable of overcoming the two positions? As many authors have noted—and Bourdieu himself seemed to recognize—his theoretical construction is only partially successful in this sense, especially when put to work in the field. Most of the empirical data used to instantiate his theory of practice derives from extensive research in northern Africa aimed at illustrating that Kabyle culture is regulated by a matrix of oppositions (male/female, high/low, warm/cold) that organize independently several spheres of social life (housing, yearly rhythms, and ceremonies, etc.). As noted by Theodore Schatzki (1997), if one interprets his text rigidly, he can be found guilty of the very error he attributes to the intellectualist:[27] first he constructed a representation of Kabyle practices in terms of oppositions, then he accounted for the generation of these practices structuring Kabyle's habitus in a homologous way (p. 127). The same issue, moreover, reappears in a different guise but on a grander scale in relation to Bourdieu's claim about basic human nature and the primacy of competition. In some texts, in fact, Bourdieu argues that the principle of all social energy within a social field is the competition for symbolic advantage, and that '... all practices, including those purporting to be disinterested or gratuitous, and hence non economic, [are in fact] economic practices directed towards the maximizing of material or symbolic profit' (Bourdieu 1977, p. 183).[28] But isn't this the sort of generalization that the detailed study of habitus was supposed to supersede? Can't one argue that substituting economic profit for agents' local sense of practice is again positing a historically, socially, and geographically situated academic theory as a social cause, this time at a global scale?

As I said, Bourdieu seems fully aware of these problems and claims that the only way out is for sociologists to embrace a 'reflexive' stance toward sociology that, if not capable of eliminating the problem, at least can keep it under control. To the extent that the researcher is aware of his or her own practices as well as the position in the field with respect to that of the subject of study, the unintentional substitution of one set of categories with another becomes less likely (see Bourdieu and Wacquant 1992, for a discussion).[29] There are suggestions, however, that this kind of reflexivity alone may not be enough. Luntley (1992), for example, argues that the contradiction in Bourdieu's position stems from his somewhat limited notion of what counts as social theory. Bourdieu is, in fact, a prisoner to the idea that the normality of practices depends always on something else, on a hidden structure that ought to become the object of inquiry.[30] The notion that in order to produce valid social knowledge we need to reveal more than is contained in the agent's subjective description, and unveil some kind of hidden structures of practice, inevitably contains 'the seed of the turn to grand theory' (Luntley 1992, p. 455). Dreyfus and Rabinow (1993) add that Bourdieu's problems stem from the fact that he is attempting to do two very different, and partially incompatible, things at the same time: to describe the ontological structures of human beings; that is, the mechanism through which the world offers itself to us as it does, *and* to prescribe a metaphysics; that is, to tell us what it is to be a human being. After having successfully accomplished the first task using habitus, Bourdieu switches to a completely different vocabulary to address the second. The result is a metaphysics of man as capital gainer, which the author developed within a sociologically invariant discourse that is at odds with the former. The mistake, argue the two phenomenologists, is simply in thinking that in order to make good science we need to generate this sort of claim, without admitting that practices may have a different meaning for different groups of agents and, hence, the notion of a universal will for symbolic capital accumulation may be the correct representation of the logic of practice of a particular group—Bourdieu's own.

The most vivid criticism of Bourdieu 'split theoretical personality' comes however from Michel De Certeau. This author discusses Bourdieu's habitus side by side with Foucault's discourse, to signal both their common descent and similarly totalizing tendency. According to De Certeau, in fact, both notions only deal with prevailing, predominant practices, and are mostly incapable of capturing the micro-tactics of resistance, local deformations, and reinvention that both habitus and discourse undergo in the act of everyday practical consumption. 'A society is...composed of certain fore grounded practices organizing its normative institutions *and* innumerable other practices that remain "minor"' (1984, p. 48). This level of practices simply cannot be captured by theory, at least not the theory the two *'maitres a penser'* use. So, says De Certeau, while Bourdieu produces a beautifully detailed and convincing account of Kabyle practice, he considers such a study illegal with respect to the norms of sociological discipline—'a lapse' (1984, p. 52). In order to re-enter legality, he has therefore to reabsorb the distance between ethnological particularities and 'the empty space of sociology'. This produces a displacement that turns habitus into a dogmatic notion: a powerful, captivating, but nevertheless dogmatic notion. The result is that 'habitus as a theory throws a blanket... [over tactics] as if to put out their fire by certifying their amenability to socioeconomic rationality' (ibid. p. 59).

There are many indications, then, that Bourdieu's attempt to resolve completely the dichotomy between objectivism and subjectivism via the notion of habitus is only partially successful. In spite of the undeniable richness and complexity of his theory, habitus leaves too many aspects of practices largely underdetermined and unaccounted for. Moreover, the problem may not be in the type of theory but in the very idea that there is such a thing as a theory of practice. In other words, there is a legitimate suspicion that the solution is in fact the problem. The above comments, however, also suggest that Bourdieu's contradiction, which is generated in theory, can be solved in practice. As I understand it, many of the above comments indicate that the search for *a* logic of practice is self-contradictory. Praxeology as an ontology militates against the search for universal invariance: practices are always situated both historically and socially. This is not to say that some habitus, some '*sens pratique*', may become widely embraced, as the raising of the economic discourse to a global scale demonstrates. However, how such practices and their inherent habitus outgrow their original site of emergence, disseminate around the world, so to speak, and become widely adopted and apparently universal, are empirical questions. Practice theory is in this perspective to be understood as an ontological sensitivity and a set of epistemic preferences; that is, a way of theorizing, instead of a corpus of universally valid normative statements. Praxeology, if it is not to become self-contradictory, must remain a modest sociology.

3.2.4 BOURDIEU'S PRAXEOLOGY AND THE STUDY OF WORK AND ORGANIZATION

In spite of the sheer scope of his oeuvre and widespread recognition that Bourdieu constitutes one of the more influential figures in contemporary social theory, his work in general, and his praxeology in particular, have made relatively little inroads into organization studies. One might consider, for example, that for any paper quoting Bourdieu's habitus in one of the referenced journals in organization and management studies there are at least twenty articles employing the concept of tacit knowledge.[31] While the 'rediscovery' of Bourdieu by North American management scholars might change all this, it appears that praxeology particularly appeals to two types of organizational scholars: those who study occupations in which corporeality takes central stage, and those who are interested in establishing connections between different levels of social and organizational phenomena.

To the former, habitus is appealing especially because of its capacity to explain practical knowledge which is at the same time inscribed in the body and sustained within a collectivity. What makes a cook a 'cordon bleu' cook? Why do ballet dancers belonging to demonstrably different companies move in different ways? Why do publicans (those who run pubs in the UK) all exhibit similar conducts and strategic behaviours? Why do public sector workers seem to exhibit a common ethos?[32] The idea that habitus is an unconsciously acquired set of bodily and mental dispositions that profoundly affect performance is a good way of answering these questions. People act in a similar way because they carry a similar habitus and because they operate in the same field conditions—as I noted before, habitus is always the property of a group. The notion of habitus, however, goes marginally further. By building on the topological nature of field and on the idea of a 'capital market', habitus goes some way to explain why just certain aspects of work become 'second nature' to practitioners, and how and why such differences between practices exist. In this sense, habitus becomes a viable alternative to the idea of organizational culture, the catch-all blanket concept introduced in the 1980s. Not only is habitus analytically more precise and convincing, it is also historically situated, open to contestation, and sensitive to power conflicts, all aspects that the functionalist concept of organizational culture is unable to capture.

Praxeology, however, also increasingly attracts the attention of scholars interested in making bridges to macro-institutional phenomena and micro conduct. In recent years, an increasing number of neo-institutionalist scholars started to explore the co-evolutionary dynamics of logics, actors, practices, and governance using the toolbox of Bourdieu's sociology.[33] By turning their attention to the concrete manifestations of culture and power in everyday organizational life, they ended up focusing on practices as the locus where institutions and institutional effects are performed, and where institutionalization processes determine continuity or change. Habitus provides these authors with a theoretical resource for explaining how institutional structure manifests itself in the daily conduct of agents without making them institutional dupes, an everlasting problem for these types of studies.

However, these and other scholars attracted by the potential affordance of Bourdieu's theory will have to face the fact that a habitus approach fails to deal, or deals unsatisfactorily, with at least three fundamental aspects of practice which are especially important in the study of organizational phenomena: change, mediation, and reflexivity.

First, Bourdieu's sociology is fundamentally a sociology of reproduction more so than transformation. True, according to the author, habitus is deeply historically situated and contingent and therefore subject to change. At the same time, objective structures and subjective expectations can become 'out of sync', therefore revealing the unquestioned assumptions behind the former; and as I have mentioned before, this may trigger a local activity of mending in which representation of practice in practise may play a role. However, Bourdieu fails to take the next step in considering how the underlying structures or principles or fields of practice mutate overtime and with them the habitus that produces them (Crossley 2001, p. 95). Nowhere in his writing do we find a convincing account of how and why the recursive regime of habitus and field changes either incrementally or abruptly.

Scott Lash (1993) has tied this weakness of Bourdieu's work with the notable absence of technology, instruments, and material mediators in Bourdieu's theory. As Lash has noted, Bourdieu's economy is very much a cultural economy that collapses what should be considered material or economic practices into the cultural sphere. The result is that tools, technology and media are seldom mentioned by Bourdieu (apart from language, which, as a practice, plays a central role in the reproduction of habitus and field). Habitus is developed in a suspiciously ethereal world of meanings, symbolic violence, and symbolic capital, but in which objects seem to play little or no role. Bourdieu pays very little attention to the role that material artefacts play in perpetuating habitus, making possible or hampering agency, embodying and materializing hegemony and relations of domination. Bourdieu's practitioners do not get their hands dirty.

Finally, Bourdieu is also found wanting over the examination of a fundamental aspect of practices; that is, reflexivity (in the ethno-methodological sense discussed in Chapter 6). While he discusses reflexivity at length as a tool and a professional duty for social scientists, Bourdieu has little consideration for the role that reflexivity plays in the generation of practices. While habitus provides a convincing explanation of practical intelligibility (what it makes sense to do), it hardly addresses the role of the monitoring of ongoing action and the associated linguistic practices of accountability associated with it. The reluctance of Bourdieu to address such an aspect is partially understandable in the context of his criticism of phenomenology and in view of the fact that reflexivity, whenever pushed too far, becomes another name for subjectivism. But if Bourdieu is right to emphasize that most of the practices of everyday life go largely unnoticed, it is also true that monitoring our action and providing accounts are an habitual aspect of our daily concern and one of the main ways in which practices are reconnected with the existing expectation and hence reproduce the field (see Héran, 1987). In this way, Bourdieu fails to spot two main sources of change in the recursive circle of habitus-practices-field; that is, changes in practice derived from conscious monitoring, and changes in practice derived from the modification of the language and framework of accountability. Bourdieu has argued, sensibly, that it is not sufficient to change language or theory to change reality: 'While it never does harm to point out that gender, nation, or ethnicity or race are social constructs, it is naive, even dangerous, to suppose that one only has to "deconstruct" these social artefacts, in a purely performative performance of resistance, in order to destroy them' (Bourdieu 1998). In this way, however, he fails to consider the role that discourse play in derailing practices from their recursive paths, introducing innovation through surprise, creativity, and irony. This is an ingredient lacking in Bourdieu's maybe too serious and intellectual world.

Change, artefacts, and reflexivity are therefore critical aspects of practice that require the examination of different practice theories, such as cultural and historical activity theory, ethno-methodology, and the socio-materialist Foucauldian tradition, all of which are to be discussed in the following chapters.

In spite of all these lapses, which are to be expected in a theoretical construction of such magnitude, Bourdieu provides what is probably one of the most convincing ways of understanding practice and its central role in explaining social order at all levels. The author's practice-based approach paints a suggestive picture of a recursive, relational, and processual world in which practice is capable of producing and reproducing a diverse and complex word. In particular, Bourdieu directs our attention to the fact that practice is the locus of the social reproduction of everyday life and symbolic orders, of the taken-for-grantedness of the experienced world and the power structure that such a condition both carries and conceals. Practically intelligible, creative agency, and institutionalized patterns of action are not opposed and, in fact, co-exist and presuppose each other in practice: competent performance always presupposes an institutionalized and constraining context of action. However, what the context is and to what extent it is perceived as an 'external' persuasive force depends on how it is represented, translated in time and space, what patterns of interest it can mobilize in its support, and, above all, how it is appropriated and put to work in practice.

Bourdieu's praxeology also suggests that practice performs a complex array of temporalities and related epistemic positions: while habitus unfolds in the long and slow flowing time of memory and history, the generation of practices takes place in the synchronic time of the here and now of the practically engaged and committed agent. Social scientists are exposed to a number of serious fallacies by confusing or conflating these two planes. These range from intellectualism, the mistake of attributing to the agents the same mechanism social scientists use to explain their actions, to localism, limiting the scope of social science to the mere description of the performance of local world order without investigating the bigger picture that makes such order possible.

Rolling case study: Telemedicine and the nursing habitus[34]

The different positions in the healthcare field are the result of the fluctuating claims by different groups regarding cultural capital (knowledge), social capital (professional membership), and symbolic capital (prestige), and their capacity to convert such capital into economic compensation in return for their labour. The activities and tactics of specific groups such as nurses, doctors, and even managers, derive from the sense of the position they occupy within the capital economy in the healthcare system combined with the effective capital. The individual habitus silently reflects the perception of such positioning; it governs the behaviour deemed as appropriate both in relation to others in a particular sphere and a particular situation. In Western societies, medical doctors usually bear a high level of cultural and, especially, symbolic capital which they have often successfully converted into economic capital. Through the careful management of this capital, in the last two centuries they succeeded in getting the upper hand over all other groups of healthcare practitioners. The difference in status between doctors and other healthcare practitioners such as nurses and technicians, is inculcated during the socialisation of all healthcare practitioners. Although the contribution to the functioning of the system of what are significantly and (often) described as semi-professions is increasingly important, the disparity of authority and prestige between groups is sedimented at the level of the professional habitus and operates a regulatory principle in the day-to-day interactions in wards, surgeries, and elsewhere. This habitus manifests pre-reflexively as a practical sense of self and as a particular feel for the situation; it shapes the understanding and the tactics employed in a particular situation, thus often contributing to reproducing the social conditions that created it.

Of course, the habitus does not have to do only with power games. In the telemedicine centre, the habitus of the nurses was first and foremost oriented towards caring for the patients even if this implied venturing to the boundary of their accepted professional discretion. If in doubt about the well-being of the patient, they would not hesitate to recommend a change in therapy or even to urge them to go to hospital, 'telling them that our centre sent you, so that you can skip the queue at the A&E' (these were patients awaiting a heart transplant whose condition could deteriorate within minutes).

The tele-nurses carried a deeply ingrained predisposition from their general training and, in particular, from their previous jobs. Most of those who worked in the telemedicine centre had previously spent a significant amount of time in the sub-intensive cardiology unit at Garibaldi. This guaranteed that the nurses in charge of caring for patients at a distance had a sound practical understanding of the disease, its remedies, and especially its human cost and implications. Working in the sub-intensive unit, however, also shaped their professional habitus deeply. In a sub-intensive unit environment, if a patient is entering a grave crisis, one can expect the nurses to intervene with powerful drugs. In the words of one nurse: '*If you are in the coronary unit, and a patient has angina pain…you don't stand there waiting for the doctor, you try anything: a defibrillator, drugs…*'. Working in such an environment thus constituted a powerful learning experience which predisposed them to operate with great autonomy and enabled them to interpret symptoms, handle medicines, and make extremely sophisticated clinical decisions.

When transferred to the telemedicine activity, where the nurses were individually in charge of patients, such experience would predispose them (providing also that they had the necessary skills and confidence) to expand their sphere of intervention and take up more clinical work. However, the same habitus which oriented them towards caring deeply for patients also silently restrained them from doing so. As one of the nurses put it: '*You are a nurse and your job is to stay in your place, while ensuring that doctors do the same*'. In other words, the nurses' habitus also gave them a sense of the limits of what was appropriate, the sense of the point beyond which they would be 'trespassing'.

In the telemedicine centre this was manifested through a number of specific tactics and conducts. A good example is the work that all the nurses put into ensuring that all treatments could be traced to the decision of a doctor. According to one of the nurses, at the end of the most difficult telemonitoring calls, where the therapy had to be changed or when the patient was particularly hard to handle, '*the nurse should always consult the specialist, possibly the one looking after that patient. Doctors will usually be found in their offices, so you have to go there. If they are not in, you will have to look for them in the hospital and ask when they are available. Finding them may be a problem, but it is part of your job.*'

Although on many occasions it was the nurse who took the decision while on the phone with a patient, most of them took upon themselves as a matter of course to report what happened to doctors. The practical logic behind this was: if we keep the doctors informed, they can reconstruct each of their actions as a variation on a (presumed) decision they have made. And since the doctors know what the nurse is doing, they can account for it and therefore also make what the nurse does accountable. This, however, required spending time looking for the clinicians in the wards, keeping up with the schedule of the specialists, and learning the habits of the different doctors (who goes to the office when, and when is the right time to talk to these doctors without irritating them). The last resort that I observed on numerous occasions was 'ambushing' doctors in the corridors or in the cafeteria.

A second tactic had to do with the language used in the ambit of monitoring. When a nurse talked to patients (and with me) they never used the word 'diagnose' or other expressions that imply the result of a decision. Nurses would tell outsiders, as they did with me when I began my observations, that they interpreted and reported, but that it was the doctor who made the diagnosis. The terminology of diagnosis carries a specific symbolic value and hence must be reserved for doctors. This was the case despite the fact that observation showed a very different state of affairs.

Finally, the nurses also used the simplest and most radical of tactics: denial. In my observations, all the actors were always intent on denying what was self-evident as follows: the nurses were doing a job that was (and still is) entrusted to doctors. Since the nurses construed what they were doing as nothing out of the ordinary, the resulting responsibility could not but fall onto a doctor.

In all three cases, the nurses' habitus was instrumental not only in informing their conduct, but also in reproducing their field position and their level of capital. Through the habitus, the professional conduct of nurses was informed both by expertise and knowledge as well as social structure. All the practices just described contributed in fact to perpetuating the well-known hierarchical difference between doctors and nurses. The nurses' habitus, together with the active work of the doctors in charge of the telemedicine service (who were keen to emphasize that nurses always operated under strict supervision), was instrumental in maintaining the symbolic domination of one group over the other. The power of doctors was embedded at an unspoken and unconscious level within the discursive practices in the field as well as in the conduct of all those involved, including the patients. In the words of another tele-nurse: '*The patients expect and are very happy to know we have discussed their case with a doctor. One of the aims of our work is to help patients feel that they are being looked after at home almost as if they were in hospital. So it is natural that they want to know what the doctor said'*.

From the vantage point of an external observer it appears that these nurses failed to exploit the 'revolutionary' opportunity offered by the new setting. By making them more autonomous and independent, telemedicine had in many ways helped them acquire an increasing amount of cultural capital that they failed to exploit. The nurses thus did not seize the opportunity of turning the balance of forces in the field into their favour. From within the field, however, things were not perceived in this way. As one of the nurses put it: '*everything is the same, only different'*.

While the balance of forces and the symbolic domination was temporarily maintained at Garibaldi, thanks (among other factors) to the resilience of the habitus of all those involved, in other quarters the potentially disruptive effect of telemedicine on the distribution of capital in the field did not go unnoticed.

The habitus of nurses is, in fact, historically situated. A senior nurse trained thirty or forty years ago would probably find it odd to be asked to prescribe medicines or to make clinical judgments, two tasks that are becoming increasingly common in contemporary nursing. Over recent decades, thanks to a strenuous battle fought mostly through their associations, nurses have gained a significant amount of symbolic capital, sanctioned for example through the establishment of nursing degrees. The field position, and the habitus of nurses are therefore not fixed and unmovable. The field is, in fact, a field of forces in dynamic tension as well as a battlefield where capital is to be fought for and defended once acquired.

It is not a surprise, then, that the pioneering use of telemedicine at Garibaldi encountered some fierce resistance. While often prized for its innovation, the telemedicine experiment conducted at Garibaldi was also criticized at some major national cardiology conventions for giving too much space to nurses. While the people of Garibaldi were extremely careful in presenting their activity as a simple extension of existing medical practices and division of labour, other doctors were quick to observe that telemedicine could, in fact, subvert the objective conditions of the field, laying the foundation for future claims by the nursing profession.

A group that was particularly at risk from the potentially disruptive field effects of telemedicine were general practitioners. The nature of telemonitoring is in fact such that over time there is the risk of establishing direct and preferential relationships between patients and specialized centres. This is in spite of the fact that telemedicine is often conceived as an opportunity for breaking down the barriers between general practitioners and hospital consultants. At least two factors concur in producing this effect. First, chronic patients, whose well-being and survival depend on rapid access to medical attention, quickly elect to rely on the specialized centre's support instead of other health agencies such as their general practitioners. After all, this is a complex pathology and, unless general practitioners have a special interest in delving into the knowledge of this illness, it is not rare that patients become more knowledgeable on it than their general practitioners. Second, general practitioners, who are under constant pressure, are usually happy to delegate management of these patients to a trustworthy specialized centre. The result is that the centre and patients establish a fiduciary relationship that leads to a progressive bypassing of other actors, starting with general practitioners. General practitioners are thus at risk of losing out in terms of positional power within the field. Should the habitus of patients and nurses change significantly, general practitioners would find their social and symbolic capital eroded by their hospital-based colleagues and, more poignantly, by the newly emerging group of highly specialized groups.

It is not a surprise, then, to find out that the general practitioners who sent their patients to the telemedicine centre had mixed feelings. On the one hand, as regards the interests of their patients, they were relieved and reassured. After all, it is not only in the nature of the habitus of nurses, but also of all other healthcare practitioners, to put patient care first. Knowing that their patients would be monitored by one of the best centres in the country couldn't be anything but positive news. Yet, there were always subtle signs of resistance, as testified by the following words of a general practitioner: *'On those rare occasions when I speak with the telemedicine centre, the nurse picks up the phone but I ask to speak directly with the cardiologist... they seem to be efficient, courteous and competent, I can see that they are well trained. But I still prefer not to speak with nurses...'* Habitus, just like habits, dies hard. And for very good capital-related reasons, one may add!

▒ NOTES

1. The term 'social praxeology' was firstly used by Loic Wacquant for giving emphasis to the central role of practice in Bourdieu and Giddens' work (see Wacquant, 1992). The term was also used for describing the methodology of the Austrian school of economics associated with the work of Von Ludwig Mises (see in particular von Mises 1949). Von Mises' economic theory was strongly action-based and centred on the assumption that human action is always a conscious aiming toward one or more chosen goals.

2. 'The basic domain of study of the social sciences ... is neither the experience of the individual actor, nor the existence of any form of social totality, but social practices ordered across space and time' (Giddens 1984, p. 2).

3. The following somewhat long paragraph from the *Constitution of Society* (Giddens 1984) is probably the best summary of Giddens' theory of structuration:

    Structure, as recursively organised sets of rules and resources, is out of time and space, save in its instantiation and coordination as memory traces, and is marked by an "absence of the subject". The social system in which structure is recursively implicated, on the contrary, comprises the situated activities of human agents, reproduced across space and time. Analysing the structuration of social systems means studying the modes in which such systems, grounded in knowledgeable activities of situated actors who draw upon rules and resources in the diversity of action contexts, are produced and reproduced in interaction. Crucial to the idea of structuration is the notion of duality of structure ... The constitution of agents and structures are not two independently given sets of phenomena, a dualism, but represents a duality. According to the notion of the duality of structures, the structural properties of social systems are both the medium and outcome of the properties they recursively organise. Structure is not "external" to individuals ... structure is not to be equated with constraints abut always both constraining and enabling (p. 25).

4. 'This book [*The Constitution of Society*], indeed, might be accurately described as an extended reflection upon a celebrated and oft-quoted phrase to be found in Marx. Marx

comments that "Men [let us immediately say human beings] make history, but not in circumstances of their own choosing". Well, so they do. But what a diversity of complex problems of social analysis this apparently innocuous pronouncement turns out to disclose!' (Giddens 1984, pp. xx–xxi).

5. The example is from Callinicos (1985).

6. According to Giddens, in a scenario typical of what he calls 'cold societies', traditions operate as a mechanism that prevents routines from becoming the object of reflexive monitoring. Changes of major routines only happen as a consequence of external influences such as environmental changes, disasters, or the establishing of relations of dependence or conflict with other different social groups. In this case, certain traditional practices are simply replaced by others without altering the basic mechanism. Things became quite different, however, with the introduction of mass literacy and wide access to writing and, more recently, to the media. When tradition is thematized as such, it ceases to be pure social reproduction and becomes subject to interpretation; this implies the necessary emergence of divergent interpretations of established norms and hence their de-routinization. This in turn requires the adoption of an array of strategies of mending and restoration both at the level of discursive practices and social structures corresponding to what Bauman calls the rise of intellectuals as legislators (1992). This phenomenon has become particularly acute in what Giddens went on to define as the Western 'reflexive society', connoted by a systematic and progressive disavowal of all forms of legitimization, starting with tradition and ending with rationality, that undermines at the very root not only the routine-based texture of the everyday but also the associated sense of ontological safety.

7. Besides the accumulation of variation derived from imperfect reproduction and the consequent incremental drift of practices, Giddens identifies de-routinization as a second source of change.

8. Schatzki (1997), p. 290.

9. See for example Mestrovic (1998).

10. The quote is from Storper (1985, p. 419). For an analysis of Giddens from a critical perspective, see for example Willmott (1999) and Craig (1992).

11. See Gregson (1989) for an extensive discussion.

12. See Jones and Karsten (2003) and Pozzebon and Poisonneault (2005).

13. Quoted in Callinicos (1985), p. 144.

14. See Orlikowski (2000).

15. The expression is taken from Whittington (1992). For an extensive review of the influence of structurationism on strategic management research see Pozzebon (2004).

16. See Schatzki (1996; 1997) for an in-depth discussion of this weakness of Giddens' work.

17. *Le Sens Pratique*, the title of the French edition of Bourdieu (1990) has been translated in English as *The Logic of Practice*; this expression however captures only in part the many nuances of the term that '*sens*' has acquired in all in neo-Latin languages ('*senso*' in Italian and Spanish, '*sensu*' in Portuguese). '*Sens*' means in fact at the same time, direction (of a road or journey), sense (as faculty of sensation and feeling), sensation, and meaning (as in 'it makes sense', it is sensible).

18. While in his early work on practice (Bourdieu 1977), subjectivism is made to include phenomenological and ethno-methodological approaches (the latter considered as the currently active school of the former, see p. 3), the target of latter work is more extreme positions like Sartre's 'imaginary anthropology'. Although Bourdieu does not provide explanations for this change of heart, one may speculate that, being the reflective and dynamic author that he is, he hasn't remained indifferent to comments such as those made in Francois Heràn's (1987),

who clearly demonstrated the continuities between the work of Bourdieu and that of Husserl and Merleau-Ponty.

19. For an extended discussion of the historical genealogy of the idea of habit and habitus, see Heràn, 1987.

20. See Di Maggio (1979), p. 64 and ff.

21. For an extended discussion of the similarities and differences between Bourdieu, Husserl, and Merleau-Ponty, see Heràn (1987) and Crossley (2001).

22. See Bourdieu (1984), p. 101.

23. Bourdieu cautions against taking the formula too seriously. In fact, it is a very poor depiction of his complex and rich theory. For one thing, for example, the formula doesn't convey the idea of the recursive nature of all the processes under scrutiny and hence it would require at a minimum a few re-entrant paths to indicate a feedback loop between practices and field, practice and social capital, and practice and habitus.

24. See Harker *et al.* (1990), p. 7.

25. For an in-depth examination of this point, see Lau (2004), pp. 378–9.

26. Bourdieu doesn't exclude the possibility that agents make explicit their *modus operandi*, especially when automatism breaks down. However, this form of reflexivity and the subsequent use of representation of practice in practise always remains subordinate to the pursuit of a practical result, in such a way that the practical pursuit bestows meaning on the representation—something that is not available to un-engaged scholars (see Bourdieu 1990, p. 91).

27. Bourdieu is aware of his tendency to intellectualism: see Bourdieu (1977), p. 117.

28. See Dreyfus and Rabinow (1993) for a discussion.

29. 'A scientific practice that fails to question itself does not, properly speaking, know what it does' (Bourdieu and Wacquant 1992, p. 236).

30. 'The goal of sociology is to uncover the most deeply buried structures of the different social worlds that make up the social universe, as well as the "mechanisms" that tend to ensure their reproduction or transformation' (Bourdieu 1996, p. 1).

31. My calculation is based on Golsorskhi and Huault's (2006) statements that between 2000 and 2005 Bourdieu was cited in about sixty articles in organization and management journals. A rapid check on one of the available journal databases reveal that there are almost 1000 articles using the concept of tacit knowledge (while habitus generates less than fifty hits). My figure is thus very conservative but telling nonetheless.

32. Cordon bleu cooks were studied by Gomez *et al.* (2003); Wainwright, Williams, and Turner (2007) used habitus to explore ballet as both a bodily performance and an institutionalized genre; publans and public sector workers were investigated respectively by McDounough (2006) and Mutch (2003).

33. See for example Lounsbury (2003; 2008); Lounsbury and Ventresca (2003); Battilana (2006); Lawrence and Suddaby (2006); Lawrence *et al.* (2009). The affordances of habitus as a meso level concept is discussed in some detail in Özbilgin and Tatli (2005).

34. Background information on the practice of telemedicine is provided in the Introduction.

4 Practice as Tradition and Community

One of the aspects emerging from the previous chapter is that socialization and learning are indispensable elements of any coherent practice-based theorizing. Both Giddens and Bourdieu rely heavily on the mechanism of socialization for explaining some critical aspects of practice, such as its perpetuation in time, its structuring force, and its capacity to carry structure. In this sense Bourdieu's and Giddens' practice theories constitute a significant variation of, and in many ways a radical departure from, a more general and very common line of argumentation in Western social theory that tends to associate the notion of practice with that of tradition and/or community. It is this way of understanding practice that I intend to address here.

The argument that understands practice and practical knowledge as a form of tradition sustained by a community and inscribed in the body and/or mind is, of course, anything but new. The association between practice, tradition, and community goes back to Plato and Aristotle, and features in one way or another in the work of many of the founders of modern social thought, from Durkheim to Weber and Mauss.[1] Moreover, this idea is implicit in many of the arguments discussed in the previous two chapters. Nyiri (1988) points out that the equation between practice and tradition constitutes a corollary of the notion that procedural and propositional knowledge are qualitatively different. To the extent that practical knowledge cannot be translated into words, either because it is pre-verbal and personal or because it serves as a foundation for much of what we know, it can only be transmitted through custom, institutions, and processes of handing down—'that is traditions' (Nyiri 1988, p. 17).[2]

Giving prominence to the process of handing down institutionalized ways of doing and talking, the effects of such a process, and the social bonding or communitarian dimension that may result from it is, however, a risky move. While devoting too scant attention to the issue of the transmission of practice leaves us with the problem of how to justify its duration in time and its causal power, too much emphasis on practice as tradition also poses some important theoretical challenges. Notions such as socialization and community always threaten to take us back to a functionalist perspective on social phenomena; that is, in a direction which is contrary to the theoretical sensitivity promoted by most practice theories.

Accordingly, in this chapter I will illustrate and critically review the work of some of the authors who have examined practice as a form of tradition handed down through a process of social learning. I will focus in particular on the idea that practice is reproduced in time through a process of active engagement and participation sustained by a specific community. I will argue that while a coherent theory of learning and transmission is a requisite element of any theory of practice, there is a fine balance to be struck between recognizing that all practices need to be recognized by a group of practitioners, and the reification of such a collective into a social body that exists independently of the practice. Beneath the fine line between these two positions lies, in fact, one of the major fracture lines in contemporary social theory. This fracture line separates the view that the world is made of stable social entities in interaction from the view consituting the subtext of this work, that we are better served by the idea that the social world is, in fact, made through process, work, and effort.

4.1 **Practice, tradition, and learning**

According to Stephen Turner, the argument which understands practice as a form of tradition contains two aspects: (1) the notion that practice implies an element of habituation and learning; i.e. the handing down of ways of doing and being at an individual level, and (2) the notion that practice refers to something that goes beyond the individual and that persists in time; i.e. the historical part (Turner 1984). Turner, who is not sympathetic towards a practice-based explanation of social phenomena, refuses (2) above, and believes that explaining regularities, continuities, and sameness of behaviour across groups of people by recourse to 'practices' in the second sense is to appeal to obscure forces and elusive objects. Although his critical argument is, on the whole, unconvincing,[3] it can be credited with the merit of articulating the two-sided nature of the notion of practice as tradition, and of raising the issue of how the process of habituation and learning (point 1 above) can explain the part that goes beyond it (point 2 above). In other words, Turner's criticism forces us to realize that, if we are to provide a convincing account not only of how ingrained ways of doing persist in time, but also why people stick to them, we need to support the argument with a coherent theory of learning. As Jean Lave once put it, without such an element, practice theory as a radically processual (and critical) social theory is bound to collapse 'like a table without a leg'. Alternatively, we are left with an obscure notion of practice as a hidden and metaphysical collective object that exerts some form of causal power over the behaviour of individuals (Turner 1984). As I explain below, such a theory of learning is to be found in the process of socialization and apprenticeship, or, to be more precise, in some of its more recent re-conceptualizations.

The critical role that the process of handing down a tradition from generation to generation plays in explaining its very existence hasn't gone unnoticed. In fact, it has been addressed by a number of authors since Plato under the two related headings of socialization and apprenticeship.

Durkheim, for example, gave the issue a prominent role and socialization remained central in the sociological tradition that stemmed from his work. For the celebrated early sociologist, socialization through family and schooling sensitizes subjects to the different orders of society because it acts selectively on their life chances, creating a sense of the inevitability of a given social order and restricting the amount of permitted change.[4] In this way, socialization explains at the same time the existence of a societal level of phenomena independent of individual members, and the emergence of individuals within society.

Apprenticeship is the other term used to describe the capacity of practice to endure over time as the perpetuation of a tradition. Although the underlying mechanism of apprenticeship is similar to that of socialization, the term is used in a narrower sense to describe the specific process through which skills, usually those of craftsmen and artists, are handed down to the next generation. In this view, apprenticeship always presupposes (i) a relationship between master and pupil, (ii) a recognized power differential between the two, and (iii) specific learning mechanisms such as imitation, practising, and the use of discourse in practice (Gherardi and Nicolini 2002). Therefore, for apprenticeship to function as a learning process, it depends on the acceptance of the inequality of relative social positions.[5]

Although a detailed discussion of the notion of apprenticeship goes beyond the scope of this book, one should note that the traditional notion of apprenticeship restricts its scope to specific historical and societal circumstances (the craftsman's shop of the pre-industrial era) and tends to focus on the dyadic relationship. As argued by Lave and Wenger (1991), such a narrow way of understanding apprenticeship, where the fundamental process is confused with one specific historical instantiation, has prevented scholars from recognizing the ubiquity and general validity of this way of learning. Accordingly, failing to recognize the social process that underlies specific historical instantiations of apprenticeship prevents us from understanding, for example, why this way of being socialized at work persisted into the second industrial revolution and still prevails, for example, in the vocational world. To rescue the idea of apprenticeship, argue the two authors, we need to develop a theory of learning that explains apprenticeship as a particular case of a more fundamental learning process. The two authors identify such a process in the mechanism of 'legitimate peripheral participation' (LPP) and use this construct to develop a notion of learning as the socially structured process by which one absorbs, and is absorbed into, a practice.[6]

The main tenet of LPP is that the process through which the learner becomes effectively engaged is an ongoing practice characterized by a specific and identifiable social process; that is, a specific regime of participation that entails partial responsibility for the ultimate product. Through this process, the learner obtains access to the expertise that is socially sustained in the ongoing practice as well as to the sociality that grows around, and sustains, the activity. LPP therefore identifies learning not as a cognitive process as much as a social one that is about belonging, engagement, inclusiveness, and developing identities:

> Absorbing and being absorbed in the 'culture of practice' (...) might include (knowing) who is involved, what they do, what everyday life is like, how masters talk, walk, work, and generally conduct their lives, how people who are not part of the community of practice interact with it, what other learners are doing, and what learners need to learn to became full practitioners. It includes an increasing understanding of how, when, and about what old-timers collaborate, collude, and collide, and what they enjoy, dislike, respect, and admire. In particular it offers exemplars (which are grounds and motivation for learning activity), including masters, finished products, and more advanced apprentices in the process of becoming full practitioners (Lave and Wenger 1991, p. 95).

LPP refers then to the progressive involvement of new arrivals in the practice as they acquire growing competence on what is going on.

The term 'legitimate' emphasizes that a necessary condition for learning anything at all is to become effectively and recognizably part of an activity; to learn one needs both to immerse oneself in what is going on, with all the risks and emotions that this implies, as well as to become a 'stakeholder' in the ongoing practice. LPP therefore suggests that learning is both a condition for membership and is itself an evolving form of membership: 'identity, knowing and social membership entail one another' (Lave and Wenger 1991, p. 53).

'Participation' indicates that learning always takes place because of (and thanks to) the interaction with others. For LPP theory, however, the context of learning is not merely collective but more poignantly social; that is, impregnated with history and articulated according to a specific division of influence and power. Since knowledge is integrated and distributed between all the various participants in the practice, both human and non-humans, and because learning is an act of belonging, learning necessarily requires involvement in, and contribution to, the ongoing practice and its development. In other words, learning cannot take place if participation is not possible. According to the LPP approach, in fact, participation in the cultural environment and in the practices which sustain a certain body of knowledge is an epistemological principle of learning. The social structure of the practice, and the existing power relations which define the regime and conditions of participation therefore define at the same time the range of learning possibilities granted to the novice. This fact, combined with individual characteristics of the learner and the particular broader contextual conditions, determine similar but never identical learning curricula and learning trajectories (Lave and Wenger 1991; Gherardi *et al.* 1998).

By entering a practice, a novice doesn't just assimilate new competence but also confirms, sustains, and reproduces the social order that sustains it. In this way, the LPP perspective links inextricably the development of knowledgeable identities with the reproduction and transformation of the social fabric of a practice. To learn is both to join and to subvert the existing fabric of power/ knowledge. No matter how compliant and subservient the novice is, there is no such a thing as learning without conflict; any modification of the knowledge distribution is (and is often perceived) as a way of subverting the established knowledge/power relations within a social context, or, more precisely, a way of subverting the established relations which determine the power of the actors involved (Foucault 1966). For this reason, LPP always entails unresolved ambivalence, such as that between revealing trade secrets to a novice so permitting her socialization, against hiding them to preserve the status quo, and that between an attempt by the novice to worm out tricks of the trade against her search for new and emancipating ways of doing things that may affirm her autonomy.

Finally, the adjective 'peripheral' suggests the existence of a variety of positions that members can occupy with respect to the activity carried out and the people involved in it. Lave and Wenger (1991) clearly state that the notion of peripheral participation does not necessarily imply the existence of a centre, and the uniform trajectory from periphery to centre in the learning and conduct of a practice. Instead, it is more a recognition that a practice is performed in a number of social places, each of which entails different power and influence. Put differently, one may say that in the LPP process, peripherality both exempts and empowers: 'where' novices stand with respect to the responsibilities for the final product makes a big difference both to them and to others. Peripherality, for example, influences the balance between how much you can learn from others and how much others may learn from you. In fact, in this model, novices do not learn only from their mentors (as in the traditional model) but also from other participants in the practice, including other novices. At the same time, learning does not 'flow' in one direction from those who are experts to those who aren't. Every interaction is an opportunity to learn and modify the ongoing practice.

It is clear that the theory of LPP was bound to produce (and did produce) some far-reaching consequences for the study of learning. Out of the many theoretical and practical implications of this approach,[7] at least two are worth mentioning.

First, by recasting learning as a particular aspect of any social practice, LPP affirms that learning should not be separated from the activity to which it refers. In many ways, LPP states that talking about learning is just one way of talking about those activities, a way that focuses on the consequences that the different positions within the social organization of the practice bring to bear on the division of tasks, distribution of responsibility, learning trajectories, and identity of participants. With LPP theory, the analytical focus shifts from learning as an activity performed by the individual to learning as a mode of participation in the social world. Studying learning from the LPP perspective implies that instead of attempting to explain what kind of cognitive processes and conceptual structures are involved, we try to understand what sort of social engagements provide the proper context for learning. In this way we can approach the study of learning and its conditions as social phenomena rather that processes which take place 'inside' the head of individuals. Instead of using the conceptual toolkit of psychologists, we can thus study learning using the sociological imagination. Indeed, Lave and Wenger's work sparked a host of ethnographic studies of situated learning which have explored, among other things, the conditions that foster or hamper learning, the role of artefacts and narratives, the use of language and linguistic practices in the process of learning, and the relationship between the practice, the opportunities of learning; and the resulting identity of the learner (Lave and Wenger 1991; Orr, 1996; Chaiklin and Lave 1993).

Second, the notion of LPP makes clear that the handing-down process is not a smooth or friendly affair. LPP, in fact, highlights the importance of the conditions and modes of engagement in the activity as a way to understand learning and its barriers. The unfolding social activity is what gives meaning to operations and membership: who counts as a model, what are the rewards and punishments, what should and shouldn't be retained and repeated. These aspects only become apparent and acquire sense to the extent that the learner is actively participating in a practice.

Besides constituting one of the major educational theory innovations of recent years, Lave and Wenger's approach provides a critical contribution to practice theory. As Lave's comment reported above clearly indicates, this is anything but incidental. The notion of learning as LPP was explicitly intended as a contribution to a way of theorizing that puts practices at the foundation of sociality. In fact, for the authors, LPP goes beyond the notion that learning is situated in a context. The notion of situated learning, albeit constituting a significant departure from the traditional idea that learning amounts to storing information in someone's mind, is still amenable to a reductive reading that takes learning 'as...some independently reifiable process that just happened to be located somewhere' (Lave and Wenger 1991, p. 35). On the contrary, LPP intends to affirm that learning is not something that happens in a social context but is 'a descriptor of the process of engagement in social practice that entails learning as an integral constituent' (ibid.). In other words, LPP is intended to be part of a broader and coherent practice approach, and it can only be fully comprehended within this context: 'Learning is an integral part of a generative social practice in the lived-in world' (ibid.).

Returning to Turner's criticism cited earlier, LPP in fact successfully performs two functions for practice thinking. Firstly, it establishes the otherwise mysterious link between the synchronic and diachronic dimension of practices. It does so by showing that habituation sustains the perpetuation of practice which, in turn, sustains habituation. The result is a recursive pattern that extends practice in history. Secondly, as I will discuss shortly, it helps to explain the origins of the normative force of practice and hence its rule-like flavor; that is, when we follow a practice or a rule we do not choose but obey blindly, as Wittgenstein once put it (Wittgenstein 1953).

Taken in the first sense, LPP offers a convincing way to bridge the two aspects of practice (habituation and the historical part) identified by Turner and discussed above. In other words, Lave and Wenger's LPP provides an analytic description of the link between (1) and (2) that does not require the introduction of mental contents, schema, or other notions that would contradict some of the basic tenets of practice theory as intended in this work. In fact, LPP has the great merit of reconciling habituation and tradition by taking into account a third common, and too often disregarded, meaning of the word 'practise'; that is, the verbal form of 'to practise' as in 'practising an art', both in the sense of learning the ropes and refining one's skills. Many authors, in fact, tend to concentrate on the former two, glossing over the third. Consider the following:

At least three notions of practice are prominent in the current conjuncture... practising as 'learning how' or improving one's ability to do something... practice as a temporally unfolding and spatially dispersed nexus of doings and sayings... and practice as performing an action or carrying out a practice of the second sort. [The first notion] is not irrelevant to the current discussion. But it will be put aside in what follows (Schatzki 1996, p. 90).

Schatzki, who as we shall see counts as being a convinced practice theorist, fails to see that a process such as LPP constitutes the necessary link between a nexus of doing and saying, and its performance in the real world by more than one person at the time. Take LPP away, and you are left with three equally undesirable options: (1) rendering a mystery the way in which practices are 'transmitted' between people and through generations, or (2) using quasi-metaphysical intermediaries as certain constructs in the Durkheimian tradition; e.g. Moscovici's social representations,[8] or (3) discarding the notion of practice altogether, as proposed by Stephen Turner (1994).

There is, however, a second way in which LPP supports practice theory. LPP as a social process of learning helps to elucidate why practices have a normative dimension; that is, why we can only say that actors share a practice 'if their actions are appropriately regarded as answerable to norms of correct and incorrect practice'(Rouse 2001, p. 190). This is possible because, through the process of LPP, novices do not acquire just the necessary knowledge to perform the activity, but also absorb a moral way of being; that is, a model of excellence specific to that practice that determines at once an ethic, a set of values, and the sense of virtues associated with the achievement of the high standard of conduct implicit in the practice.

This aspect has been convincingly discussed by MacIntyre. The author defines practice[9] as a:

coherent and complex form of socially established co-operative human activities through which goods internal to that form of activity are realised in the course of trying to achieve those standards of excellence which are appropriate to, and practically definitive of, that form of activity, with the results that human powers to achieve excellences, and human conceptions of the ends and goods involved, are systematically extended (MacIntyre 1981, p. 187).

For MacIntyre, practices involve standards of excellence and obedience to rules as well as achievement of goods. To be absorbed in a practice is to accept the authority of those standards and to accept that the inadequacy of a given performance may be judged by them. Although these standards have a history and are therefore subject both to change and criticism, a practice without standards is not a practice. Above all, one cannot be initiated into a practice without accepting the initial incapacity to judge correctly. 'If, on starting to play baseball, I do not accept that others know better than I when to throw a fast ball and when not, I will never learn to appreciate good pitching (or to hear good music, or to recognise a nice building) let alone pitch' (MacIntyre 1981, p. 190). According to MacIntyre then, inherent in the concept of practice is the notion that its goods can only be achieved by subordinating ourselves within the practice in our relationships with other practitioners, and that we have to accept, as necessary components of any practice, both the goods and standards of excellence as well as the honesty and courage on the part of the novice in his/her attempt to achieve them. A novice who cheats, who is unwilling to embrace these goods and try, at least to some extent, to achieve them, will simply not become part of that practice.

Returning to our previous discussion, it is clear that this moral aspect is both what is passed on through LPP and what motivates and fuels the process itself. Although this aspect is rarely considered in the literature, it is fair to say that within the LPP process one cannot separate the cognitive from the moral and affective aspects of learning. More to the point, the moral aspect is crucial both to practice and to its perpetuation (see also Thevenot 2001, p. 59). That is to say, what is produced and reproduced through the LPP processes are not only ingrained ways of doing and the relationships between those who participate in a given practice, but also the normative, telic, and affective dimensions of a practice that those who are involved in it experience and report.

In this sense, LPP sheds light on Wittgenstein's notions discussed in Chapter 2, that to know how to follow a rule is something that cannot be fully articulated, although it can be communicated. It can be added that Wittgenstein himself established a relationship between this fact and social learning processes:

System communications...we shall call 'language games'...Children are taught their native language by means of such games...The boy or grown-up learns what one might call special technical languages, e.g., the use of charts and diagrams, descriptive geometry, chemical symbolism, etc., he learns more language games (Wittgenstein 1980, p. 201).

In a similar ways, LPP also explains why, when observed from the outside, practices appear to be endowed with a mix of teleology and affectivity, what Schatzki describes as the normative teleo-affective structure of practices (see Chapter 7). As affirmed by MacIntyre, the sense of good that one introjects while being absorbed in a practice includes a range of acceptable and correct ends, tasks, and beliefs, a sense of which tasks are appropriate to achieve which ends, a set of discursive resources to account for what is appropriate, and even what are acceptable or correct emotions that should accompany the practice.[10] These elements are perpetuated—which doesn't mean perfectly reproduced— through LPP. They not only play a central role in the agents' practical intelligibility, and orientate people in the same activity towards mutually recognizable ends and a communal sense of how things matter, they also constitute a resource for collective processes of identity-making and taking. This, as I discuss shortly, allows, for example, fellow practitioners to describe themselves (from the outside) as a community of practice.

If, thanks to its focus on the reproduction process, LPP gives new meaning and strength to the understanding of practice and practical knowledge as a tradition, it still bears some of the weaknesses somewhat inherent in the underlying idea of tradition. Two major weaknesses are worth emphasizing here.

In the first place, like all other theories of tradition, LPP is much more effective in explaining persistence and perpetuation than it is in explaining change. That is to say, LPP tends to explain change as the incremental result of imperfect reproduction and of the micro-conflict inherent in the relation between generations. As I noted above, learning a practice involves, by definition, a conflict between continuity and displacement: 'newcomers are caught in a dilemma. On the one hand they need to engage in the existing practice, which was developed over time...On the other hand they have a stake in its development as they begin to establish their own identity in its future' (Lave and Wenger 1991, p. 116). The ensuing conflict is what puts 'practice in motion' (ibid.) and what makes change one of its fundamental properties. Without repeating some of the criticisms applied to the notion of habitus, and that can be also applied to LPP, it is worth noting that while this incremental model has some appeal when applied to traditional practices (West African tailors, midwives) as studied by Lave and Wenger, it is much less convincing when applied to other, more rapidly changing activities and contexts. This aspect is exacerbated by the theory's marginal attention to the role of mediating artefacts. The result is that it is quite difficult to explain some of the profound and stepwise changes affecting practices in post-industrial society simply as the outcome of the incremental changes generated by the socialization of newcomers.

The latter point is strictly connected to the second major source of criticism towards this approach; that is, its incapacity to take into account the relations between practice and its wider socio-historical context, including broader issues of power, ideology, and domination. The issue has been extensively discussed by Contu and Wilmott who note that history and conflict have only a minor role in the theory (Contu and Wilmott 2000; 2003). While power, conflict, and contradiction are discussed and do play a role in the perpetuation and change of a practice, their role is always interpreted at the level of micro interactions. In this way, say the authors, the dynamics of identity construction and maintenance are not situated within a wider institutional context of struggles associated with forms of domination and exploitation. There is a risk, in other words, that focusing on practices as the result of a process of imperfect reproduction through LPP distracts us from the fact that such a process takes place within a wider political economy of sense, and that practices do not exist, emerge, or perpetuate in a vacuum but play instead a role in broader discursive formations that concur to determine both the conditions of legitimacy of novices, the nature and content of the teleo-affective structure of practices, and the level of conflict generated in the process (Contu and Wilmott 2000).

4.2 **Practice and community**

A different way to summarize Contu and Wilmott's criticisms presented above is to note that LPP ambiguously stands at the boundary of two different ways of conceiving the relation between practice, learning, and tradition. These are the processual and constructivist view discussed above, and one that is more functionalist in character and exists side by side with the former.

This underlying ambivalence became especially visible during one of the developments of the original work on LPP, in particular the strand of work focusing on the relations between practice and community, and which came under the heading of 'community of practice'.

The notion of 'community of practice' was first introduced by Lave and Wenger in order to identify the network of actors involved in the LPP process (Lave and Wenger 1991).

The authors define community of practice as

a set of relations among persons, activity, and world, over time and in relation with other tangential and overlapping communities of practice. A community of practice is an intrinsic condition for the existence of knowledge, not least because it provides the interpretative support necessary for making sense of its heritage. Thus, participation in the cultural practice in which any knowledge exists is an epistemological principle of learning (Lave and Wenger 1991, p. 98).

The notion was, first and foremost, used to confute the traditional idea that apprenticeship was a two-person business—between master and apprentice. In fact, the notion of an LPP process extends the range of learning opportunities available to novices. These opportunities include a variety of previously disregarded sources such as other experts, advanced novices, other apprentices; as well as the artefacts used within the activity. However, this de-centring strategy also implies an extension of the notion of mastery to become a notion of mastery as residing no more in the master alone but 'in the organization of the community of practice of which the master is part' (Lave and Wenger 1991, p. 94). The notion of 'community of practice', then, extends to knowledge of the social and historical character that the LPP bestowed on learning.[11] Knowing is, therefore, understood as a socially and historically situated phenomenon:

Knowing is inherent in the growth and transformation of identities and is located in relations among practitioners, their practice, the artefacts of that practice, and the social organization and political economy of communities of practice (Lave and Wenger 1991, p. 122).

In the original formulation, the notion of 'community of practice' mainly denotes the pattern of sociality performed by a practical regime through its reproduction process:

[community of practice] implies participation in an activity system about which participants share understanding concerning what they are doing and what that means in their lives and for their communities (ibid.).

The notion, moreover, was meant to attract attention to the fact that 'knowing' is an effect of such sociality, and that the structure of relations as well as the existing power inequalities play a central role in the distribution, reproduction, and change of such knowing. The 'common' aspect here is mainly the activity in which participants are involved and that they contribute to, sustain, and perpetuate. It is this practice that allows them to understand each other and to act in a recognizable way. The common practice also constitutes a resource for identification vis-à-vis other practices and communities. That is to say, participation in a practice and a recognizable history of learning can be used as a resource in the process of identity making and taking. In summary, practice performs community and sustains identification processes.

It is worth noting that when they introduced the notion, Lave and Wenger went to some length to caution that in using the term 'community' they didn't imply 'some primordial culture sharing entity' (Lave and Wenger 1991, p. 98), and that '...participation at multiple levels is entailed in membership in a community of practice'. Nor did the term 'community' necessarily imply 'co-presence, a well-defined identifiable group, or socially visible boundaries...' (ibid.). Why all this caution?

The captivating power of the notion of community of practice stems from the risky juxtaposition of two terms, practice and community, each of which has a distinctly different lineage. Community is a term with a long, and somewhat troublesome meaning, both in current parlance and social science jargon.

Since the work of Tönnies (1887/2001), the notion of community, just as that of tradition, has been used ideologically; that is, in such a way that a prescriptive use of the term is hidden behind a descriptive one. Tönnies, it is worth recalling, used the term to introduce a value-laden distinction between *Gemeinschaft* (community) and *Geselleschaft* (society). *Gemeinschaft* is the traditional community. It was presented as the pre-industrial phenomenon, which resulted in enduring, genuine, and intimate relationships rooted in family and kinship, and the creation of bonds arising from shared language and customs. Under conditions of Gemeinschaft members of the community find strength in their similarities, and operate under a collective conscience. Communication consists of face-to-face interaction, and ideas are transmitted through an oral culture. *Geselleschaft*, on the other hand, was defined as the newer industrial concept—a superficial, transitory artefact which was contractual in nature and where all relationships were impersonal and individualistic. These relationships were based on, and carried forward by, self-interest.

Almost a century later, Hillery (1955), when reviewing academic studies of community in the mid-1950s, found ninety-four different definitions of community. Many of the definitions had at least one of three elements in common: a reference to some defined and limited geographic area; the existence of social interaction among people; and that people in the community have some common tie, such as social life, a consciousness of their homogeneity, or some norms, means, or ends (Hillery 1955). Hillery found that 'interaction' and 'ties of interest' were the features most commonly shared by academics working in the area, followed by 'geographical proximity'. Almost all of them, however, referred to community in positive terms, as the locale of solidarity, mutual understanding, shared interests, or common endeavour. Within a century, community, or, to be more precise, its romanticized image, had come to represent social scientists' idealized form of sociality.

This moral aspect survived the demise of the geographical constraint as a definitional character of community—a tendency that pre-dates the recent interest in virtual communities. When Anderson (1983) describes American 'imagined communities' as any community that is (a) larger than the smallest village, and (b) imagined, 'because most people never know most of their fellow community members or know anything about them' (Anderson 1983, p. 6), he posits a unified sense of union (he called it a 'selfless feeling of unisonance') as the common ingredient. Although community members may never meet in person, 'in the minds of each lives the image of their communion' (ibid.).

Historically then, the notion of community carries with it a real or imagined sense of the 'doceure d'être inclu'[12] which obscures power, conflict, and differences. Far from being a descriptive term, community therefore constitutes a 'discursive formation' (Foucault 1969); that is, a power/knowledge apparatus which controls what can be talked about, and who is allowed to speak/write about it, and which dictates rules for proper forms that concepts and theories must assume in order to be accepted as knowledge. The notion of community emphasizes stability, commonality, reciprocity, what can be shared, boundaries, and rules of inclusion/exclusion. It makes talk of conflict and inequality anti-communitarian; that is, a morally unacceptable sign of selfishness and betrayal of the common bond. At the same time, traditional community thinking introduces a style of social science that is necessarily anti-processual in character. To function and to bond their members together, communities have to pre-exist their constituents, who need to be socialized into their rules and 'culture'. More than this, in order to legitimize the criteria of inclusion and the moral values that supposedly bond people together, traditional, but also modern communitarians, need to naturalize community, turning it into a 'res nata' instead of a 'res facta'. As a consequence, a traditional perspective on community promotes a naturalistic, as opposed to a discursive, understanding of identity. According to the former, 'identification is constructed on the back of the recognition of some common origin or shared characteristics with another person or group, or with an ideal, and with the natural closure of solidarity and allegiance established on this foundation' as opposed to the latter which conceives of identity as a temporary effect of discursive practices (Hall 1996, p. 3).[13] In summary, as Rubin (1983) makes clear, community thinking is a necessary ingredient of structural-functionalist social science.

It should now be clearer why the juxtaposition of two terms to form 'community of practice' is risky, and why the two authors were concerned about possible misuses of their notion. In many ways, the notion of community can neutralize the philosophical effects introduced by the notion of practice as discussed in the Introduction, which is more or less what has happened 'in practice' (see e.g. Handley *et al.* 2006 for a review).

Evidence of the effects of traditional community thinking on the notion of 'community of practice' are already identifiable in the development that one of the authors bestowed on the idea in the years following the publication of *Situated Learning*.

In his 1998 book, Wenger explores the concept of community of practice and proposes a framework for thinking about learning in terms of communities, their practices, the meanings they make possible, and the identities they open. The complex essay, with a strong, symbolic, interactionist flavour, is mainly a study of the social formation of identity through learning; that is, how identity emerges as the result of different forms of engagement in communities of practice. Social practice is defined as 'doing, but not just doing in and of itself. It is doing in historical and social context that gives structure and meaning to what people do. In this sense, practice is always social practice' (Wenger 1998, p. 47). The community of practice becomes 'the prime context in which we can work out the common sense through mutual engagement' (ibid.).

It is defined by the following characteristics:

- Mutual engagement: 'practice resides in a community of people and relations of mutual engagement by which they can do whatever they do' (ibid., p. 73).
- Joint enterprise negotiated by the community: 'the enterprise is joint not in that everybody believes the same thing or agrees with everything, but in that it is communally negotiated' (ibid., p. 78).
- Shared repertoire, which constitutes a major 'source of coherence': 'I call a community's set of shared resources a repertoire to emphasise its rehearsed character and its availability for further engagement in practice . . . it reflects a history of mutual engagement and remains inherently ambiguous' (ibid., p. 83).
- Shared histories of learning: 'learning in practice includes . . . evolving forms of mutual engagement, understanding and tuning the enterprise . . . developing their repertoire, styles, and discourses [. . .] Learning is the engine of practice, and practice is the history of that learning' (ibid., pp. 95–6).

To these aspects, which were present although not fully developed in previous works, Wenger adds a few others that are significant for our discussion and symptomatic of the drift of the notion of community of practice over time.

First, according to the author, histories of learning create discontinuities revealed by the learning involved in crossing them. In other words, practice defines boundaries and 'while these boundaries form, communities of practice develop ways of maintaining connections with the rest of the world' (ibid., p. 103). These ways include the use of boundary objects (Star 1989), brokering activities, complementary connections, and boundary encounters. Practice itself becomes a potential 'connection between communities' through boundary practices, overlaps of practices, and 'opening of peripheries' (see Wenger 1998, Ch. 4).

Second, having established the community of practice as a 'something' with defined boundaries, Wenger needs to spell out some criteria to distinguish between a community of practice and something else. This is done by listing a number of categories (see Wenger 1998, p. 126) that, according to the author, render communities of practice something more than simple 'analytic categories' (Wenger 1998, p. 126); that is, a *social structure* that 'reflects shared learning'. These categories allow, for example, discerning between a community of practice and a constellation of interconnected practices—a configuration that is 'too far removed from the scope of engagement of participants, too broad, or too diffuse to be usefully treated as a single community of practice' (ibid.). Constellations of practices are aggregates of bounded communities of practices kept together 'by interactions between practices' (ibid.) which allow a rethink of distances not (only) in terms of locality, proximity, and distance but, above all, in terms of sharing similar histories of learning.

Even from my short rendition, I believe it is apparent that Wenger's argument entails a progressive reification of the notion of community which ceases to be conceived as a process and becomes a well-identifiable social 'thing' connoted by detectable boundaries, specifiable characteristics, and systemic relations. The text itself makes use of a number of terms (boundary, members, social system, locality) that contravene Lave and Wenger's earlier recommendations not to fall for the fallacy of believing that the term community (in the expression 'community of practice') necessarily implies a well-defined identifiable group, or socially visible boundaries (see earlier).[14] Finally, the relative balance of importance between terms seem to change during the discussion, shifting from what at the outset Wenger calls a relation of synonymity ('The term community of practice should be viewed as a unit . . . when I use the term community or the term practice by itself, it is just an abbreviation', Wenger 1998, p. 72) to a relation of dependency of the latter on the former, so that community comes first and contains practice ('practice resides in a community of people', Wenger 1998, p. 73).

The takeover of the notion of community of practice, so to speak, opened the gate for other well-known issues associated with the former concept. Critics note how the functionalist parable of the notion of community of practice, which partly coincides with its appropriation within managerial discourse,[15] has been accompanied by the disappearance of organizational politics and power and change from the debate (Cunliffe and Easterby-Smith 1998; Contu and Wilmott 2000, 2003; Fox 2000). Cunliffe and Easterby-Smith, for example, note that several of the developments of the notion of community of practice 'contain no political component and are therefore unable to deal with the substantial issues of power' (Cunliffe and Easterby-Smith 1998, p. 2). Fox adds that while wider issues of conflict and power are safely tucked away in the footnotes, 'communities of practice theory tells us nothing about how, in concrete practice, members of a community change their practice or innovate' (Fox 2000, p. 860). Contu and Wilmott (2003) conclude that the parable of the 'communities of practice' approach corresponds with a shift from an early discourse in which the enhancement of mutual understanding is conceived as an emancipatory practice to a discourse that is primarily pre-occupied with improving prediction and control for purposes of improving performance: 'we encounter an (unacknowledged) shift or slippage from an earlier representation of learning as praxis fashioned within a discourse of critique to a formulation of learning as technology conceived within a discourse of regulation and performance' (Contu and Wilmott 2000, pp. 272–273).

4.3 Withdrawing the phrase 'community of practice'?

What can we make of all this? As I said, and as other authors have also made clear (see Contu and Wilmott 2003), looking at practice as community (but also as tradition, as I explained above), is fraught with risks. In particular, once we couple the notion of practice with a 'stronger', more entrenched notion, such as community, the former tends to lose its main processual, social, temporary, and conflictual character.

To prevent this, perhaps a solution would be to withdraw the notion of 'community of practice' as an analytic concept, and use 'practice' instead. If two terms are synonyms, as Wenger seemed to believe (see above), we could simply drop the word 'community'. As I have discussed in the previous chapter and above, it is practice, not community, that sustains joint enterprise and mutual engagement. It is the process of perpetuation through learning that endows those who are engaged with specific capabilities and a repertoire of communal resources (routines, sensibilities, artefacts, vocabulary, styles, etc.) that Wenger and other authors identify with as communities of practice. Put differently, practice produces sociality and network effects; it sustains stabilized regimes of saying and doing which constitute a resource for the discursive constitution of individual and collective identities. As Wenger himself recognizes, a community of practice 'need not be reified as such to become a community: it can enter into the experience of participants through their very engagement' (Wenger 1998, p. 84). This is because, as I showed above, it is through learning that practices constitute a contexture of commonality that allows people to connect with the history of learning, to understand each other, and to act in a coordinated manner. There is no need for a voluntaristic notion of community, where it is understood as a self-conscious, self-proclaimed entity to sustain the connectedness bestowed by practice. On the contrary, the sense of community that has fascinated social scientists, politicians, and ideologues of all times reveals to be itself the *result* of specific practices. These practices, as all practices, are not value- or interest-free, and they are indeed integral to the repressive discursive formation discussed above. As Swan *et al.* (2002) have documented, the process of acquiring a practice-related identity and of developing an awareness of 'belonging to a community of practice' is the result of specific intentional practices and specific identity-making and awareness-promoting doings and sayings. These community-making practices are sponsored by specific configurations of interests and facilitated by community-making practitioners in view of the extension of managerial control over the professionals and their competence. In the Swan *et al.* (2002) case, through the use of this performative notion, managers sought to exploit both the performative qualities of the community of practice in relation to the sharing of knowledge, and its associated discursive qualities of consensus and solidarity in relation to the mobilization of commitment for the pursuit of business strategies and commercial objectives. In other cases, the notion of community of practice is heralded by semi-professions in order to gain power through the creation of 'postulated communities (of practice)' supposedly marked by feelings of sharedness and community but which, in fact, are propelled by economic and legitimacy interests (see, for example, Barley and Orr 1997).[16]

However, the suggestion of withdrawing the phrase 'community of practice' is both impractical and, to some extent, counterproductive. For one thing, the term, safely reinterpreted within the functionalist paradigm through the process discussed above, has been enthusiastically endorsed by large sections of management studies and has acquired a currency and acceptance. Not only does the term now appear in most recent editions of the main organizational behaviour textbooks, it has also been turned into a thriving consulting opportunity. Withdrawing the term would amount to closing the proverbial stable door after the horse has long gone or, seen from a different perspective, after the horse has been seized by the not-so-obscure forces of capitalism always in search of a new buzzword to be sold in the thriving market of management consultancy.

There is, however, another reason why withdrawing the term is not a good idea. The notion of a community of practice is critical in emphasizing that a practice counts as such only for those who are capable of recognizing it. 'Recognizing' is, of course, intended here both in a cognitive and normative sense. I may fail to recognize a practice either because I have no idea about what is going on (a sensation that we have all experienced as novices), or because I do not want it or cannot accept it (because we 'do things differently here'). In both cases, however, as suggested originally by Wittgenstein (1953), the implication is that the notion of a private or arbitrary practice is a nonsense. Practices are by definition social, because it is only at this level that morality, meaning, and normativity can be sustained. For this reason, in this text I have omitted the qualification 'social' from the term 'practice'. The term 'social practice' says the same thing twice. It is therefore a tautology.

Accordingly, there is something to be lost if we dispose of the term 'community of practice' which, as I have already discussed, had a precise function in the economy of the processual theory put forward originally by Lave and Wenger (1991). The only way forward is thus using the term in a strongly qualified way, emphasizing that the 'community' in the expression is, if anything, a form of commonality performed by the practice and not vice versa. Communities of practice are thus social structures that do not live up to the criteria of the communitarian ideal. They are one among the many forms of post-communitarian structures which populate the knowledge society. As such they are inherently communities without unity.[17]

A different way of expressing the same concept is to emphasize that communities of practice are, in fact, communities of practitioners constantly busy positioning themselves within the ongoing practice. Practitioners, as in the vignette discussed at the end of the chapter, do not need to share the same occupational background, the same interests, or some kind of feeling of unisonance in order to be part of the community of practice. It is the practice itself that provides the common background: as I described above, it is practice which performs community and not the other way around. In this sense, the practice which brings practitioners together also divides them, as all practices have by definition a plurality of positions and voices. As much as sharing some inexistent substance, knowing how to be a good practitioner implies knowing how to interact with different 'knowings' and the power positions that go with them. This requires, in turn, an appreciation of the different perspectives based, for example, on the understanding of the practical concerns that guide other people's conduct. It also requires the establishment of discursive and material practices of mutual positioning and alignment. The result is that the practice consistently looks much more like a dissonant pattern of voices in search of a precarious point of alignment than a canon sung in unison by all those involved.

In summary, learning and tradition explain some fundamental aspects of practice and practicing while leaving others in the background. As I have shown, these two concepts conjure up a static and ahistorical view of practice, one in which perpetuation prevails over change, and the associations between humans overshadow the inherent materiality of all practices. One can note, in fact, that even when amended from some of its functionalist overtones, the idea of community of practice still performs the specific discursive effect of attributing the inherent sociality of practices to human agents. This notion, however, is scarcely credible, especially in a society where artefacts constitute both the trigger, the media, and often the reason for the emergence of both transient and stable forms of sociality (Nicolini, Mengis, and Swan, 2012). Artefacts, both the tools we use and the spaces we gather in, often sustain our sociality as much as the intentional conduct of human actors does. This aspect, however, is scarcely considered in this particular way of understanding practice. In order to make room for artefacts, conflict, and materiality in the understanding of practice we need to turn to a different thought tradition which can accommodate such aspects in their theoretical understanding. Accordingly, in the next section, I will introduce cultural historical activity theory, a form of practice-based theorizing firmly rooted in the Marxian tradition. My argument will be that by developing some of Marx's original intuitions, cultural historical activity theory developed an approach which addresses many of the issues left unresolved by the notion of habitus and the 'practice-as-tradition' approach which I discussed above. Resolving such issues—from materiality to change and conflict—is critical for a sound understanding of practice.

Rolling case study: Becoming part of the practice of telemedicine[18]

All practices need to be learned and telemedicine is no exception. This applies not only to those who, in common parlance, are described as practitioners (nurses, doctors, and other healthcare specialists), but to patients as well.

The nurses who are new to this activity undergo a short period of apprenticeship, during which they are taught how the telemedicine process works, the canonical form of telephone calls, as well as other fundamental 'tricks of the trade'. They are required first to occupy a legitimate peripheral position, observing for a short period the work of one of their senior colleagues. This takes three to four weeks in the case of a junior nurse from a hospital ward, and slightly less when the newcomer is a practitioner from the sub-intensive unit. The nurses are later allowed to take phone calls and deal with lighter cases. In this phase, they interact a lot with the senior nurses and the consultant cardiologist, both to ask questions and to confirm their decisions. Only later can they deal autonomously with some less serious cases. Through a process of social learning, the newcomers internalize some of the practical knowledge and tricks of the trade which are typical of the way in which telemonitoring is practised at Garibaldi. For example, they learn that:[19]

- After you report to work and before going to the telemedicine room you should pass by the nurses' office. You need to check to see if there are any messages for you (some patients may have called during the night) or any other news. You then collect the list of patients to be discharged over the next few days who have been placed on the telemedicine list. You chat briefly with other ward colleagues, ask who the doctors on duty are, who is doing what that day (e.g. exercise tests, echocardiographs), and who did the night shift. In this way you find out who to ask in case of need and which doctors to avoid because they are in a bad mood.
- Once you get to the telemedicine room, check the faxes to see whether your patients' test results have come in. Your patients know that before the scheduled phone calls, they have to do tests and send the results via fax. If they are there, you put them on a pile of records in the room.
- The first thing to do is reply to urgent requests. If the patients have called during the night you must call them immediately. For routine contacts it is

pointless to call too soon because many of the patients still have to get up from bed, or measure their blood pressure, weight, etc. Many others will be out shopping or with their doctor. Since it is summer, you will be aware that the patients prefer to go out when it is cooler.

According to the more senior staff, it takes at least six months to become a good tele-nurse, or at least to become as good a tele-nurse as possible. Not only the nurses but also the patients need to be socialized into the practice of telemedicine. As it is for nurses, theirs is in fact a re-socialization which builds on previous knowledge on how to 'be' a patient.

Becoming an expert patient is something that we all learn from an early age— by going to the doctor, being examined and cured, visiting sick people in hospitals, and perhaps by being admitted to one. Through this long process of experiential learning, we learn the conducts that makes for a good patient in Western medicine: we learn to respond to the physician's questions; we learn to open our mouths when the dentist bends towards us holding her instruments; we learn to take prescribed medicines when we return home. For not-so-lucky individuals, for example, those who suffer from a chronic disease, the apprenticeship lasts so long that they become experts. In the case of telemedicine, most of the patients knew more about their ailment and remedies than their own family doctors—with all the complications that this entailed.

When a patient becomes part of a complex practical regime like this which allows nurses to monitor a life-threatening condition from a distance, she or he must put to use all the expertise acquired in the past, plus learn something new. Enrolment, the military term used when the patient joins this type of service, is a critical aspect of this organized activity.

The enrolment implies first an effort at socializing the patients so that they know about their disease, and above all become accustomed to self-managing their condition. This educative aspect includes distributing leaflets, constant work to make clear to patients the symptoms and the effects of the drugs they will have to take, and more generally the dynamics of chronic heart failure itself. The patients learn these things not only from the staff but also from other patients via the small talk that goes on in the wards. In this way they become increasingly knowledgeable about their disease, a knowledge that they often willingly pass on to the next cohort of patients.

Through this combination of formal training and incidental learning, the patients and their families are socialized into the discourse of active involvement in the process of care and its specific moral and disciplinary regime. By learning about the disease and the way it is controlled, they become their own doctors and controllers. The process also connotes the relationship between staff and patients in explicitly moral terms. From then on, the nurses' injunctions proffered at a distance (more exercise, stop smoking, etc.) will be construed as a way of reinforcing a partnership against the disease, instead of as a disciplinary and coercive action. Any form of non-compliance will in turn be connoted in a moral sense as something deviating from the practice, thus generating a sense of wrong (and possibly guilt) in the patient.

The second phase of the enrolment into the telemedicine practice takes place inside the hospital in the telemedicine department or, less frequently, at the patient's bedside on the hospital ward. The process generally only takes about twenty minutes, as the people involved are frail and ailing. The nurses concentrate on the aspects of fundamental importance: carefully explaining how the service operates, helping the patients get used to the portable cardiograph (not just using it but also how to send the trace), setting the date for the first contact, enrolling the patient in the register of callers, and opening a medical file. This represents an important opportunity for the nurses to establish personal contact with the patients because after this they will only be speaking to them over the phone.

Practicing with the portable ECG is a key aspect of enrolment. Telemonitoring involves the patient gathering and sending his or her own ECG data. The patient or a family member must place the device directly on the central part of the chest (sternum) and start it by pressing a small button. To send the trace, it is enough to place the ECG device against the telephone receiver and press another button. Both these procedures convert electrical signals into sounds. This means that, with experience, both nurses and patients can become familiar with the sounds and 'hear' the ECG so that they can tell if the recording is good, or if it needs to be repeated because the device was in the wrong position. In this case, the signals will be inadequate or affected by interference so the recording will have to be repeated. The nurses call this ability 'learning to hear a good trace'. To help patients follow these practical procedures correctly within the telemonitoring routine, nurses must simulate the whole procedure personally with the patients during the enrolment process. The nurses observe this phase attentively because while other aspects can be modified 'remotely' after the patient is discharged, this one cannot. So the patients' ability to use the device properly must be consolidated before their departure. Often the nurses will return to the ward to simulate a recording with the patients before their discharge.

Finally, the learning process continues once the patients return to their home. The new patients have now to learn when to contribute to sustaining the practical regime of telemedicine, which requires work and discipline. For example, they have to learn how to prepare for the calls and to obtain the vital data that the nurse will ask for. This requires, for example, having their blood pressure measured, checking their weight and urination, and keeping a log of the results (liquid retention is major early sign of worsening condition for these patients), and sending the ECG trace to the office in time for the nurse to check it before the scheduled call takes place. They also have to learn how to collaborate during the call: they have to learn the flow of the questions, to interpret the nurse's technical expressions (which include names of medicines, names of lab tests, and technical terms such as 'creatinin level'), to report their symptoms and their general state (cardiology is a discipline still firmly based on direct observation of the patient and their physical appearance), and to help the nurses gather all the data they need for monitoring necessary vital parameters. With time and practice (patients can be monitored weekly or fortnightly for years on end), patients become extremely skilled in keeping the practice going, so that the interactions with the nurse become more equal and informal.

The process of socialization thus brings nurses, patients, cardiologists, family doctors, and other 'practitioners' together. The practice of telemedicine makes them knowledgeable members and establishes direct or indirect connection between them. Although patients tend not to go to scientific conferences and are, for this reason, seldom accepted as legitimate members of this particular practice, telemedicine is impossible without their knowledgeable collaboration. Thus, for telemedicine at Garibaldi, there is a precise community of practitioners. That these practitioners work together does not mean, however, that they are joined by some sense of unity. Consider the following exchange observed during a meeting:

> Nurse: (reading from her therapy sheet) *'I spoke with Ms ****...she talked about Lasix with her family doctor...now she takes it all very early in the morning because her doctor told her that what matters is the dosage...'*
> Cardiologist: *'What?!? Absolutely not, no way!'*
> Nurse: *'That's what she has been told (opening her arms, an Italian gesture of discouragement)...she also told me that she is not using the sticking plaster because it makes her dizzy...'*
> Cardiologist: *'What dizziness! She must not change her own therapy... and ensure that she's using the plaster.'*

A critical dimension of making telemedicine happen is drawing on, and working with, different and often dissonant knowledge. Consider, for example, the patient's refusal to assume the prescribed medicine in the light of what one of the family doctors told me: *'Specialist cardiologists are very aggressive about clinical parameters...in order to reduce your overall body pressure of the ventricular diameter to their standards, they often go beyond what an improvement is for the patient. I am thinking of a patient whose life was prolonged by two months, but who had her last year so completely disrupted and such a very low quality of life'* (extract from interview).

In the fragment above we have three very different knowledge abilities— that of a legitimately expert doctor; that of a seemingly expert patient; and that of the clinical and practical skill of the nurse. These 'knowings' do not necessarily converge, yet they have to be worked together. Knowing how to be a good tele-nurse, but also a good cardiologist, patient, and family doctor, implies knowing how to interact with different levels of knowledge and the power positions that go with them. This requires, in turn, an appreciation of the different perspective on which each knowing is based; for example, on the understanding of the practical concerns that guide each other's conduct. It also requires the establishment of discursive and material practices of mutual positioning and alignment. 'Being a nurse' requires working around other levels of knowledge, and continuously negotiating the boundaries with these other levels. The result is that the practice of telemonitoring consistently looks much more like a dissonant pattern of voices in search of precarious points of alignment than a canon sung in unison by all those involved.

■ NOTES

1. See Eisenstadt (1973) and Turner (1994) for an in-depth discussion.
2. For example, says Michael Polanyi: 'By watching the master emulating and his efforts in the presence of his example, the apprentice unconsciously picks up the rules of the art, including those which are not explicitly known to the master himself' (Polanyi 1958, p. 53).
3. The main target of Turner's criticism is the notion of practices as hidden collective objects that exert some form of causal power over the behaviour of individuals. Having locked himself into a language of psychological causality that necessarily requires 'something' capable of exerting such influence, he argues that practices as shared presupposition can hardly play such a role because persistence, sameness in time, and sharedness become very difficult to account for. His proposed solution is therefore to drop the transindividual dimension of practices ('practices without sharing') and to revert to individual habits (1994) and more recently to connectionism (2001) to explain why people do very similar things all the time. Responding to his criticisms, Joseph Rouse (2001) argues that Turner's otherwise flawed argument has the merit of revealing the fundamental ambiguity in the use of the notion of practices between practices as simple regularities and a stronger, normative view of practices. I would add that, by the same token, Turner also highlights some of the difficulties inherent in the association between practice and community.
4. The role of socialization in the reproduction of social order and related inequalities is also a central theme in the work of Bernstein (1975) and Bourdieu and Passeron (1990).
5. Imitation requires that the 'source' is recognized as authoritative for the mechanism to work. As Polanyi put it '[The] hidden rules [of an art] can be assimilated only by a person who surrenders himself (sic) to that extent uncritically to the imitation of another' (Polanyi 1958, p. 53). It is worth reiterating that historically apprenticeship has always been a very authoritarian and exploitative social practice. For centuries apprentices were often reduced to the role of semi-slaves and subject to all sort of harassment—often reduced to beg to survive.
6. See Lave 1988; Lave and Wenger 1991; Chaiklin and Lave 1993.
7. I have discussed these themes in detail elsewhere. See for example Gherardi et al., 1998; Gherardi and Nicolini 2002.
8. Moscovici argued for the existence of socially determined universes which operate at both the cognitive and behavioural level (Moscovici 1969; Farr and Moscovici 1984). He called such constructs, reminiscent of Durkheim's collective representations, social representations. Social representations are cognitive systems with a logic and language allowing the members of a community to organize the conditions and contexts of their interactions. On

the one hand, social representations allow individuals and groups to construct a coherent vision of reality which they use to orient their behaviour. On the other, they are the outcome of mental activity modulated by the features of the social situation in which they are produced.

9. Please note that, for MacIntyre, agriculture and architecture are practices, while planting turnips and laying bricks are not (MacIntyre 1981, Ch. 13).

10. For an illustration of this aspect, see Gherardi and Nicolini 2002a, in which we describe that, to become a site manager in the construction industry, one has to learn to fear and not fear certain aspects of the practice.

11. Studies on organizational cultures have developed the similar concept of the occupational community (Van Maanen and Barley 1984; Kunda 1992; Barley 1986), focusing on the growth of local cultures, the socialization of their members, and the 'organization' as resulting from negotiation within communities and between the communities external and internal to a given organization.

12. Morineau (1983), quoted in Bauman (1999) p. xxxi.

13. In his essay, significantly titled 'Who needs identity' Hall suggests that [The concept] of identity does not signal that stable core of the self, unfolding from the beginning to end through all the vicissitudes of history without change...Identities are never unified and, in late modern times, increasingly fragmented and fractured: never singular but multiple, constructed across different, often intersecting and antagonistic, discourses, practices and positions: (Hall 1996, pp. 3–4; see also Bauman 1999 for a discussion).

14. It must be noted that when the concept of community of practice loses its critical and post-functionalist flavour, it also forfeits much of its theoretical appeal. A non-processual version of community of practice becomes in fact very similar to other, better established and better developed concepts, such as that of profession and semi-profession, two notions with a long and robust legacy in the sociological tradition. For example, many of the more functionalist notions of community of practice circulating in the literature closely resemble Goode's defining characteristics of professions. Consider, for example, the following definition of community of practice:

[a COP is] a group of people who are informally bound to one another by exposure to a common class of problem. Most of us belong to more than one, and not just on the job: the management team; the engineers, some in your company and some not (Steward 1996).

The resemblance with Goode's definition of profession is uncanny. In fact, almost half a century ago, Goode defined profession as follows: '(1) its members are bound by a sense of identity. (2) Once in it, few leave, so that it is a terminal or continuing status for the most part. (3) Its members share values in common. (4) Its role definitions vis-à-vis both members and non-members are agreed upon and are the same for all members. (5) Within the areas of communal action there is a common language, which is understood only partially by outsiders. (6) The community has power over its members. (7) Its limits are reasonably clear, though they are not physical and geographical, but social. (8) Though it does not produce the next generation biologically, it does so socially through its control over the selection of professional trainees, and through its training processes it sends these recruits through an adult socialisation process' (Goode 1957, p. 194). Please note that the same resemblance applies also to other recent definitions of community of practice, such as those to be found in Lesser and Prusak (1999) and Wenger and Snyder (2000).

15. This has become even more pronounced in later writing on community of practice aimed at practitioners or prescriptive managerial use (see e.g. Wenger and Snyder 2000; see also Swann *et al.* 2002 for a discussion).
16. This is implicitly recognized in the recent merger of the debate on community of practice with that of 'social capital', see e.g. Lesser and Prusak (1999); Lesser and Everest (2001).
17. The idea that the contemporary knowledge society is populated by a variety of post-traditional communities has been discussed by Knorr Cetina (1999). The expression 'community without unity' was coined by Corlett (1989).
18. Background information on the practice of telemedicine is provided in the introduction.
19. The fragments have been obtained using a method called 'the instruction to the double' (Nicolini 2009a). This is a projective technique which relies on mimicking the instructional conversations which occur during the socialization of novices; it requires interviewees to imagine that they have a double who will have to show up at their job the next day. The informant is then asked to provide the necessary detailed instructions which will insure that the plot is not unveiled and the double is not unmasked.

5 Practice as Activity

In the previous chapters I have suggested that the growth of interest in practice in Western contemporary debate is very much the result of the coming together of a number of thought traditions among which Marxism plays a central role. As I have shown in Chapter 2, Marx's thinking had a significant influence on most practice-oriented authors who built on his twin notions of the primacy of practice in human life and the direct relation between practice and power phenomena.

While most practice theories utilize only some aspects of Marx's thinking, one in particular, activity theory, has systematically developed the implications for practice thinking from Marx's work. Over the course of almost a century, authors from this tradition constructed a sophisticated and far-reaching practice approach which retains several fundamental and distinctive characters of Marx's thinking, such as a strong materialist flavour, attention to the role of objects in human activity, and a sensitivity for the conflictual, dialectic, and developmental nature of practice. These features, which are absent or scarcely considered in many of the theories discussed elsewhere in this book, make activity theory a unique and fundamental addition to the contemporary practice-theory toolkit.

Activity theory is one of several lines of thinking and research which stemmed from the work of the Russian psychologist Lev Vygotsky during the 1920s and early 1930s. Trying to develop a new approach which would adhere to the principles laid out by Marx, Vygotsky introduced a host of innovative concepts which gave rise to the 'cultural-historical' school of psychology. However, because of political and linguistic reasons, this line of research remained fundamentally segregated from the Western academic world. During Stalin's era and the Cold War, exchanges between scholars were rare and difficult. The problem was compounded by the fact that most texts were only available in Russian. It was not until the end of the 1970s, thanks to an improved political relationship between the Soviet Union and the West, that exchanges began to be established between scholars from the two political blocs, including those working on Soviet psychology and other Western research traditions, such as pragmatism and the genetic school of Jean Piaget. Beginning in the late 1980s, and thanks particularly to the work of scholars such as Michael Cole, Yrjo Engeström, and James Wertsch, the basic tenets of activity theory were reintroduced into the West and extended to the study of education, individual and social psychology, and work and organizations.

As a consequence of this long evolution and complex circulation, activity theory, especially in the West, never became a single unified theory. The term covers, in fact, a family of related, but not completely overlapping, research programmes and approaches which span child psychology to the philosophy of mind and research methodology. Accordingly, in this section I will focus in particular on one specific variety of activity theory known as cultural and historical activity theory, or CHAT (Engeström 1987, 1999, 2000, 2001, 2005; Engeström, Miettinen, and Punamäki 1999; Miettinen 2006). This is, in fact, the strand of activity theory that tackles more explicitly the issue of theorizing practice, and which has been translated into organization and management studies.[1]

Prior to addressing these basic tenets of CHAT, it is worth briefly recapping Marx's original view on work and activity, so that the continuities between the two approaches can be fully appreciated.

5.1 The Marxian roots of cultural historical activity theory

In *Das Kapital* (1867), Marx provides a seminal description of work as an enduring unity of exertion and will directed toward the realization of an end. Marx saw human work as a complex phenomenon which needs to be understood as comprising the following six distinct moments or elements:[2]

(i) the worker.
(ii) the material upon which he or she works.
(iii) the instrument used to carry out the work.
(iv) the actions carried out as a worker.
(v) the goal toward which he works. and
(vi) the product of his work; that is, the new form of the material upon which he or she worked.

All these elements are indispensable for a human activity to be considered as work. Moreover, they interpenetrate and influence each other and need to be addressed as a unity. For Marx, then, work needs to be understood as a complex phenomenon and studied accordingly. Thought alone, for example, is still not work. To become work, thought needs to lead to material action; i.e. to a concrete practice which inscribes the world. Similarly, work cannot be thought in the absence of instrumentality, a broad category which for Marx includes language and all the other material conditions which are necessary for work to take place (Rossi-Landi 1975). Instruments are critical both because they make work materially possible, and because they establish relationships between different forms of work and different workers. Tools and artefacts are, in fact, the outcome of previous work, and when used in a new context they manifest the original work in the new situation. In this way they connect the worker with his of her object and establish a relationship between workers, so making work a collective and inherently social endeavour. It should be noted that relationships are also established through the consumption of work. Through the act of consumption, the results of an activity enter the practical sphere of another subject, thus establishing yet more direct or indirect relationships through work. In summary, the fact that the result of one type of activity may become the raw material for another makes work the fundamental grounding of sociality as well as one of its outputs. Work is thus not only material, but also inherently social.

Another important element emerging from Marx's holistic view of work is that what and who the workers are (what we would call today their identity) need to be considered as emerging out of this complex configuration. For Marx, workers are shaped by their work and instruments into something else 'like the caterpillar is transformed into a butterfly' (Rossi-Landi 1975). Hence, the category of 'the worker' cannot be abstracted from, and made to pre-exist, the category of work itself. The two emerge together and cannot be understood in isolation, as they would be were identity be addressed as something with a separate existence.

Finally, work is never merely physical behaviour. Work depends necessarily on a background of beliefs and intentions as well as a set of surrounding circumstances, including those set out by the relations of consumption in which work is necessarily implicated. Take these conditions away, says Marx in *Das Kapital*, and work loses its meaning. However, the goal of the work processes, like that of other elements, cannot be conceived in isolation. The goal is not an independent metaphysical reality, but the consequence of a particular articulation of all other aspects. The objective of work is partly internal and partly external to it, and neglecting one of these two aspects leads to misunderstanding and antinomies.

In summary, Marx develops a view of work as an inherently social, collective, and material endeavour, and one which should not be confused with the operations that go into performing it. When we speak of work, we therefore always need to take into consideration the entire configuration of elements. For it is only within such an integrated whole that we can understand and make sense of instances of instrumentality, goals of work, or products of work.

5.2 The central tenets of cultural and historical activity theory

While Marx's view of work was extraordinarily insightful, he mainly provided a general and abstract set of categories that were in need of further development. It was up to later scholars to bring these far-reaching intuitions to fruition. This task was undertaken by, among others, Lev Vygotsky and his successors. Over several decades they developed Marx's original view into a philosophical, psychological, and cross-disciplinary framework for studying different forms of human practice.

Five main tenets are particularly useful when describing more generally this distinctive approach, and the interpretation given by CHAT scholars in particular. These tenets are: the mediated nature of practice; the notion of an activity system; the object-oriented nature of human activity; its historical and contradictory nature; and the necessarily interventionist and developmental nature of the study of practice (Engeström 1993, 1999, 2001, 2005; Blackler *et al.* 2000). I will briefly address these tenets in the following.

5.2.1 THE CENTRAL ROLE OF MEDIATION

Mediation constitutes, both historically and logically, the point of departure of all strands of activity theory. Historically, the notion originates in Lev Vygotsky's attempt to reform psychology according to non-Cartesian principles. According to Vygotsky (1978), humans never react directly to their environment. The relationship between humans and their environment is instead always mediated by some cultural means such as signs and artefacts (i.e. material devices skilfully built by humans). Mediated means here that all practices are carried out through, and are made possible by, a range of ideational and material apparatuses, devices, and 'utensils' that we draw from our cultural heritage or social milieux. Language in particular plays a fundamental mediatory role, and is for this reason considered by Vygotsky as the 'tool of tools' (ibid. p. 25 and ff). During the course of human evolution (both as individuals and as a species), mediation moved from an external to an internal plane, a drift that Vygotsky called internalization. By participating in common activities with other humans during development, young individuals internalize language, theories, techniques, norms, ways of acting, and other forms of culture. Mediation therefore comes to depend less on external artefacts and more on signs and symbols. Although individuals now master tasks and functions without the use of visible artefacts, their competencies are in a very real sense distributed and anchored in the social milieu in which they were developed and learned. Higher psychological functions are thus transactions that include the biological individuals, the cultural mediation of artefacts, and the culturally structured social and natural environments of which people are part. Humans are historical and social beings through and through.

The concept of mediation, which Vygotsky developed from the Marxian view of work discussed above, set the scene for a profoundly innovative approach to the study of human affairs. The idea of mediation suggests in fact that consciousness and intelligence do not reside in individual heads or minds, but 'in the interaction—realized through material activity—between the individual and the objective forms of culture created by the labour of mankind' (Miettinen 1999, p. 2). 'Mind' and 'being' cease to be a property of the individual and become inherently social and cultural historical phenomena. This in turn has several striking theoretical implications (Cole and Wertsch 1996; Engeström 2001; Kaptelinin and Nardi 2006).

First, all psychological functions begin, and to a large extent remain, culturally, historically, and institutionally situated and context-specific. Different forms of mediation carry history and sociality into all human situations, even the most individual and private ones. In a poignant sense, there is no way *not* to be socio-culturally situated when carrying out an action, even in perfect solitude. Second, artefacts are recognized as transforming mental functioning in fundamental ways. For activity theory, artefacts do not simply facilitate mental processes that would otherwise exist; they fundamentally shape and transform them. As already asserted by Marx, what we do and what we use deeply influences who we are and how we perceive ourselves. The mediating artefacts thus make us, and transform us, just like Marx's workers are metamorphosed by the tools they use. Finally, the meaning of action and the context in which it happens are not independent of each other. As in Marx's conception of work, objects and contexts arise together as part of a single bio-social-cultural process of development. The proper unit of psychological analysis and of human action is thus necessarily 'action in context', and it is the separation of these two aspects that creates many of the problems that have occupied philosophers during the last three centuries.

As noted by Blackler (1993), the notion of mediation thus lies at the heart of this approach, and in at least two fundamental ways. Firstly, it supports the principle that symbol-mediated activity 'should not be studied as if it were for the "mind alone"' (Blackler 1993, p. 870). Mediation makes practice, all practices, even those carried out in isolation, a historically situated and profoundly social phenomenon. Through mediation, history, culture, institutions, and power are all concretely manifested in human action. While this explanation bears some obvious similarities to those discussed in preceding chapters, it has the great merit of reintroducing a strong materialist flavour into the discussion of practice. At the same time, the idea of mediation injects a fundamental developmental flavour into the discussion of practice. Artefacts are not only a way of conveying the past into what we do. They are also the main way in which we can expand our practice—and ourselves. The creation of mediational artefacts, either material or symbolic, can become therefore a very practical strategy which, as we shall see below, makes this theory a powerful tool both for thinking and intervening.

5.2.2 THE ACTIVITY SYSTEM AS THE BASIC
UNIT OF ANALYSIS

While Vygotsky's reflections remained fundamentally at the individual level, it was up to subsequent generations of activity theorists to extend his insight at a collective level. This was mainly achieved by advancing the idea that the fundamental unit of analysis for understanding human conduct is not individual behaviour (or configurations of it), but collective and mediated activity. Another way of stating this is that the key for understanding and explaining a variety of phenomena, from mind to sociality, from organizing to identity, is to foreground the regimes of mediated activity in which people are involved. In this way, activity or practice (the two being synonyms in this context) acquires a foundational ontological status: activity theory is first and foremost a practice-based theory of mind and action.

The concept of activity was advanced especially by Leont'ev (1978), who built on Marx's original idea that work is always a collective endeavour. For Marx, as we have seen above, work is always carried out in relation to other people (directly or through the products of their work). The mediated effort to relate to nature thus always implies some form of sociality and organized community, and it is only within such a framework that work acquires its sense. From this it follows that communal activity, not individual behaviour, is the proper unit of analysis for understanding human conduct.[3]

In order to foreground the difference between individual behaviour and the collective activity that makes it possible, Leont'ev introduced a hierarchical distinction between automatic operations, goal-directed actions, and activity.[4] His view was that actions and operations are a relatively subordinate unit of analysis which can only be understood when interpreted against the background of a collective activity.

Operations are the basic level of human action. They are the 'well defined routines used subconsciously as answers to conditions faced during the performing of an action' (Kuutti 1996, p. 24). If you want to boil a pot of rice, you have first to pick up a pot. Or move the pot onto the top of the stove. Or pour the rice in the water (or vice versa, depending on your custom). While operations may be conducted 'heedfully', they depend on actions and activity to take up a specific meaning. The same operation (turning on a tap, turning on a stove) can thus be used in the context of different activities.

Goal-directed actions, e.g. cooking a pot of rice, are composed of simple operations. However, they have a relatively short temporal span and a clearly identifiable beginning and end. Although they can form chains, actions thus depend on larger, historically situated activities to acquire meaning. It is only at this higher level of analysis that we can fully grasp the meaning of human action as well as a variety of social and organizational phenomena. Turning on the stove and cooking a pot of rice thus only acquire meaning in the context of the historically situated activity of home cooking, a culturally situated, complex, mediated, meaningful, and usually strongly gendered (that is, power-laden) effort.

Actions, activities, and operations are not completely segregated, and there is an inherent dynamic and movement between the levels. An often-used example, first introduced by Leont'ev (1978), is learning to use the manual gearbox of a car. At the beginning, every step in the process of changing a gear is a conscious action that requires thought and specific orientation. Soon, however, these conscious actions turn into automatic operations (as in Heidegger's hammer) and gear-changing becomes an operation within broader driving-related actions such as accelerating, stopping at given places, and ascending steep grades. The opposite is also possible. An action can be expanded, or a new action formed, by 'unfolding' the constituent operation, bringing it into the level of conscious action and assembling them differently.[5] As Kuutti (1996, p. 24) states, 'this action-operation dynamics and the broadening scope of actions is a fundamentally typical feature in human development'.

In summary, while an activity realizes and reproduces itself by generating actions and operations, it is only by focusing on the collective effort that we can understand both the object and the motives that give coherence to actions. Each concrete activity thus organizes a specific and specifiable system of collaborative human practice (Holt and Morris 1993, p. 98) which constitutes the minimal meaningful unit of analysis. In this sense, activity refers to actual, identifiable activities and practices, as opposed to a generic notion of 'human activity'. The term activity corresponds to, and partly clarifies, what other authors examined in this book such as Giddens (Chapter 3) or Schatzki (Chapter 7) would call a social practice.

While Leont'ev had the merit of articulating the concept of activity, its elaboration was still lacking a clear and explicit social dimension. It was thus up to Engeström (1987) and his colleagues to include an explicit attention to rules, patterns of relationships, and what is being done by whom toward the object in the model, so that it can be used to study not only learning and development (the traditional areas of interest for Vygotskian pyschology), but also work and organization. Starting in the 1990s, the CHAT group of scholars introduced the idea that activities and social practices can be studied in terms of a small number of basic interrelated analytical elements and the fundamental forms of mediation between them. In order to emphasize that these analytical elements were mutually related and strongly interdependent, Engeström (1987) introduced the idea of an 'activity system' as the basic unit of analysis for the theory. In his words, 'the first principle [of Activity Theory] is that a collective, artefact-mediated and object-orientated activity system, seen in its network relations to other activity systems, is taken as the prime unit of analysis' (Engeström 2001, p. 136).

All activities can hence be described in terms of a *subject*, either individual or collective. Unlike in more traditional Cartesian approaches, the idea of subject here defines quite neutrally the person or group engaged in the activty, without assuming that this is the only, or even the main, source of agency (although in the approach it often remains the primary rhetorical perspective for the analysis).

An activity also comprises an *object*, either Marx's raw material or a more symbolic 'problem space' (Engeström 1987), which is transformed or shaped into an *outcome* with the help of some form of *instrumentality*; e.g. tools, language, or other kind of material and symbolic artefact. Please note that the object and the outcome are two different sorts of things as the transformation or materialisation of the object into an outcome is what motivates the existence of an activity.

All activities also generate and depend upon a *community* composed of those who share in some way the same object of work, some form of *division of labour* which specifies both different tasks and different power, and status positions, and access to resources for different members, as well as the balance of activities among different people and artefacts in the system.

Finally, all activities imply a set of *rules, norms,* and *conventions* that regulate actions and interactions within the community.

The notion of 'system-ness' urges us to focus on the systemic nature of the whole instead of limiting our attention to the separate elements or the connections between them. Following Marx, the idea of an activity system emphasizes that practice is a collective, systemic, object-oriented formation that has a complex mediational structure and which produces actions and is realized by means of actions, but it is not reducible to actions and operations (Engeström 1987, 2000).

In the effort to systematize and advance the theory, Engeström (1987) introduced a now well-known graphical rendition of CHAT's theory of practice (see Figure 5.1).

The characteristic triangular picture emphasizes the dimension of 'system-ness' and suggests that each element performs a specific mediating function between the other two. Take, for example, the relation between the subject of work and the community. The picture suggests that this relation is mediated by the existence of a set of rules, expectations, conventions, and constraints. These are partly externalized in artefacts such as organizational charts and written codes, and partly internalized in the form of tacit codes of conduct. The picture thus indicates that the coexistence of a subject and a community depend on the presence of these mediating artefacts. It also suggests that the nature of these mediating artifacts is involved in determining the shape and form of the community and what/who counts as a subject. Finally, the picture also implies that a change or shift in any of these three poles is likely to reverberate on the other two. A change in the community (say, a new expert

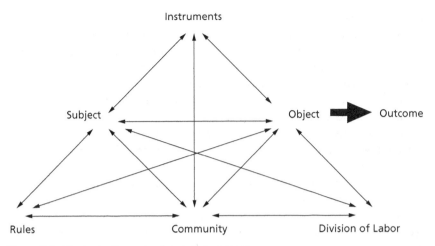

Figure 5.1 The basic elements of an activity system

member in a project) is likely to trigger a renegotiation of both the rules and expectations as well as a redefinition of the nature and identity of the acting subject (the project team has now changed). The 'system-ness' thereby becomes the source not only of relationships but also of imbalances and conflicts which, in turn, form the condition for the activity to expand and evolve.

5.2.3 THERE IS NO SUCH A THING AS AN OBJECT-LESS ACTVITY

One of the fundamental tenets of activity theory is that all practices are inherently object-oriented (Engeström 1995; Engeström and Escalante 1995; Miettinen 2006). Activities have an inbuilt directionality which derives very much from the objects towards which they are oriented. As in the expression 'what is the object of this discussion?' collective activities that have no object usually stop or fade out—unless a new one can be found or a non-visible one was at work all along (the so-called hidden agenda). The idea of an object is already implicit in the very concept of activity, to the extent that it is hard to imagine an object-less activity.

The object of an activity can be a material thing, but it can also be a less tangible (like a problem space), or totally intangible element (like a common idea). The critical aspect of the object is that it can be shared for manipulation and transformation by the participants of the activity, thus establishing (causal) relationships among the different elements which constitute the activity systems: 'the motive is formed when a collective need meets an object that has the potential to fulfil the need' (Engeström 1999, p. 65). To the extent that it embeds the motives for the communal actions, the object thus acts as the main organizer of the different elements of the activity system. The object of an activity is both the internal engine and the source of coherence and energy of the activity. As Engeström (2000, p. 964) writes: 'the object and the motive give actions their ultimate continuity, coherence and meaning'.

Three characteristics define the object of all practices: they are emergent, fragmented, and evolving.

First, for CHAT activity, its object, the agents involved, and all other aspects emerge together and define each other (Miettinen and Virkkunen 2005). For example, the way people will be involved in the activity, the way in which labour is divided, the rules and tools to be used, the position and identity each member will assume in the local social context, all depend very much on the nature of the object of work. At the same time, what counts as the object of the collective activity is dependent on the interests of those who compose the community that gathers around it. The object is, in this sense, partly given and partly emergent, both socially constructed and objective. It is socially constructed in that the object is actively constructed through the negotiation, alignment, or ignoring, of the different motives, interests, and aspirations represented in the community. It is also objective in that the object of any activity is materially instantiated in, and through, the product and services constituting the outcome of the activity. These instantiations have the capacity to 'bite back', revealing the contradictions that, as we shall see later, all activity objects carry with them.

Second, from the above, it follows that the object is inherently fragmented. For one thing, the object is not visible in its entirety to any one of the participants. At the same time, because it is composed of heterogeneous entities that are embedded in different practices and discourses, the object is inherently multiple and may hold together orientations, interests, and interpretations that are potentially contradictory. This means that the socio-material community performed by the object is unlikely to be an integrated whole in which parts move in harmony, and will more likely look like a community without unity where contradictions and conflicts abound.

Finally, the object of an activity is also evolving. In any practice, the object emerges in the course of activity and may well undergo changes during the process. Moreover, because activities are always mediated by artefacts, the objects of an activity are always understood and manipulated within the possibilities and constraints set by the instruments. The object and motive of an activity is hence both a 'moving target' (Engeström 2001, p. 136), which will reveal itself only in the process of the activity, and a 'horizon of possibilities', which tends to escape once intermediate goals are achieved and so needs to be reconstructed and renegotiated (Engeström 1999, p. 65). In this sense, the object of an activity is always partly given and partly anticipated; it is intimately related to the mediating factors through which it is constructed; it is always subject to social processes of interpretation and negotiation, and is therefore always contestable and (often) contested.

Objects thus provide both a telic dimension to the activity and the fundamental horizon of meaning for all the elements comprising the activity system. There is, however, a third way in which objects are critical to CHAT's theory of practice. Besides orienting the effort, providing meaning, and acting as the main organizer of the elements of the activity system, objects also establish relationships between activity systems, practices, and wider societal phenomena. Because of their emergent nature and inherent interpretive flexibility, activity objects not only 'keep together' the heterogeneous elements of a single activity system, but also tie together several activity systems (Engeström *et al.* 1999). The object of one activity becomes, in fact, an element for (or a hindrance to) another, thus instituting a thick web of interdependencies and/or conflicts among practices. In this sense, 'third generation' CHAT scholars (Engeström1999, 2000) increasingly take not one but at least two or more interacting activity systems as the minimal unit of analysis: 'a historically evolving collective activity system, *seen in its network relations to other activity systems* is taken as the primary unit of analysis' (Engeström 2000, p. 964, emphasis added). At the same time, and by the same token, the object situates the practice in a specific historical context. The interests, aspirations, and desires which enter the definition of the object of collective activity are usually derived from broader discursive formations and circuits of discursivity. In this way, the idea of the object helps us take into account both the contrived nature of purposive organisations, the main place in which work is carried out (Blackler 1993), and the fact that the modern post-capitalist society is increasingly based at all levels not on the fulfilment of needs as much as on the attainment of consumption-related desires. By focusing on the object instead of on the need, the theory allows for a broader range of objects and social processes to drive the communal activity.

5.2.4 THE CONFLICTUAL AND EXPANDING NATURE OF ACTIVITY SYSTEMS

While CHAT shares the idea of 'system-ness' and the principle that human conduct is always object-oriented with a host of post-functionalist theories of the social, one of its characterizing aspects, which descends directly from its Marxist legacy, is a special sensitivity for the inherently conflictual, dialectic, and developmental nature of practice. Activity systems are, in fact, by definition internally fragmented and inconsistent. The tensions and conflicts emerging from such contradictions constitute the origin and the source of energy for the continuous change and expansion of activity systems and their components.

One can first note that all activity systems comprise, by definition, a multiplicity of points of view, traditions, and interests. Division of labour creates different positions for the participants, and different mediation tools and symbols bring into the system multiple layers and strands of history embodied in rules, conventions, and artefacts.

It should be added that such multi-voicedeness is amplified by the inter-action of different activity systems. According to Engeström *et al.* (1999), one of the characteristic features of post-industrial work is the emergence of networked and co-configuration models of production. While the former is based on the establishment of long-term negotiated relationships, the latter involves the pulsating creation of contingent and localized forms of cooper-ation. These forms of organizational cooperation, that Engeström *et al.* (1999) call 'knotworking', are based on the weaving together of different activities around the emergence of a partially shared object of work which keeps them together while also keeping them distinct. Co-configuration and knotworking emphasize how activity systems are never isolated from each other, and consequently provide a continuous reciprocal source of modification and change. History and society, therefore, constitute two inexhaustible sources of contradiction which fuel a continuous and never-ending process of change within activity systems. It is important to note that unlike other theories, these contradictions are not considered to be mistakes, problems, or deviations from a set norm. On the contrary, contradictions and conflict are integral to activity systems, which must therefore be considered as disturbance-producing systems (Blackler 2003).

Engeström (1987) identifies several forms of contradiction that may arise and accumulate within activity systems. A first form of contradiction can be found within each of the elements of the system.

Because of the multi-voicedeness of the activity system and the historical stratifications of views and ways of doing, different and contrasting concep-tions of the object of the activity, or different practical interpretation of norms and rules, or diverging understandings of what tool is appropriate as a form of mediation can and will likely exist within an activity system.

A second form of contradiction may emerge between elements. This can be a consequence of the internal modification of existing elements or the importing of new elements from the outside (i.e. a new device or a new safety rule). The introduction of a new technology or the adoption of a new set of rules will most likely conflict with one or more of the existing elements. Also, the adoption of a new and cultural notion of the object of work which may be formally implemented is likely to produce internal misalignment and tension. Finally, contradictions may also emerge from the fact that activity systems are interconnected and depend on each other to achieve their desired result. The shifting of the object of work in one activity system can, therefore, trigger conflicts and misunderstandings with other connected and interdependent activity systems. It should be added, however, that underlying these secondary contradictions lies the primary, and fundamentally unresolved, contradiction between the value of use and exchange upon which capitalism is built. This historical contradiction is used both as the matrix and the model of all the contradictions that affect activity systems, and it is used to support the idea that activity systems can never attain equilibrium, and that practices are always and necessarily evolving.

Following a well-known Marxist approach, CHAT sees contradictions as accumulating within activity systems, and triggering dialectical processes of resolution. Quoting Ilyenkov, another Russian scholar, Engeström often reiterates that 'contradictions are not just the inevitable features of activity, they are the principles of its self movement and the form in which the development is cast' (Engeström 1987, p. 45). Activity and practice are thus, by definition, movement and change. 'Expansion' is Engeström's (1987) metaphor for the process of change in which activity systems and practices are, by definition, constantly involved. An expansive transformation is accomplished when the object and motive of the activity are reconceptualized to embrace a radically wider horizon of possibilities than in the previous mode of the activity. Although the transformation is necessarily achieved by the emergence and institutionalization of new forms of mediation, the object of expansive learning is the entire activity system. Expansive learning thus produces culturally new patterns of activity. The identification of contradictions and the production of exapansion are, therefore, not just merely analytical tools: they also constitute the opportunity and starting point for intervening.

5.2.5 THE INTERVENTIONIST NATURE OF CHAT

Unlike many other contemporary social theories that take Marxism as a mere historical antecedent, CHAT proponents also made a practical attempt to remain faithful to the original practical intent of Marx's work summarized in his famous adage that while philosophers have only interpreted the world, the point is actually to change it (Marx, 1845/1977). In this sense, CHAT contrasts significantly with most other theories of practice surveyed in this work, and particularly with the ethno-methodological movement which posited the principle of practical indifference as one of its basic tenets.

From early on, Engeström (1987) conceived CHAT as a form of engaged scholarship: 'In the approach advocated here, research aims at developmental re-mediation of work activities ... research makes visible and pushes forward the contradictions of the activity under scrutiny, challenging the actors to appropriate and use new conceptual tools to analyse and redesign their own practice' (p. 6).

The reason for the engaged nature of CHAT is thus both moral and epistemological. CHAT scholars need to get involved not only to respond to the moral obligation to act as Gramsci's organic intellectuals,[6] but also because they cannot abstain from entering the fray if they want to get a secure grasp of what is going on. Activity, in fact, cannot be understood from outside; it can only be appreciated from within. This descends from the observation that the direction of expansion of all activity systems is never determined in advance. Expansion implies, in fact, that activity systems take shape and get transformed over lengthy periods of time through the emergence and resolution of their inner contradictions (Engeström 1987). As there is no such a thing as a universal direction of development or progress, which way is up needs to be determined in relation to the situated contextual conditions in which it takes place. This, in turn, means that in order to fully comprehend the expansion of an activity system, one cannot sit outside it. Instead he/she necessarily needs to be involved in its dynamic (Blackler *et al.* 2000).

This Marxian reading of Kurt Lewin's principle that you cannot understand a human organization until you attempt to change it is reflected in the way in which the intervention itself is conceived. Expansive learning always originates from small fractures, deviations, and individual exceptions, and proceeds in cycles or spirals, through multiple phases and over lengthy periods of time. As Engeström (1987, p. 84 and ff.) describes it, the theory and practice of expansive learning is based on the dialectics of 'ascending from the abstract to the concrete'. This is a method of grasping the essence of an object by tracing and reproducing theoretically the logic of its development, and its historical formation through the emergence and resolution of its inner contradictions (Engeström 1987). It is through this process that the local and invisible 'innovation germ cells' are taken up by others and become universally accepted as new forms of activity. The development work thus necessarily follows the same pattern. Engeström (2000, 2001, see also Virkkunen and Ahonen) suggests that expansive interventions need to proceed through a number of steps which are likely to include questioning historical and empirical/ethnographical analyses of the emerging contradictions and disturbances; modelling the new solutions (often new material or symbolic instruments); examining the model and/or the new artefact in use; implementing the new model/solution; reflecting on the process; consolidating the new practice, and appreciating which new contradiction the applied solution stirs up somewhere else in the system. This developmental work thus uses the theory of the activity as an analytical compass, and makes significant use of ethnographic and other reserch methods capable of providing 'thick descriptions' of the activity, its tools, and the contradictions they generate. For the same reason, one of the main contributions of researchers is feeding back their results as a means to bring to the surface some of the existing contradictions, thus triggering the search for remediatory forms of mediations—instruments, rules, and division of labour (Engeström 2000, 2001).

The interventionist nature of CHAT therefore builds on the traditional Marxist historical form of explanation which assumes that a genetic understanding of the internal dynamics and contradictions of the activity system will 'provide the key to understanding the laws which govern social change' (Blackler 1993, p. 872). However, the approach stays clear of the usual determinist implications of this approach, tapping instead into the well-established framework of the Scandinavian action research tradition (Gustavsen 1996) and the pragmatist tradition (Miettinen 2006). CHAT interventions conducted through a methodology that Engeström and colleagues named 'Change Laboratory' (Engeström *et al.* 1996; Virkkunen and Ahonen 2011), are, in the main, based on dialogue between researchers and practitioners. In accord with the theory's tenets, interventions are thus mainly focused on producing the expansion of the activity at hand through 're-mediation or re-instrumentation' (Engeström 1999, p. 158), a process that inevitably solves some problems while bringing to the fore new contradictions which become the object of a new cycle of work.

5.3 **The weaknesses of a strong theory**

The tenets summarily illustrated above established CHAT as one of the most radical theories of practice available to date. CHAT offers a highly innovative perspective on the understanding of practice by convincingly tackling several issues left unresolved by other theories.

In the first place, CHAT gives ontological pre-eminence to social material practices as the explanations for social (and psychological) phenomena. The main assumption of this approach is, in fact, that the fundamental unit of social—and also organizational and work—studies is an indissoluble, molar complex of active agents' heterogeneous mediatory tools, and motives. Like other strong performative theories of the social, such as actor network theory (Latour 2005, Law 2009), it suggests that much is to be gained if we address social and organizational phenomena (and problems) as resulting from a network of practices organized around an emerging object of work. At the root of the sensitivity of the third, and more recent, generation of activity theorist, there is, in fact, the realization that to account for the nature—their elements and their object of work—of activity systems, we need to follow the relationships which connect activity systems together. The internal multivocality of the activity system is thus multiplied across the network of interacting activity systems. Understanding activity systems requires both investigating their inner history, and unfolding and attending to the way in which activity sytems are knotted together (Engeström *et al.* 1999).

Besides supporting a strong performative and heterogenous view of the social, CHAT also offers an interesting and balanced way of addressing the issues of agency. The projected and aspirational nature of the object of the activity implies, in fact, the presence and residual centrality of human agents. In other words, for these authors, activity remains fundamentally a human endeavour. What prevents CHAT from falling into the old individualist position is the observation that the nature and identity of the agents depend on the activity system(s) they are invoved in, and the mediational tool they use. Although humans and artefacts are different, and activities need people to happen, human subjects, like all other elements of a practice, do not pre-exist the activity system in which they are involved. Although human agency remains central, this is made to depend on the practice from which it emerges. The individual is not a substance that precedes the activity for doing. Being human means first and foremost operating as a social being, a 'doer' within a social context.

Further, CHAT offers an interesting way of dissolving the distinction between micro and macro phenomena in the study of organization. By proposing to start the analysis in the middle of things (activity is already an integrated whole), the approach bridges the study of micro and macro phenomena, suggesting that an understanding of the fine details of the activity are a necessary requirement for understanding both the source of rupture and conflict, and the possible remediation initiatives. In a similar way, the theory addresses the traditional opposition between change and stability. One of the great merits of the theory is to provide strong support to the idea that, from a practice-based perspective, change and not stability is primordial. CHAT stories are necessarily stories of local attempts at repairing and stabilizing systems which are, by definition, moving targets and conflict-producing machines. From a CHAT perspective, stability and permanence, not conflict and change, make the news.

Finally, CHAT offers a powerful and innovative view on the phenomenon of organization through the concept of the object. The object of the activity offers in fact a convincing explanation of both why and how organization happens without introducing unwarranted simplifications. The idea of a common object makes organization possible even in the absence of perfect alignment or sharing. Unlike other approaches, in CHAT mutual understanding and agreement are not necessary for human organization to happen. All that is needed is a common object of work which can be only partly shared and is often conflicted. In this way, the approach can successfully explain both coordination and collaboration without agreement, and the emergence of temporary and transient forms of coordination (from why a group of people becomes a crowd, to how people who have never met before can work together, caring for someone who falls ill in the street, only to disband once the ambulance has departed).

In summary, the notion of activity puts particular emphasis on several aspects—e.g. the role of artefacts, the historical and ever-changing nature of practice, the central role of conflict, and the organizing capacity of objects—which are scarcely taken into consideration by other theories. By offering authentically innovative answers to some old and vexing theoretical problems, it constitutes 'one of the best kept secrets of academia' (Roth and Lee 2007, p. 218). Its particular strengths come from combining a radically processual approach to the study of practice with a sensitivity for contradiction, development, and change derived from the Marxist tradition. Unlike other theories, CHAT is founded on a practice-based and processual 'generative code' (the social and processual idea of mediation and the socio-material notion of object of work) which allows it to successfully bypass both some of the traditional antinomies such as that between subject and object, and micro and macro, but also some of the residual dichotomies between structure and agency found, for example, in Giddens. Moreover, the strong materialist approach avoids some of the pitfalls of Bourdieu's approach for whom, as we have seen in Chapter 2, objects and artefacts (other than the body) seem to play a minor role in the performance of practice. In this way, CHAT is particularly suitable for making sense of the distributed and heterogenous nature of mind and expertise, the centrality of learning, and the fluid and inherently technologically mediated nature of organized work practices in the new millennium.

Interestingly enough, however, some of the aspects that make CHAT a particularly robust and immediately usable theory are also the root of its main weakness or, at least, its main sources of criticisms. Three, in particular, are worth mentioning here: the risk of a functionalist misunderstanding of the approach, the limitations of its teleological underpinnings, and the accusation of endorsing a 'California style' of Marxism.

As I have noted above, the idea of the complex and systemic-like nature of activity is one of the central and defining aspects of the theory. This dimension is captured in Engeström's triangle that has become not only a powerful intermediary for the theory but also something of a brand. For example, the picture constitutes a powerful analytical tool of immediate utility for all those who need to analyse and describe practice for different purposes (for example, those who are in the business of designing systems for integrating work practices: see e.g. Nardi 1996), and as such it has effectively supported the circulation and take-up of the theory.

The problem is that an excessive emphasis on the notions of 'system' and 'system-ness' combined with the use of closed representations such as the 'magic triangle' and other spatial metaphors (e.g. expansion) risk emphasizing the wrong thing, so to speak. Given that there are no neutral words and forms, the risk is that such imagery foregrounds the structural elements of the practice to the detriment of its processual dimension. In fact, these linguistic artefacts offer a way[7] into the theory from an attention to boundaries, elements, and interdependencies that at times obfuscate attention to the poietic, improvisational, uniquely-performed and uniquely experienced nature of practice. By following the complex patterns of mediation and relationship within and between triangles, we thus risk losing sight of the fact that CHAT is, first and foremost, a conceptual apparatus for talking about everyday doings and sayings, and how these combine to conjure the world we live in. In other words, the risk is that of hypostatizing practice, i.e. turning the activity system into a 'thing', a real entity 'containing' the different elements (objects, rules, etc.) that someone will, before long, try to measure or reduce to a series of factors. The signs are already there. When authors start to raise questions about the boundaries of the activity system (Thompson 2004) or revert to the old distinction between *praxis* as an event and practice as that which persists in time (a distinction that reintroduces yet a new dualism in the place of those we have just managed to eliminate),[8] alarm bells should start ringing, and one wonders if the theory would be better served by weaker models and more neutral terms such as 'nexus' or 'arrangement' (see Blackler and Regan 2006, 2009 for an interesting attempt).

A second weakness stemming from what is otherwise one of the main strengths of the approach is the insistent and almost exclusive emphasis on the object-orientedness of activity. As emerges from my description above, an activity is mainly a form of doing directed towards an object. It is the transformation of the object into an outcome that motivates the activity and the agents. While this explanation makes the theory all the stronger, in that it explains both the how and the why of collective practice, it also gives prominence to purposive action. In so doing, argue Smolka *et al.* (1995), the theory emphasizes one type of social interaction—teleological collaborative activity—over others. While providing a strong model of why people work together in the presence of different motives (the same object can bring together agents who have different and divergent personal goals and needs), this view risks discounting other forms of social interaction such as conflict, opposition, and resistance, and other non-instrumental sources of activity, such as desire, fear, passion, and indoctrination. At the same time, the theory assumes that humans have a sort of horror *contradictionis*, an innate dislike and fear of contradictions, not unlike the supposed 'horror of emptiness' postulated by Aristotle (see Chapter 2) which prevented scientists from discovering the vacuum until well into the eighteenth century. Stories by CHAT scholars often tell, in fact, of members anxious and willing to address the contradictions emerging in the system, which is in stark contrast with the observation that living in a fragmented and partially contradictory world is the fundamental existential condition of the postmodern man and woman.

While some of these aspects can, and have been, accommodated in the theory (for example, through the observation that the object is always project-ive and conflicted, and can thus be the source of desire, passion, and conflict while still keeping practices together), the fact remains that the approach tends to foreground the collaborative and problem-solving orientation of the members. One has to force the theory to make room for these new aspects that are, at times, hard to accommodate in such a strongly integrated model.

Finally, and strictly related to the above, is the observation that CHAT's adoption of system theory concepts combined with the endorsement of the principles and practices of action research risk diluting the original Marxist antagonist imprint of the theory. As observed by Avis (2007), while Engeström continues to place Marxist categories such as commodity, use versus exchange value, and contradictions at the core of CHAT (see e.g. Engeström 2005), the focus in both his writings and his interventionist work is almost exclusively on secondary contradictions (those emerging within the capitalist system). According to the author, the interventionist project stemming from CHAT is predicated on 'a version of consensus that seems to legitimise and resolve differences enabling the system to function' (Avis 2007, p. 169). The interest is, therefore, more about resolving the local contradictions which act as disturb-ances and require remediation than it is about foregrounding how these contra-dictions reflect the capitalism that is in us, and in the situation we encounter. In Avis's words, 'primary contradictions... are effectively bracketed... [and] al-though the notion of social practice is fully theorised, with respect to the activity system(s) under investigation, in its application it is truncated and veers towards a conservative practice [reminiscent of] Gramsci's transformism'. He continues, that 'while change occurs, it secures the interest of capital rather than being forcibly tied to an emancipatory project' (Avis 2007, p. 163).

There are, of course, good reasons (or justifications) for this apparent marginalization of a radicalized agenda. Engeström (1999), for example, claims that the move away from grand theorizing and the emphasis upon intervention in concrete situations is part of CHAT's explicit endorsement of a strong form of radical localism. The idea is thus that 'fundamental societal relations and contradictions of the given socio-economic formation—and thus potentials for qualitative change—are present in each and every local activity of that society' (Engeström 1999, p. x). The interventionist stance of CHAT would therefore follow the principle of acting locally and thinking globally, the hallmark of many postmodern antagonist movements. While the position is coherent with the overall bottom-up ontological project of 'practices all the way down', it exposes the approach to being accused of, and possibly becom-ing, simply another form of consultancy aimed at improving work practices. The lesson is thus quite clear. The radical project of practice theory (whether theoretical, political, or both) is less about providing a toolkit for zooming in on the local practice and more about making a connection between what is local and what is global. When such a connection is severed or not developed, it is likely that we end up with an advanced version of something else.

In conclusion, CHAT enriches the toolkit of practice theory, suggesting that practice should be conceived as a form of doing oriented towards an object, that both organizes all the elements of a practice and distinguishes it from all others. CHAT locates practical action in a process which is collective, recurrent, systemic, and self-organizing. It emphasizes that activity is always 'social, rooted in history, and reaching out to the future' (Blackler 1993, p. 875). By foregrounding the issue of how people can shape the contexts that shape their activity, CHAT suggests that practice should be studied as a transformative activity. In so doing, the theory offers a new and engaged position for the researcher. By highlighting disturbances within activity systems, researchers can, in fact, help those they are studying to recognize, reflect upon, and perhaps rebuild their activity systems (Blackler *et al.* 2000). By arguing that capacities are embedded and expressed in collective action, that mastery is a processes distributed in (and emergent from) daily material interaction, and that social order and epistemological norms are achievements jointly established, maintained, and transformed in ongoing process instead of *a priori* entities, CHAT comes closer to another tradition which is partly responsible for the contemporary return to practice; that is, ethno-methodology. Although the different historical roots of the two approaches means that they diverge on some significant points, e.g. on the scope of the analysis (inherently local for ethno-methodologists, necessarily historical for CHAT scholars), and on the issue of change (ethno-methodology focuses on the reproduction of social order, while CHAT emphasizes possibilities of change), the two theories agree on the assumption that practice and practical action must constitute the starting (and end) point of all good social research. As I shall show in the next chapter, what ethno-methodology adds (or added, given that some of its tenets have been incorporated by CHAT authors such as Engeström and Escalante 1995) to the other practice theories surveyed here, is an attention to the fine-grained aspects of the practicing as well as the methodological discipline of grounding the theorization of practices and social order in the empirical analysis of the actual practicing.

Rolling case study: Telemedicine as an activity system

Until a few years ago chronic heart failure (CHF) was typically treated through a recurrent pattern of hospitalization, intensive therapy, discharge, deterioration of condition, and subsequent new hospitalization. As noted before, this activity conflicted with emerging evidence that addressing crises after they had happened was ineffective. In order to resolve this major contradiction in existing practice, in the mid-1990s, health practitioners in different parts of the world introduced the practical innovation of using day hospitals as preventive measures. Patients went to the hospital for a few hours on a regular basis. Once there, they would be seen by nurses and doctors who monitored their state, adjusted their therapy, and prevented the deterioration of their condition. They would then return home until the next appointment.

While day hospitals constituted a great innovation, they still required patients to travel considerable distances with the ensuing aggravation and cost. Because of this, some practitioners started to explore the possibility of monitoring patients from home, moving information instead of people. In Italy, the idea of expanding the traditional medical practice in this sense was first tested at the centre in Garibaldi, a branch of a national medical foundation specializing in the care of chronic heart conditions (see Figure 5.2).

The centre in Garibaldi had a long track record of dealing in innovative ways with CHF. They could also count on the recently established Telemed Centre, a specialized company that provided specialized cardiology second-opinion consultation to general practitioners. Telemed gave general practitioners portable ECG transmitters that allowed a heart rhythm to be sent through a normal phone line. They then provided facilities and infrastructure for relaying the ECG to specialists on a 24/7 basis. Staff at Garibaldi reasoned that if they gave the portable ECG transmitters to the patients, using the Telemed facilities they could monitor their patients from home. They thus set up this new way of caring for CHF patients at a distance.

The attempt at stretching in time and space the existing traditional ways of caring for CHF patients soon encountered difficulties that could be interpreted as a major contradiction. The expansive effort conflicted, in fact, with one of the most entrenched, and hence seldom-noted principles of traditional medicine. Medical work is, in fact, still mostly organized around the convention of

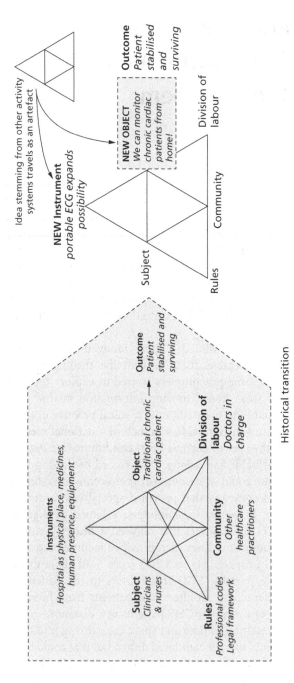

Idea stemming from other activity
systems travels as an artefact

NEW Instrument
*portable ECG expands
possibility*

NEW OBJECT
*We can monitor
chronic cardiac
patients from
home!*

Outcome
*Patient
stabilised
and
surviving*

Subject

Rules

Community

Division of
labour

Historical transition

Instruments
*Hospital as physical place, medicines,
human presence, equipment*

Object
*Traditional chronic
cardiac patient*

Outcome
*Patient
stabilised and
surviving*

**Division of
labour**
*Doctors in
charge*

Community
*Other
healthcare
practitioners*

Subject
*Clinicians
& nurses*

Rules
*Professional codes
Legal framework*

Figure 5.2 Telemedicine as an historical expansion of traditional hospital cardiology

the physical co-presence of the two parties, and spatial co-location has a practical, cultural, and legal importance. For example, direct observation and perception of nuances constitute two fundamental resources of diagnostic practice. Analogously, proximity is a cornerstone of nursing, the practice being historically based on the assumption that direct human interaction has a therapeutic effect. In CHAT terms, one could say that the hospital as a physical (and symbolic) space constitutes a key mediating artefact in the medical activity. This composite artefact (which includes not only the rooms but also the way in which people and equipment populate the spaces) mediates the activity between the subjects (the healthcare professionals), and the object (the patient). When the mediatory artefact is substituted (or, as in this case, removed), a number of contradictions are bound to ensue. Doing medicine in the hospital is, in fact, a strongly institutionalized and multi-vocal practice or activity system. In addition to a host of healthcare practitioners, subjects, and artefacts, hospital medicine also includes a variety of specific norms (for example, the hospital routines that require patients to wake up and eat at certain established times), a well-defined community of workers (all the support personnel), families, and those who benefit from it in different ways (from the catering companies to the taxi drivers), and a precise and hierarchical division of labour. When taken as a whole system, this strongly institutionalized arrangement of people, activities, artefacts, norms, and relationships performs a specific way of conceiving the patient and what it is to 'do' medicine. We all experience this view when we become 'patients'. As the word suggests, in fact, this particular activity system requires that when we enter a hospital, we subject ourselves to medical discipline and temporarily trade a bit of our autonomy and personhood in exchange for the benefits of modern scientific medicine.

Introducing distance between provider and client in medical encounters was, therefore, bound to problematize certain conventional assumptions of this well-established arrangement and upset some deeply entrenched practices. Two main problems soon became evident to the group of Garibaldi's practitioners who tried to establish the new practice of telemonitoring. First, they discovered that the construction of the history of the patients—a necessary step for monitoring their condition—was obtained in practice through the combination of actions and artefacts, some of which had remained almost invisible. Not only did constructing a history of the evolution of a patient's state implying recording in writing certain measurements such as changes in temperature and blood pressure, but building a patient's history also depended on the mainly discursive practice of 'handing over cases' to personnel on the next shift. This is a critical passage that determines whether a patient's local trajectory is constructed or not, as it is impossible for staff on the wards to write absolutely everything down. By taking co-location away, so to speak, telemedicine had made visible one of the tacit principles of the existing practice but also created a rupture that needed repairing.

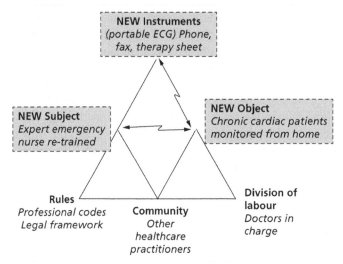

Figure 5.3 First wave of contradictions and remediatory actions (contradictions are traditionally represented with broken arrows, after Engeström 1987)

During the effort of establishing telemedicine at Garibaldi, it emerged that not only memory but also expertise was socially distributed. When nurses proactively intervened in the cure of patients (as illustrated at the end of Chapter 3), they did so relying on the fact that they could always double-check things with their colleagues or doctors who were never too far away. This condition too, however, was upset by expanding the activity in a 'tele' way and required some remedial intervention (Figure 5.3).

Both contradictions were addressed in a classic Vygostkyan way; that is, by introducing new expansive mediatory instruments. The first contradiction was addressed by introducing or updating new trajectory-making tools, the most notable of which was a therapy sheet developed by the nurses on the basis of their own needs (Figure 5.4).

This was the real trajectory-making tool that the nurses used to plan and record all their calls. It recorded the reading of the patients' vital signs, changes in dosage of medicine, and, in the expanded note filed at the bottom, all sorts of useful information that helped the nurses make sense of any minute variations. This instrument soon became a pillar of the new activity. The artefact allowed, in fact, one to reconstruct at a glance the patient's history, and it gave the operators an overview of all the patient's critical parameters which could then be compared extremely effectively, so revealing any anomalies.

The second contradiction was addressed by combining the use of artefacts and training. The nurses underwent a period of specialized retraining, while several protocols were developed to support their work. Of course the expansion of the activity also shuffled the priority and importance of certain goal-directed actions. For example, at Garibaldi, nurses routinely answered patients' queries over the

Surname and first name	Date of arrival					Tel.					Diagnosis				

	Date of call								Date of call								Date of call								Date of call								Date of call								Date of call							
	8	10	12	14	16	18	20	22	8	10	12	14	16	18	20	22	8	10	12	14	16	18	20	22	8	10	12	14	16	18	20	22	8	10	12	14	16	18	20	22	8	10	12	14	16	18	20	22

FC

PA

Weight

Doctor's signature

Notes | Notes | Notes | Notes | Notes | Notes

Blood test results

Figure 5.4 Therapy sheet used by the nurses

phone. But this activity was necessarily residual and unstructured. However, the introduction of telemedicine brought call making and handling to centre-stage. In the new setting, making and responding to calls became a well-identified practice with its own structure, rhythm, and rules that was soon one of the main things that was handed down from expert to novice nurses.

On the one hand, the new activity challenged the division of labour between doctors and nurses. Within Garibaldi, this was addressed by establishing a new division of labour as well as new practice that would support it; for example, a regular review meeting of all cases. This 'secondary' (e.g. between elements) contradiction necessarily reverberated outside the system as it had to do with the broader issue of the shifting professional identity of the nurse in the Italian healthcare system. While the centre at Garibaldi was criticized by other doctors for the extended role granted to the nurses, the emergence of tele-nurses contributed to the wider debate and effort to establish in Italy 'expert nurses' who can legally carry out some of the duties traditionally reserved for doctors.

Please note that it was not only the identity of the nurse that shifted. One of the defining characteristics (and challenges) of healthcare work is that the patient is both the object and a subject in the activity. What it means to be a patient also radically changes within the context of the new activity. Telemedicine, in fact, depends on the active and knowledgeable work of the patients to succeed. In order for telemedicine to happen the patients need, among other things, to weigh

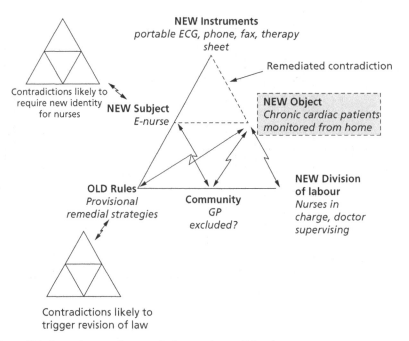

Figure 5.5 Second wave of contradictions and remedial actions

themselves; regularly measure their blood pressure; book, carry out, and transmit results of tests to the centre; record the ECG and transmit it to the centre; and answer the phone and provide all information required. Most of these actions would not be carried out if the patient was lying in a hospital bed and, in fact, patients, like the nurses, needed to be trained and to learn how to become members of the telemedicine activity. In a very real way, then, telemedicine created a new type of expert and autonomous patient as a way of solving some of the emerging ruptures in the system. It is worth adding that the emergence of this new type of patient is, in turn, bound to generate contradictions somewhere else; for example in the traditional practice of general practitioners who often have to deal with patients who know more than they do.

While some of the initial disturbances were addressed through remediation and the introduction of innovations in practitioner's everyday actions, a new set of disturbances and conflicts soon emerged (Figure 5.5).

The new activity in fact generated a 'tertiary' contradiction (e.g. within one of the elements) between the existing and the new tacit rules of conduct. While the existing tacit rules of conduct and the legal framework required a doctor to be always formally in charge, the new rules generated by the new object of work required, on the contrary, that the nurse acted swiftly in order to prevent the deterioration of the situation. The capacity to react rapidly is a critical factor for success in the effective management of decompensation. Any strategy that does not take into account this aspect will see its effectiveness reduced drastically. The local solution at Garibaldi was the introduction of a host of new tactical ways of dealing with this internal contradiction described in Chapter 4. These span from reporting to a doctor after an event has taken place, to discursively constructing the decision-making process in such a way that the appearance that 'the doctor was always in charge' was saved.

Also, in this case, the legal implications of telemedicine, which at Garibaldi emerged as a tertiary contradiction, were revealed to be the manifestation of much wider issues and conflicts that are still widely discussed at national and international level, and are bound to generate new innovations and expansion elsewhere. Finally, the potential sidelining of the general practitioners discussed in Chapter 3 can also be considered as one of the contradictions generated by the stretching of medical practices in space and time.

Most of the above contradictions emerged within the activity system in the attempt to establish the remotely monitored patient as a new object of the medical activity at Garibaldi. However, a whole new wave of issues surfaced when staff at Garibaldi tried to export their model to the rest of their region, convincing the health authority to endorse telemedicine as an accepted way of handling CHF. The move would make Garibaldi the centre of the new realm of telemedicine, attracting funds and enhancing its reputation. However, this plan had to deal with the fact that the same original idea (stretching the existing practice of caring for CHF patients in time and space) had been developed in different ways in other localities, particularly at the clinic at Z, another cardiology centre in the same region, and which is famous nationwide.

For years, the clinic at Z used telemedicine practices to look after its recently discharged patients who had gone through open heart surgery. The practice established at Z applied a form of 'hybrid' telemonitoring, partly face-to-face and partly distance monitoring. From its inception, the clinic at Z, unlike Garibaldi, sent nurses on housecalls at set times. The clinic thus aligned similar elements to Garibaldi in a different way. The result was to have nurses who were experts at handling patients face to face but not over the phone, and

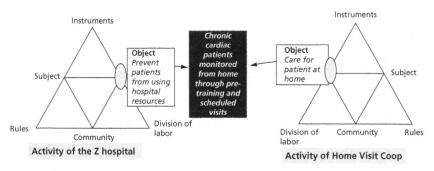

Figure 5.6   The network of interactive activity systems behind the telemedicine at Z

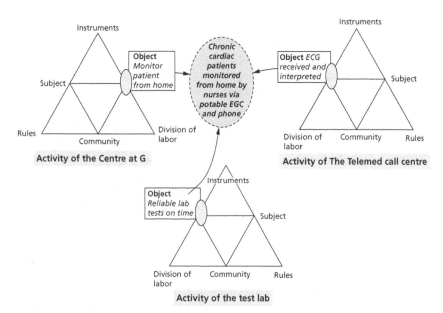

Figure 5.7   The network of interactive activity systems behind the telemedicine at Garibaldi

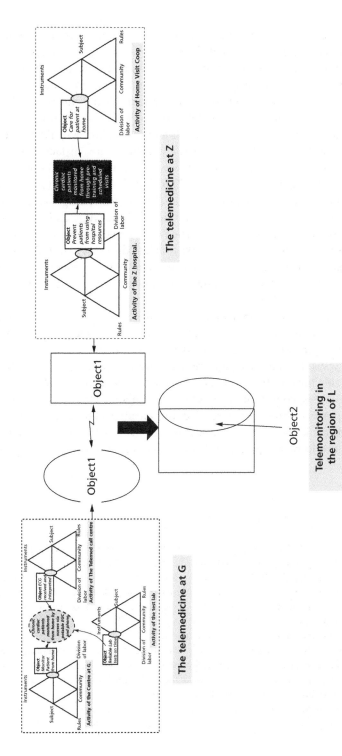

Figure 5.8 The new object and activity system emerges at the encounter/clash of two networks of interactive activity systems

infrastructures capable of reacting to an emergency but which did not involve supporting daily supervision, as at Garibaldi. For example, they did not have dedicated full-time staff, a room, or computers, and their patients were not educated to be independent (the nurses did the tests during housecalls). The encounter and clash of these two activity systems clearly illustrated that the 'telemonitored patient', who constituted the object of work of both activity systems, had been an object-multiple all along. As shown in Figure 5.6 and Figure 5.7, the two local practices of telemedicine were, in fact, already the result of the coming together of two networks of interactive activity systems.

At Garibaldi, this network (Figure 5.7) included, at a minimum, the centre of Garibaldi, the Telemed Company, and the lab test. Things were different at Z (see Figure 5.6), where the network included the clinic and the cooperative that took care of the home visits. The two telemedicine practices emerged thus from two distinct activity networks that had different historical components. The different nature of their objects could only be understood against their own specific history, and how tools, opportunities, and ruptures had shaped them.

The practice of telemedicine in this region thus emerged at the encounter of these two different histories and heterogeneous assemblages (Figure 5.8).

Through a process that cannot be described in detail for reason of space, these two ways of doing telemedicine were eventually reconciled in order to create a stable form of telemedicine through the development of a new series of artefacts, rules, community, and division of labour. On this point, the new resulting practice, duly tested so that the ensuing contradiction could be ironed out, could be used as a model for the rest of the region, where it is bound to lead to new ruptures and contradictions, and hence new expansion and change.

■ NOTES

1. See for example Blackler 1993; Holt and Morris 1993; Blackler 1995; Engeström *et al.* 1996; Blackler *et al.* 2000; Engeström 2000, 2001; Blackler 1993; Miettinen and Virkkunen 2005; Engeström and Blackler 2005. Other areas where activity theory made significant inroads include human–computer interaction and information system design (Nardi 1996; Kaptelinin and Nardi 2006), education (Daniels 2001; Hedegaard 2001) and of course 'western' psychology (Cole and Engeström 1993; Cole 1996; Wertsch 1998).

2. Marx, *Das Kapital*, Book 1, chapter VII, section 1.

3. Leont'ev famously illustrates his thesis using the example of the practice of hunting; 'A beater, for example, taking part in a primeval collective hunt, was stimulated by a need for food or, perhaps, a need for clothing, which the skin of the dead animal would meet for him. At what, however, was his activity directly aimed? It may have been directed, for example, at frightening a herd of animals and sending them toward other hunters, hiding in an ambush. That, properly speaking, is what should be the result of the activity of this man. And the

activity of this individual member of the hunt ends with that. The rest is completed by the other members (. . .) What unites the direct result of (his) activity with the final outcome? Nothing other than his relation with the other members of the group. This relation is realised through the activity of other people . . . the connection between the motive and the object of an action reflects objective social relations, rather than natural ones' (Leont'ev 1981, p. 210, quoted in Engeström, 1987, p. 54).

4. In Leont'ev words: 'This result, i.e., the frightening of game, etc., understandably does not in itself, and may not, lead to satisfaction of the beater's need for food, or the skin of the animal. What the processes of his activity were directed to did not, consequently, coincide with what stimulated them, i.e. did not coincide with a motive of his activity; the two are divided from one another in this instance. Processes, the object and motive of which do not coincide with one another, we shall call "actions". We can say, for example, that the beater's activity is the hunt, and the frightening of the game his action' (Leont'ev 1981, p. 210, quoted in Engeström 1987, p. 56).

5. A similar process also applies between the level of action and activity. An activity that loses its motive and object can become an action.

6. 'Our research did not aim to produce analytical academic reports only. It aimed to grasp developmental potentials and dynamics by initiating, supporting, and recording qualitative changes in the practical work activity itself. That is why this approach is called developmental work research.' (Engeström 1990, p. 72).

7. CHAT intellectuals, of all people, should be aware that the conceptual artefacts they use in their practice of theorizing are bound to change the theory, not simply to represent and communicate it!

8. '*Praxis* denotes the moments of real human activity that occur only once . . . which distinguishes it from the notion of practice, which is used to denote a patterned form of action, inherently a theoretical signified' (Roth and Lee 2007, p. 190).

6 Practice as Accomplishment

Although ethno-methodology (EM) is not, strictly speaking, a *theory* of practice, it warrants careful discussion because it constitutes one of the most important ways of understanding practice and practical action. EM was, in fact, set squarely from the beginning as a way to 'treat practical activities, practical circumstances, and practical sociological reasoning as topics of empirical study' (Garfinkel 1967, p. 1).

According to Lynch (2001), key to the praxeological orientation of the ethno-methodological tradition is treating phenomena such as language, reasoning, knowledge, work, and organization as 'situated accomplishments by the parties whose local practices assemble the recurrent scenes of action that make up a stable society' (p. 131). Hence, ethno-methodology is first and foremost a praxeological orientation characterized by being concerned with all practices involved in constituting knowledge in the world.[1] That said, one should add that the notion of practice and the way of understanding it promoted by ethno-methodologists differ in substantial ways from some of those surveyed in preceding chapters. Ethno-methodologists take, in fact, a radical stance and consider practices both as the inescapable texture of everyday life and the contingent, ongoing accomplishment of the same practices. EM therefore investigates practices not as instances of something else (e.g. habitus, tradition, community, or mind), but as spatio-temporal accomplishments obtained by knowledgeable actors who use a variety of (ethno) methods, tools, techniques, and procedures. These practical methods and procedures through which we constitute our daily scenes of action, in other words the actual competent 'doing' of something, constitute the object of study in this approach. Other things—such as society, history, mental categories, and social theories—are not denied or forgotten, they are simply bracketed and programmatically ignored unless they play a visible role in the conduct of an actor. In this sense, the aim for EM and all ethno-methodological-related research programmes, such as the EM-inspired study of work, the study of technology in action, and more recently workplace studies (all briefly discussed below), is not to produce a theory of practice which would encapsulate its sense and logic, or display its fundamental elements, or outline its general process. On the contrary, EM's aim is to provide convincing accounts of the methods used by members to produce and reproduce organization and society, and to uncover the work necessary to the concerted production of intelligible forms of activity. The business of EM is thus re-presenting the accomplishment of (work) practices 'from within'.[2] As I shall show, this has important consequences not only for how we understand practice, but also for the ways we go about learning and writing about it. EM, in fact, carries with it not only a new theoretical approach, but also a peculiar way of practising research and a recognizable literary genre.

In the following, I will summarize some of the main tenets of EM in order to pave the way for a subsequent brief discussion on the implication of EM for the study of practice, especially work and organizational practices. Following Lynch (1993) and Fele (2002), I take the four key notions of accountability, reflexivity and indexicality, and membership to be those most consequential for understanding EM's praxeological orientation. I organize my discussion accordingly.

6.1 **Ethno-methodology's view of everyday activity**

6.1.1 ACCOUNTABILITY

Most of the basic policies and objectives of EM as an inquiry into the practical accomplishment of sociality were recorded and codified by Garfinkel in his 1967 collection (Garfinkel 1967). Accountability features prominently in this text.

'Account' and 'accountability' were not new terms in social science when Garfinkel chose them as the cornerstones of his approach. As shown by Orbuch (1997), the concept of 'account' has a solid foundation and history in early sociological analysis and research. However, unlike previous authors, Garfinkel refused to consider accounts merely as occasional adds-on to our daily activity produced in case of breakdowns. On the contrary, he regarded them as a constitutive and continuously exhibited property of ordinary activities and practice. As the author put it in his somewhat ornate style:

Ethnomethodological studies analyse everyday activities as members' methods for making those same activities visibly-rational-and-reportable-for-all-practical-purposes, i.e., accountable, as organisations of commonplace everyday activities (Garfinkel 1967, p. vii).

EM, therefore, is not interested in accounts per se as much as in the fact that social activities are always produced with an eye on the fact that we may be asked to explain them verbally. Lynch (1993) suggests that, in order to appreciate the many implications of Garfinkel's convoluted expression, it is useful to understand it in terms of a set of proposals that taken together configure new programmes of inquiry. Accountability comes thus to mean that:

(a) social activities are orderly; that is, they are both non-random/recurrent and meaningful/coherent;
(b) this order is public and hence observable: it can be witnessed and comprehended;
(c) the intelligible orderliness is also ordinary: 'the ordered features of social practices are banal, easily and necessarily witnessed by anybody who participates competently in those practices' (Lynch 1993, p. 14);
(d) this ordinary, intelligible orderliness is orientated. Participants orientate to the sense of one another's activities, and in this way they contribute to the temporal development of those activities (ibid., p. 15). Lynch uses the example of a pedestrian who, with a gesture or a glance, can display her intention to cross the road. This display is available to all other actors at the scene (drivers, other pedestrians) and is therefore embedded in the organization of 'traffic' in the street;
(e) this being orientated to public orderliness is rational; that is, it makes sense to those who know how to produce it;
(f) this 'rationally orientated ordinary observable orderliness' (ibid.) is describable by all those who master the relevant natural language. They can talk in practice and about that practice, hence making (sociological) descriptions a feature of the same action which constitutes the object of the professional attention of sociologists.

Accountability emphasizes that social conduct and practice is experienced normatively, although in no sense can one say that rules cause or determine human behaviour. While Garfinkel's source is the phenomenological tradition and the work of Husserl and Schutz, his understanding of rules comes extremely close to that developed by Wittgenstein and already discussed in Chapter 2 (see also Lynch 1993 for an extensive discussion). For Garfinkel, human interaction depends, in fact, on a texture of tacit assumptions which are not, and cannot be, rendered completely explicit, let alone described in terms of a set of rules. As for Wittgenstein, the normative dimension of human intercourse is already implicit in the moral and emotional character of the 'methods' for acting in the world. Conforming to the normal way of conducting an action is both morally required and morally expected from all participants in any social scene. As Wittgenstein would put it, and as Garfinkel has demonstrated by his well-known 'breaching experiments' (Garfinkel 1967), we follow the methods that allow us to accomplish our daily activity (what EM authors call ethno methods) 'blindly', as a matter of course. While rules neither determine 'externally' such morality nor can they really describe it, they are however an important aspect of the language of accountability that all actors learn to draw on for making themselves accountable and intelligible at all times. The language of rules, as well as that of motives, aims, aspirations, and explanations, are hence typically used by members to account for the rationality of their action both retrospectively (after the fact) or prospectively. Rule-talking and motives-talking are, therefore, deeply implicated in making our action intelligible and interaction possible, as well as in achieving what Lynch calls the 'instructable reproducibility of social action'; that is, enabling members to reproduce and recognize the same action on different occasions (Lynch 1993, p. 15).

Accountability and accounts are, therefore, both constitutive and continuously exhibited properties of ordinary activities, and are reflexively involved in the production of conduct. Hence, for EM, accounts do not hold special status when it comes to penetrating the world of causes, motives, or goals which trigger people's actions. Accounts are a fact of life, an ordinary resource— among many—used to create and sustain organized conducts. Uncovering verbal justifications is a weak way to investigate human practice. This leads to the second key concept in EM, that of the reflexivity of accounts.[3]

6.1.2 REFLEXIVITY

EM conceives of reflexivity and reflection in a way that is substantially different from other thought traditions. The prevailing current usage of the idea of reflexivity refers, in fact, to the self-conscious view of social science's activities and practices. As we have seen in Chapter 3, authors such as Bourdieu and Giddens use the notion of reflexivity as a way of emphasizing the need for social scientists to take into account their position in the world, and what effects this produces on their accounts of that world. Such an epistemic-moral-political appeal is distinctly different from Garfinkel's use of the term (Macbeth 2001). For Garfinkel and other ethno-methodologists, the term 'reflexivity' describes how the sense of a question, an indicative gesture, or a silence in conversations, are achieved as part of the setting in which they occur (Lynch 1993, p. 35). Reflexivity hence points to the fact that the 'incarnate' or reflexive achievement of sense is an endogenous property of the practice under consideration. As Garfinkel put it:

The central recommendation [of EM] is that the activities whereby members produce and manage settings of organised everyday affairs are identical with members' procedures for making those settings 'account-able.' The 'reflexive' or 'incarnate' character of accounting practices and accounts makes up the crux of that recommendation (Garfinkel 1967, p. 1).

Accountability and reflexivity are therefore inextricably connected. Actors who participate in social interaction both rely upon and use the order they 'find' as the basis to develop current courses of action or to initiate another. Heritage (1984) uses the example of a person who walks down a corridor in a building and is greeted with salutes. The greeting completely transforms the scene for that person, who is now caught in a located form of organization that binds the participants in a web of mutual expectations, but which does not absolutely determine their behaviour. The person can respond to the salute, or can ignore it, therefore strategically exploiting the possibilities afforded by the normative expectation associated with the particular scene, what we could call the rule associated with the interaction. Such a rule is not something external, but is instead reflexively constitutive of the unfolding circumstance in which it is applied. If the salute greeting was unreturned it will reflexively trigger some further considerations on the part of the other participants to the action, who will account for this unusual behaviour (e.g. 'she's angry because I didn't call her last night') and develop the scene accordingly. For EM, then, through reflexive accountability of actions, members find themselves in a world in which whatever one does is likely to be intelligible and accountable as a way of sustaining, developing, violating, or changing some order of activity. A world, to use Merleau-Ponty's words, in which members 'are condemned to be meaningful' (quoted in Heritage 1984, p. 110).

Accountability and reflexivity conjure up a world in which perceived normal courses of action need to be continuously reproduced locally and accountably through the use of seen, but unnoticed, procedures and 'practical' knowledge. This is a world in which participants' practices are reflexively both context-shaped and context-renewing. To capture this inherent open-ended and time-bound characteristic of everyday actions, Garfinkel used the notion of 'indexicality', which constitutes another key notion of EM's praxeological orientation.

6.1.3 INDEXICALITY

Indexicality refers to the embeddedness of meaning in practical action; i.e. to the fact that 'the stability of sense, relevance and meaning does not arise from the form of propositions but from the circumstances of their use' (Garfinkel and Sachs 1970). Seen from a praxeological perspective, however, all expressions and actions are indexical. This is true not only for EM but also several of the perspectives—including those of Wittgenstein and Heidegger—discussed in this book.

What is new in the EM project is that how actors are able to deal with indexicality and 'get by' in the face of it becomes the central object of inquiry. The problem of the gulf between the abstract and general on the one hand, and the concrete and situational on the other, can, for ethno-methodological purposes, be *respecified* as a problem that members of society solve as a matter of course in their everyday activities (Lynch 1993; Fele 2002; ten Have 2002):

I use the term 'ethnomethodology' to refer to the investigation of the rational properties of indexical expressions and other practical actions as contingent on-going accomplishments of organised artful practices of everyday life (Garfinkel 1967, p. 11).

'How people do it?' is then the main question which really fuels EM research. How do people make definite sense of indefinite resources? How are accounts and descriptions used? How do accounts and descriptions work, and how they are put to work?

EM is not interested in whether these descriptions are right or wrong, or consequential for practical purposes, as much as how members make out what these descriptions refer to, or more specifically, which competencies are necessary to claim that 'a collective member is entitled to exercise that he is capable of managing his (sic) everyday affairs without interference' (ibid., p. 57).

6.1.4 MEMBERSHIP

The notion of membership, the last of our key concepts, is thus critical for the EM project. For EM, the focus of attention in the study of practice is not atomic and well-formed individuals such as those in the methodological individualist tradition. For EM, what takes centre stage are instead the capacities or practical skills to perform competent membership. EM is not in the business of endowing humans with competencies and other psychological attributes that generate a practice, but seeks to identify what sort of ethno methods are necessary for a person to participate actively and competently in the accomplishment of an activity, and therefore to become a member. The focus is not on individuals as such, but on the capacities or competencies to perform competent membership. In the words of Garfinkel and Sacks (1970), 'the notion of member is the heart of the matter. We do not use the term to refer to a person. It refers instead to mastery of natural language ... We ask what it is about natural language that permits speakers and auditors to hear, and in other ways to witness, the objective production and objective display of common-sense knowledge, and of practical circumstances, practical actions, and practical sociological reasoning as well' (p. 342).[4] For EM, then, being a member is a state of affairs generated by the activity, regardless of it becoming the object of discussion. In other words, for EM, just as in the legitimate peripheral participation theory examined in Chapter 4, activity performs membership.

In summary, what fuels the EM programme of research is not that practical indexicality exists, but *how* it is that people manage to deal with it in such a competent manner that they become recognized members of a practice. As

Lynch (1993, p. 18) puts it, the ideas of indexicality and membership, therefore, constitute just 'a ticket that allows entry into the EM theatre, and is torn up as soon as one crosses the threshold' (Lynch 1993, p. 18). It constitutes a watershed which separates EM and EM-inspired research traditions from other forms of social theorizing, generating in the process a whole new set of issues and problems, which the notions of accountability, reflexivity, indexicality, and membership help raise and clarify, not solve. That is to say, these concepts open up a space for discursivity to re-specify what the study of practice and sociality may look like. But the onus of responding to the questions they set was left to the empirical study of practices.

6.2 **The implication of ethno-methodology for the study of (work) practices**

From my discussion above it follows that for ethno-methodologists, our stable, constraining, and orderly reality, made of recognizable and rational properties, is nevertheless a local accomplishment achieved through a combination of linguistic and non-linguistic, seen but not noticed, competencies. These competencies, their formal properties, and how they unfold in time constitute the actual object of study of EM. As Psathas stated: 'we can characterise the EM approach as being concerned with making a topic of study, any and all practices for constituting knowledge in the world of everyday life' (Psathas 1980, p. 15).

Historically speaking, the task of describing the accomplishment gave rise to two related, but nevertheless distinct, lines of research—conversation analysis and the ethno-methodological study of work.

Conversational analysis (CA) aimed to elucidate the rational properties of indexical expressions by investigating the sequential structure of naturally occurring conversations. These studies described the regular procedures for turn taking, adjacency-pairs organization, referential placement and correction, story structure, and other aspects of talk in interaction. The overall aim became to develop a grammar of conversation that describes how different speakers coordinate their actions to produce coherent sequences of conversation. CA constitutes a specific template for understanding practice, and I will have more to say about this line of research in Chapter 8.

The ethno-methodological studies of work were, on the contrary, aimed at showing how practitioners in various settings made their activities objectively accountable. Garfinkel's interest was not in work as a phenomenon to be studied, as much as it was in work as an instantiation of methods used by members to carry out courses of action in an accountable way. The analytic interest was in how that work was accomplished within the setting in which it was performed, and the detailed scrutiny of just what makes an activity what it is. The focus was therefore on work as a material, bodily, and linguistic activity carried out within specific local contexts. Ordinary activities were therefore examined for the ways they exhibited accountable work practices, as viewed by the practitioners.

Several studies of work were conducted as part of the first generation of EM studies.[5] For example, two of the chapters of Garfinkel's Studies (1967) are focused on work-related issues, and investigate the activities of employees at a suicide-prevention centre and clinical records centre. Significantly enough, many of the studies of this period were conducted at sites in which accountability was the heart of the matter both for members and the observing social scientist. Among others, one can cite Wieder's study of a half-way house for narcotic offenders on parole (1974), Bittner's analysis of police conduct (1967), and Cicourel's work on police contact with juvenile offenders (1968). The quest to find work sites in which a particular issue is of central concern for practitioners and can therefore be studied '*in vivo*' by social scientist has become a programmatic feature of EM studies of work. This quest became known as the search for 'perspicuous settings'. Perspicuous settings are real-world settings where the topic in question is a prominent feature of a day's work. A perspicuous setting allows researchers to investigate situated material production practices and the work that goes into them:

A perspicuous setting makes available, in that it consists of, material disclosures of practices of local production and natural accountability in technical details with which to find, examine, elucidate, learn of, show, and teach the organizational object as an in vivo work site (Garfinkel and Wieder 1992, p. 184).

If one is interested in studying how categorization works in practice, the best setting to investigate is one in which members do 'classification' all the time— as in the statistics office studied by Garfinkel. Given that accountability and rules are at the heart of EM reflection, it is therefore not surprising that many of the studies have been, and continue to be, conducted among occupations in which members are mundanely concerned with the selfsame topics, such as police and law practitioners. For similar reasons, medical settings also figure prominently among early EM studies of work. Medical practice is, in fact, characterized by everyday concerns for categorization and accountability. For example, Sudnow's study of death and dying in hospital settings, which demonstrated how several categories used in hospital life (e.g. life, illness, terminal patient, dying, and death), need to be seen as constituted by the practices of hospital personnel as they engage in their routine interaction within their organizational milieu (Sudnow 1967).

It is fair to say that the interest in work settings somewhat subsided during the late 19070s and early 1980s, which was possibly correlated to the growing attention to CA and its methods. Because of its pursuit of fundamental devices in talk-in-interaction, CA in fact developed a preference for less special material to work on, and focused mainly on ordinary conversation in ordinary settings.

When the EM interest in work and organizational settings was revived at the end of the 19080s, the phenomenon was partly framed, rightly or wrongly, as a reaction to some of the formalistic excesses of CA which had, in the meantime, come to be considered as co-extensive with the EM programme (Lynch 1993).

This new generation of EM studies of work was construed as a response to what was considered a major shortcoming in contemporary studies of work and organization, including studies which included an ethnographic approach to these phenomena.

In fact, according to Garfinkel and other EM practitioners, most contemporary studies of work and organizations failed to address the interactional 'what' of the occupation they studied. This failure applied not only to traditional sociology of work phenomena and to functionalist-oriented organization theory, but also to the emergent interest in an ethnographic study of organizational processes. Lynch (1993), for example, reports that Garfinkel often observed that Howard Becker's famous study of dance-band musicians (Becker 1963) did not address the interactional and improvisational work of playing together. Instead it focused on other more general aspects of the culture of the performers. EM's aim would therefore be that of addressing such a vacuum, so providing a new stream of studies which depicted the core practices of occupational worlds and uncovered the 'missing what', 'haecceity', or 'just-thisness'—to use some of Garfinkel's expressions[6]—of the different specialized practices in ordinary society.

Garfinkel and Wieder (1992) advocated, in particular, the use of what they called Sack's Gloss as a primary procedure to examine the 'concerted vulgar uniquely adequate competencies of order production' (Garfinkel and Wieder 1992, p. 184). Sack's Gloss was illustrated through narration:

In 1963 Sacks and Garfinkel were at the Los Angeles Suicide Prevention Centre. One day Sacks came into Garfinkel's office: 'Harold, I have a distinction.' It is relevant to this story that Sacks had finished Yale Law School two years before, because the distinction at first sounds very legalistic. 'I have a distinction between "possessibles" and "possessitives". By a possessable I'll mean *this*; I might as well mean this; I'll mean this for the time being with which to learn from others, by having them teach me, just what I'm really talking about: You're walking down the street; you see something; it looks attractive; you'd like to have it; and you see of the thing, that you'd like to have, that you can have it. You *see* that of the thing. As compared with: You're in the street; you see something attractive; you'd like to have it, but seeing the thing you'd like to have you see about it that you can't have it. You *see* it belongs to somebody. I'll call that a "possessitive". Now, Harold, what do I mean by that distinction? That is what I want to *find out*. I don't want you to tell me. I don't want to settle it like that. *I could* go to the UCLA law library; I know how to use it. I could find discussions that would bear on what I might as well mean, but that's not the way I want to learn what I mean.' He trusted himself to write definitions, 'but I don't want to write definitions; and I don't want to consult authorities. Instead, I want to *find* a work group, somewhere, perhaps in Los Angeles, who, *as their day's work*, and because they know it as their day's work, will be able to teach me what I could be talking about as *they* know it as the day's work.'

One day he came in with a great grin; he'd found such a group. In the Los Angeles Police Department are police who, in riding around their territories, as part of their work, spot cars that have been abandoned. Other cars look equally bad, but it could be found out that they were not abandoned. You call the tow truck for one of these cars; the other you ticket. As their day's work the police must make this distinction; make it fast; make it subject to supervisory review for the truth, correctness, and other adequacies of the recognition; make it in each particular case; do so within the bureaucratically organized Los Angeles Police Department; and having among its consequences that various parties, who as members of populations that can properly become involved, become forensically interested parties to issues of truth and correctness (Garfinkel and Wieder 1992, p. 185).

This story not only explains quite effectively what the authors mean with terms such as 'missing interactional what', 'haecceity', or 'just-thisness', it also constitutes an almost programmatic statement about the what and how of EM interest in work and work settings.

First, it suggests that the object of EM inquiry ought to be the incarnate nature of the lived work of real time, real-world work practice, and accountable orderliness of mundane events. Garfinkel and Wieder do not give us a definition of what a lived practice means. Instead, through the story of the Sack's Gloss they instruct us to consult a perspicuous setting and to immerse ourselves in the practicalities of the daily work of a work group who will be able to teach us what we could be discussing. As noted by Llewellyn (2004, 2008), however, it is not the object of study as much as the underlying analytic mentality that distinguishes EM from other apparently cognate approaches. Unlike other qualitative or interpretive approaches, EM is not satisfied with allusions and elliptical descriptions of work activities and organizational phenomena. Descriptive claims and attribution of motives, intentions, emotions, interest, etc. need to be empirically substantiated using detailed and almost forensic evidence. EM would thus find insufficient a typical ethnographic description that, say, during a meeting, participants were induced to confess, with expressions of culpability and remorse, their failures and mistakes.[7] An EM-orientated analyst would, in fact, ask how was the perception of culpability and remorse obtained, how did the participants observably display such 'culpability' through bodily motions and discursive practices, and how did the observers discerned remorse in their colleague's conduct. Such a forensic approach should be applied to all the aspect of other organizational life and work. The task for the social scientist, the so-called Garfinkel's 'awesome mystery'[8] is not just to register the existence of authority, or hierarchy, or surveillance, but to describe in painstaking details how authority, hierarchy, and surveillance are performed in specific situations and interpreted in practice by members.

The above story of Sack's Gloss also reiterates that what is at stake is the public, visible work of performing an orderly state of organized conduct, and not an investigation into things that happen 'behind' the backs of participants in the scene. Work practices and occupations are, therefore, understood not as the product of conventions, beliefs, or tacit assumptions, but 'primordially, as the self-organizing domains of recognizably competent work practices which compose themselves through vernacular conversations and the ordinariness of embodied disciplinary activities' (Heritage 1984, p. 302). The policy is, thus, that of refusing to 'ironicise' members' accounts, either by discounting them as subjective reports or by trying to explain them as the result of something else (habitus, class position, subconscious, etc.). The policy is central in setting EM apart from most other forms of social research. For the approach, in fact, social scientists should avoid using categories, theories, or constructs unless members are demonstrably orientated towards them (Berard 2005). For example, they should avoid stipulating the existence of, say, organizational structure, unless such a structure (1) has some demonstrable relevance to a particular occasion; (2) is exhibited as a phenomenon for members, in the sense that it makes a difference; and (3) all this is documented in or recognizable from the data, for instance, because one member visibly uses a different way of approaching different colleagues based on their publicly recognized hierarchical positions.

Finally, the above points imply that competencies can, and should always, be treated from within; that is, they should be described from the perspective of the members. Hence, familiar organized phenomena such as road traffic should not be described in terms of rules or prescriptions as much as the ongoing accomplishment of a number of drivers who can only see (or not see) a car in front, vertical and horizontal signals, and a number of other situated features (no oncoming vehicles on the other carriageway which is usually busy, and no progress of the car in front: why might this be the case?). They may hear about queues and gridlocks on the radio, but they can never step outside the car and fly over the city to get a glimpse from above—the position that, according to EM, is implicit in traditional social science. This means that (1) documenting the mundane activities composing an organizational domain can only be achieved by immersing oneself in that domain, and (2) that such immersion implies acquiring a vernacular competence in those practices. Thus in order to develop an appropriate understanding of work practices, an analyst *must* acquire vulgar competence in the phenomenon he or she is studying. Only in this way will it be possible to recognize the endogenous sense of the practical actions under scrutiny and to generate descriptions which can be understood by the practitioners themselves.

This aspect has, in fact, become central to Garfinkel's view of the study of work practices, and it has been renamed as the principle of 'unique adequacy'.[9] In its stronger formulation, the unique adequacy principle is a methodological injunction which requires (a) that social scientists acquire specific membership competencies, in order to gain access to the competencies that are actually used in specialized local practices, so that (b) the results of the investigations be fully intelligible and meaningful for members of the site under consideration. When combined with the strong analytic and evidentiary style of inquiry, the principle sets out some stringent conditions for embarking on EM studies, turning this form of research into a life-long endeavour. As two eminent EM scholars put it, albeit somewhat dramatically, the unique adequacy principle connotes EM 'not as a body of finding, nor as a method, nor a theory, nor a world view ... but as a form of life' (Mehan and Wood 1975, p. 3). These strict conditions for EM explorations also constitute a practical device which often determines its topics of study. Because of its evidentiary and analytical orientation, which translates into high labour intensity and time-consuming activity, EM traditionally ends up focusing on narrowly bounded settings and delimited activities, leaving wider phenomena as unexplained or simply unaddressed. As I shall discuss below, this practical constraint ended up becoming a characterizing trait of EM studies which meant that EM became pigeon-holed as a micro sociology, a label that ethno-methodologists have been at times willing to carry in order to differentiate themselves from other types of sociologists. However, in the process this led to some serious misconceptions.

It should also be added that such a strong version of the EM programme of radical studies of work became hard to adhere to in practice. Lynch, for example, notes that a strict observance of the principle would amount to the development of a number of 'wild sociologies', each capable of 'grasping the genetic essence of each praxeological species' (Lynch 1993, p. 276), and each requiring social scientists to become fully competent in the practices they studied. While this may work for some,[10] there are several of stories of EM apprentices who got so involved in their observation field that they never found their way back, nor wanted to return, or were unable to then find a place in the academic world (Lynch 1993).

6.3 The new generation of EM-orientated studies of work and organization

For a long time, ethno-methodologists were known as a relatively isolated and esoteric group of converts who claimed that EM was 'incommensurable and asymmetrically alternate' to all other forms of social analysis (Flynn 1991;

Garfinkel and Wieder 1992). What is less widely known, however, is that such a professed and often reiterated distinctiveness of the EM programme was not only the result of specific intellectual choices, but also the defensive strategy of a small cohort of scholars under attack from the sociological establishment (Mullins 1973; Flynn 1991). As documented, for example by Clayman and Maynard (1991), EM was, at least for two decades, the object of fierce controversies that resulted not only in the sidelining of its practitioners from the wider sociological community but also, and more importantly, in their near-total exclusion from the academic job market in US universities.[11]

The resulting partly self-imposed isolation, reinforced over time by the development of an esoteric way of researching and writing, was inevitably to become less tenable as EM became progressively accepted as a legitimate form of social research, and became reintegrated into the social science community. In recent times we have witnessed a sort of rapprochement of EM and other branches of social science, especially those surveyed in this book. It is not that EM has relinquished any of its original assumptions, rather that its message has attracted increasing interest and acceptance. At the same time, social and organizational studies have undergone a linguistic and practical turn, partly due to the incessant stimulus of EM criticisms,[12] which has certainly made this rapprochement much easier.

As a consequence, EM has in recent years become conversant with several of the post-functional approaches that together feed the 'practice turn in contemporary theory' discussed in Chapter 2. This is evident, for example, in the increasing number of studies carried out in the last two decades in a host of related areas, such as the study of science as a practical endeavour (see e.g. Lynch 1993), technology in action (Suchman 1987; Button 1992; Heath and Luff 2000), real-time work practices to inform system design (Dourish and Button 1998; Crabtree *et al.* 2000; Heath *et al.* 2000), and work and organizing processes (Hindmarsh and Pilnick 2002; Samra-Fredericks 2003, 2005; Llewellyn 2004, 2008; Llewellyn and Hindmarsh 2009). In all these cases we observe the establishment of fruitful exchanges between EM and other sociologies which resulted in the application of EM's analytical approach and methods to a host of traditional conversations and topics.

A case in point is the EM-inspired studies of work activities carried out particularly in Europe under the umbrella term of 'workplace studies' (Luff *et al.* 2000; Heath *et al.* 2002; Llewellyn and Hindmarsh 2009). These studies, which make cooperation and technology central themes for EM investigation, stem in fact from the conversation between EM-inspired studies of specific work practices and more established themes in organizational studies (see e.g. Heath and Button 2002; Suchman 2003; Llewellyn and Hindmarsh 2009, for a discussion). These studies suggest that only through a proper EM analysis can we shed light on how collaborative arrangements emerge in particular circumstances (Heath and Button 2002, p. 159), and discuss how technologies impact the life and work practices of organizational members. In this way, workplace studies introduce two novel focuses for EM scholars and pave the way for EM to have a bigger impact on organization and work studies.

All these studies, conducted in diverse settings such as call centres, printing firms, architectural practices, scientific labs, banks, and control centres, present a rich picture of the variety of ways in which one can capture and convey the accomplishment of particular activities, the range of practical resources that people bring to bear in such an accomplishment, as well as how these activities are shaped with regard to the practical circumstances. In this way, they constitute not only attractive examples of a particularly rich way to portray work and organizational practices, but they also demonstrate how to go about theorizing them which will appeal to other organizational and work scholars. EM-orientated workplace studies are not limited, in fact, to claiming in principle—as other theories do—that actors are bricoleurs, that they improvise and construct their world, that there is power and hierarchy. Rather, such studies go to great length to present living instances of bricolaging, improvisation, and power and hierarchy making and unmaking. They are not limited to claiming that organizations and society are socially constructed, that decisions and conducts are context-dependent, and that knowledge is practical and situated. Instead, they set out to provide evidentiary empirical substantiation to these claims, describing in detail how ordered and organized scenes of action are accomplished, how members build on 'contextual' clues for accomplishing their activities, how knowing is visibly exhibited in what members actually do or refrain from doing. In keeping with the EM programme, they thus strive to make work and organizational practices perspicuous objects of inquiry, thus treating them analytically instead of descriptively (Llewellyn 2004), hence offering a new way of conceiving the program of investigating work and organizational practices from a constructive and processual perspective.

EM is therefore appealing because it proposes a way of theorizing practice which significantly diverges from most other approaches surveyed in this book. EM is not a theory as much as a set of theoretical questions which 'have the edifying effects of cultivating sensibilities that are closely aligned with the goal of disinterested, naturalistic, non-reifying, non-ironicising closely empirical research into members' methods of practical reasoning and practical action, what can be called the indigenous, observable logic of practice' (Berard 2005, p. 215). While all the other approaches discussed in the rest of this book attract abstract theory, EM isolates a new order of phenomena and develops new methods for its study. In this sense, an EM sensibility runs against the idea of formulating a theory of practice, claiming that this customary move, typical of traditional social theory, would substitute theoretical constructs for the 'real thing'. As an alternative, EM suggests that the only legitimate way of theorizing practice is by providing exemplars and instructive descriptions. In relation to the former, analyst effort is directed at capturing 'the concreteness of things' (Garfinkel 1996), and making the actual process of practising available to inspection in and through the text (or other media). The aim is to convey the procedural accomplishment of these activities as actual, concerted conducts. In relation to the latter, the analyst explicitly provides a minimal set of instructions that replicates the method actually used by members so that readers can do it for themselves. The aim here is to allow, at least in principle, reproducibility of the same conduct. In both cases, focus is exclusively on the methods that are called, interchangeably, 'procedures', 'methods', and 'practices' (Maynard and Clayman 1991, p. 387). In other words, EM does not see itself as being in the business of providing idealizations, or constructing non-empirical theoretical entities that can be used for explaining why the world is as it is in one way and not another. On the contrary, it proposes to re-specify theory in terms of 'methodography'; i.e. 'a search for the practices or methods by which substantive features of the setting are made available' (Boden and Zimmerman 1991, p. 95).

EM's theatrical stance towards practice (in the sense of being orientated toward describing the staging of practices) is thus mainly to be found in its analytic mentality and its way of conducting and communicating research. At the core of the EM programme is the aim of representing practice from the member's perspective as a way of making it capable of analysis and revealing its formal properties. To achieve this, EM builds not only on the methodological dispositions described above, but also on a literary genre carefully engineered to foreground practice. Such a literary genre responds to the challenge of engaging with the minutiae of practical conduct instead of only alluding to them. Although its thorough analysis goes well beyond the scope of the present work, a few features are worth noting. In particular:

- EM's praxeological accounts are necessarily data-driven.[13] For EM authors, the formal and recurrent features of practice need to be made visible and recognizable in and through the data. EM accounts, therefore, traditionally start from, or rotate around, a report on a piece of empirical research which is taken both as an illustration of the phenomenon at hand and the object of the subsequent analytical work. Practice is first exhibited for everyone to see, and then it is patiently and thoroughly dissected in search of the micro procedures, processes, and moves that make it the way it is. EM's literary genre is often inspired by the natural sciences rather than other brands of social theory (Heritage 1984).
- EM's praxeological accounts do not require specific sociological techniques to be employed. The rendering of practices is carried out using members' natural language which, as I have shown above, already embodies the vernacular understanding of what is going on.

- Such accounts need to capture both the concerted and time dimensions inherent in lived practices. Courses of action develop in time, and such an emergence needs to be captured by describing in some way the sequential order of activities.

- Talk is, of course, a central feature of organizational life, and it needs to figure prominently in accounts of practices. In fact, EM as a programme shows that talk and practice are two different aspects of the same phenomenon and cannot be separated, not even for analytic purposes. Instead, how discursive and non-discursive practices co-exist in the pursuit of situated practical concerns becomes an empirical issue to be thematized in the research. On the other hand, however, EM also warns that attending to talk alone, as for example in certain linguistic interpretations of organizational phenomena (see e.g. Westwood and Linstead 2001), is insufficient for understanding practices: any account which doesn't also pay attention to bodily movements, interactional choreographies, material landscapes, spaces, and tools cannot but provide a sensorially deprived and scarcely-recognizable rendering of practices. To the extent that the architectures, machineries, and bodily techniques such as those identified by Foucault make up coherent order of practices, these need to be taken into account in the description.

- There is a need to assemble entire scenes. Lynch (1993) and Cicourel (1981) noted that practices cannot be understood by extracting a small segment out of a larger meaningful segment in that this contradicts the basic notion of indexicality according to which all practices are both context-dependent and context-renewing.

In conclusion, EM offers a powerful way of approaching practice as a topic of study. It alerts us that practice can only be understood and described as a publicly available accomplishment based on the situated assembling of a number of discursive and non-discursive practices. Enumerating the resources that enter into this accomplishment (e.g. rules, formal descriptions, categories, narratives, technologies, and other artefacts) is insufficient, as it is to claim that social structures, inequalities, power, and meaning are 'constructed'. Once we have accepted that the world is the result of an incessant process of social construction, we have begun our task, and we then need to work to provide convincing instances of what this means in practice (Lynch 1993). EM therefore suggests that no descriptions of traditional categorical features of organizational or social life is complete without the 'alternate' description of how they are lived through in practice; that the division of labour is experienced not as a coherent and integrated phenomenon but as a fragmentation of activities and tasks; that authority is performed through mundane acts of getting this and this paper signed off 'just in case'; that hierarchy is achieved through waiting for one further minute before starting the meeting. EM's praxeological accounts are, therefore, not only noted for their style of investigation but also for the style in which they are reported to, and offered for, readers. Although risks of a theoretical empiricism and realism are inherent in such an approach,[14] this practical and rhetorical apparatus promises to enable us to reproduce the 'just this-ness' and the concreteness of lived practices to which other approaches cannot aspire.

6.4 **An unfinished task**

The question of to what extent EM is capable of doing this is, of course, a different matter. Garfinkel and Wieder (1992) and Lynch (1993) have alerted us to the fact that EM renderings of real-time practices simply situate descriptions in materially embodied practices, in contrast to rules of method, bodies of ideas, formulae, formal structures, generic formats, and other theoretical and meta-theoretical formulations of orderliness. EM accounts of the practice of others are thus to be viewed as 'corrigible claims written as sketch accounts [which are to be] read praxeologically . . . ' (Garfinkel and Wieder 1992, p. 181). There is no claim that this type of representation can access the 'just this-ness' of the *in vivo* activity in an unmediated way, only that the mediation used by EM is more convincing and less abstruse than that of a traditional formal constructive social analysis. Just like the descriptions produced by the actual actor for all practical purposes, praxeological accounts are never right or wrong but only more or less defensible, more or less rectifiable.

While this argument settles the score with regards to possible claims that EM is naïve empiricism, EM is however still liable to Bourdieu's criticism discussed earlier. As we have seen, for Bourdieu, practice as such is available to agents who are not only competent but also authentically implicated in the consequences of their actions. Habitus make agents feel what it is that makes sense to do, and what is doable; agents do what they feel like doing or decide the right thing to do while being aware of the consequences, or not, of their actions. Practice only exists in the temporal dimension of the urgency of engagement and cannot survive either in the reversible universe of rules and formal logic, or in the semi-engaged world of the professionally orientated sociologist who can claim, but never occupy, a coherent and unique adequacy position. The 'unique adequacy principle' and the notion of instructable reproducibility, which together are supposed to resolve the issue of accessing and describing common sense, hence run into familiar troubles. Although they provide a thoroughly convincing way of both investigating and reporting practices, they cannot but provide a thick allusive account of the engaged practices of members. The allusive account may be thicker than in other approaches, but it is still an allusion *qua* account. In this way, and not necessarily negatively, EM is just an unfinished project, as are all other fields of social science.

There is, however, another way in which EM, taken as a way to describe work and organizational practices, is unfinished business, or, more precisely, just a beginning. I am referring to the unofficial but strictly observed commitment of EM to focus exclusively on localized phenomena and abstain from addressing all phenomena which do not constitute local scenes of action. I call this unofficial because this policy does not stem from any of the assumptions of the approach, and derives instead from a combination of tradition and the effect produced by the tools of the trade used by ethno-methodologists.

EM usually frames the strict observance of the 'we only do local here' principle as a contrast between the inherent tendency of functionalist sociology 'to address society as a big thing that contains the action and events that we witness in daily life' (Lynch 1993, p. 30), and the EM focus on the local accomplishment of social order. For EM, the distinction between micro and macro means that the global is simply left behind. It is not that EM denies the existence of social structural phenomena *per se*; it is that EM refuses to take them as an object of study unless they are visibly manifested in the actual social practices of members. In this sense, for EM, the so-called 'macro' is squarely contained in the local, and because there are no scenic overlooks of the global, we cannot but focus on situated local practices.

Historically speaking, this assumption led to the identification of the local as the proper domain for ethno-methodology, and in time, led to a limitation of scientists' observations to what could be seen or empirically witnessed (Garfinkel, Lynch, and Livingston 1981). This radical local focus went hand-in-hand with the already discussed political focus through which EM carved a niche in the sociological market by claiming to be alternative to all essentialist sociologies. In other terms, other social scientists could go about their usual business of talking about gender, class, power, and society, while EM scholars (without interfering with, and possibly arguing with, other social scientists) would continue to focus on local order and the accomplishment of intelligible scenes of action. This emergent localism was further reinforced by the fact that most of the analytical tools used by EM scholars were developed for the purpose of examining narrowly bounded settings and specifically delimited activities; this in turn created a self-fulfilling prophecy as to what concerns the type of phenomena that were considered by the approach.

The result, however, is that EM ended up exposing itself to the risks of turning the principle that social order is a local product into a form of localism, what Levinson (2005) calls 'interactional reductionism'—the tendency of reducing all social phenomena to self-organizing local interactions. This reductionist risk is exhibited, for example, in the belief that the discoveries of EM in general, and CA in particular, are subject to growth by accumulation. The argument implicit in many EM works is that if we pursue our research long enough, at some point we will discover *all* the ethnomethods for producing conversation and so will achieve the complete reproducibility of human discursive interaction (see Lynch 2001 for a discussion). The problem with this position is not only theoretical but also eminently practical. Embracing localism or interactional reductionism as a policy prevents, in fact, EM from turning its gaze towards a number of interesting phenomena and issues, such as how different scenes are related, and what are the observable effects that these relations produce in the practice of members. EM's effort to differentiate itself from traditional social theory, which tends to substitute grand theoretical cathedrals for real life, thus becomes a degree of abdication from addressing phenomena of a larger scope. However, as I mentioned above, such a programmatic abdication, similarly to localism and interactional reductionism, does not necessarily stem from EM's basic assumption. Nowhere in the approach does one find good theoretical reasons not to focus, say, on the interaction between practices, how micro events are linked in chains or nets, and how these associations produce particular effects in the actual activity of members. To the extent that all these events can be addressed as observable and reportable empirical activities, there are no reasons why they cannot be addressed using the EM sensibility and toolkit. As long as one does not substitute an idealized order for the ordering activities actually emerging in and through the data, there are no reasons to uphold the traditional view that EM should only address what can actually be seen or otherwise empirically witnessed here and now. By endorsing a more nomadic version of EM, and following the practices and their connections (as suggested by Collins 1981), and the intermediaries that carry such practices around the world (as proposed more recently by Latour 2005), one can thus extend the heuristic power of EM to a variety of topics until now largely ignored by this approach. Disregarding the connections that link not the local and the (idealized) global, but the local with other translocal instances of accomplishment, looks less like the consequence of a choice and more the result of a shortcoming covered by an ideological argument. The contribution of EM to the understanding of social phenomena in general, and work and organizational work in particular, could be much enhanced if we conceive this approach as the building block of a general programme of interactional constructivism,[15] an approach in which practice and its relations, and not practices in isolation, become the main topic of study. This is what I have tried to do in some of my studies, as I will explain in Chapter 9 (the final chapter of the book) which offers a very preliminary outline of how such approach may look.

Rolling case study: Accomplishing monitoring[16]

Offering patients and their family telephone assistance on all aspects of their condition, is an essential (albeit not the only) aspect of telecare. Telephone contact thus takes up a substantial proportion of nurses' time. This takes precedence over all other activities, which the nurses abandon as soon as the phone rings. Phone activity is thus a good place to immerse ourselves in the practicalities of the daily work of the tele-nurses. At the same time, the phone call also constitutes a perspicuous site where we can observe at work one of the healthcare practitioners' critical skills—classifying and making distinctions.

6.5.1 How to tell if a call is urgent before you hear what the patient has to say

Telemonitoring is accomplished through a variety of phone contacts. On an institutional level, as for example in official documents and scientific reports, telephone calls made by nurses are clearly separated from those made by patients. The former are always classified as part of telemonitoring, the latter as tele-assistance. In reality, there are many more types of telephone contacts, and nurses tend to classify calls more according to what they involve and what the requests are for, than to whom initiates it. Moreover, although all calls are important, some are more important than others. By its very nature, in fact, heart failure requires swift and urgent action. The typical progression of the disease means that an attack is more serious the longer it takes for medical staff to intervene. The capacity to react rapidly is a critical factor, and any strategy that does not take into account this aspect will see its effectiveness reduced drastically. In one case a patient called to complain of a terribly bad night with much swelling and localized pain. Suspecting a cardiac arrest, the nurse immediately told the patient to send through his trace which indicated an incipient heart attack. She then called the patient again, asking him to contact his doctor and at the same time to go to the nearest emergency ward where the diagnosis was confirmed.

If one observes the nurses long enough, one gets the clear impression that they have a method for recognizing urgent calls just by knowing who is calling when, even before they actually hear the content of the call. However, when pressed to explain how they do it, nurses provide vague answers often using the word 'depending' in their answers. So how do they practically solve this 'it depends', or conditional, issue that social scientists would describe as the 'context' of the call?

To solve this mystery, we need to observe that nurses tend to classify calls according to what they involve and what the requests are for, rather than who initiates them. In the first place, they distinguish between patient and non-patient calls. This is done for them by the set-up of the service, in that they have one dedicated line for talking to patients and another for other business. When the 'black' phone rings they already have a good idea who is calling. They also tend to distinguish between 'check-up', assistance, or information seeking, follow-up, and urgent calls.

Planned 'check-up' calls follow an agreed schedule established collaboratively between the nurse and the patient. These calls are made at precise times during the day, usually mid-morning or early afternoon, when nurses expect they will have had enough time to prepare for the calls, to talk with the patients without interruption, and to end the conversations appropriately. Planned calls are thus recurrent and important appointments allowing operators to close one brief cycle and start a new one. They also weave together many of the activities carried out in previous calls into a sequence marked by regular intervals. This, in turn, creates the temporal flow necessary for monitoring to take place.

Not all calls are planned, though. Patients also call to ask questions or to report non-urgent anomalies. The number of these calls varies according to the type of patients, because people in a more critical condition or novices to the service are generally more anxious than those in other groups. As one nurse put it: 'People having had serious heart failure call two to four times a day, particularly at the beginning... these are often people who have never taken drugs... and know nothing about their side-effects.'

Although nurses take a lot of time to support and reassure patients, assistance calls, when patients only call in search of psychological support, are fairly rare. Patients can access a special psychological support line, and whenever patients call 'just for a chat' the nurses take the occasion to ask specific questions about the physical condition of the patient and other health parameters. One of the critical features of all these types of calls is that they create a sequence and generate need for a follow up. In other words, a single call often does not close a conversation segment or settle the matter. For example, during check-up calls, patients often make arrangements which require follow-up calls:

'Well, look, let's try to increase your medicine dose by half a tablet. Try it tomorrow and
    Sunday. Take it right after breakfast. See how you go and we can talk on Monday...'
'OK, then Monday.'
'I'll call you in the morning.'

When the patient is contacted on Monday, the nurse picks up the conversation where it left off, often reinforcing the link with the previous conversation as if there had been no break between the two: *'Hello, I wanted to know how you went with the medicine we discussed Friday . . . '*. Similar arrangements are also made when patients call for information or for support (the 'just to talk' calls are thus actively subverted by the nurses). Most calls therefore generate a significant appendage of follow-up contacts and short calls, like a tail of fragments of interaction which continue after the originating event. This renders the work of the nurses highly complex and apparently chaotic. But there is a clear method at work in this apparently fragmented landscape. The fact that all check-up and assistance calls are conducted in such a way to generate a follow-up is used, in fact, as a practical resource which allows nurses to distinguish unexpected from more likely calls. When they receive calls that cannot be immediately linked to any previous conversations, and when they originate from patients who are not known to customarily call the centre for support 'all the time', nurses know that something may be happening, even before they hear the tone of voice or content of the call. Classification is thus made on the basis of the formal property of the call vis à vis the sequence created by other calls. These 'out of place' calls are, in a way, a non-sequitur and as such they signal some potential deviation from the norm, which is what the nurses fear most. These 'totally unexpected' calls therefore often take precedence over others, even if only by a couple of minutes.[17]

6.5.2 Monitoring as a bodily choreography

The strategy whereby a texture of activities becomes the background or 'context' against which deviations and anomalies emerge is, of course, well known and widely discussed as it constitutes the gist of any monitoring and control activity.[18] Speaking in ethno-methodological language, we could state that monitoring thus thrives upon reflexivity. The telemonitoring calls are particularly interesting in that they allow an appreciation of how this background is built in practice through a variety of discursive and materially mundane activities. More specifically, the close analysis of the calls during the telemonitoring activity makes it visible that the 'context' against which the information provided by the patient acquires sense is skilfully created through a choreography which combines discursive practices, bodily activities, and the use of a variety of artefacts.

Consider the following reconstruction of one of the scheduled calls of one of the tele-nurses.

On her desk, the nurse has placed her agenda and two large ring binders with clear plastic envelopes. She looks at the agenda and tells me that she is about to call one female patient. She opens one of the two binders, looks through the envelopes in alphabetical order and retrieves the one belonging to the patient she wants to call. She turns and takes two fax sheets from a pile on her desk: an ECG trace received earlier and a fax with the results of the laboratory tests the patient has undergone. She takes her ruler from the coat pocket, measures the ECG, and shakes her head. She puts the sheet back on the table. She takes a look at the plastic envelope containing a variety of sheets, and pulls out a big A3-sized sheet that she places on the table under the computer. The large 'therapy' sheet (see Figure 5.4 in Chapter 5) contains a number of columns as well as a heading, and some of them are already filled. The date of the call is indicated at the top of each column on the sheet. In the first column with a heading, each line carries the name of a drug. Lower down there are three lines for heart function, pressure, and weight. At the bottom of the sheet there is a line for the doctor's signature and a large notepad. The different columns next to each call, indicate the dosage of each drug, weight, and pressure data, with occasional notes in their respective fields.

Therefore, the nurse has in front of her an agenda, the two tests, the binder, and the large open sheet which sits in the middle of this configuration at the centre of her desktop. The nurse then takes the binder. In the envelope the first sheet is divided into printed boxes. In each, and written in pen, there is information that the nurse wants to have 'always ready'—name, telephone number, family doctor, diagnosis, ultrasonograph results, objectives, some tests. She places it on top of the large therapy sheet and uses it to dial the patient number. What happens next is described in the table below. On the left I report the conversation transcribed verbatim. On the right I describe what the reader would see if on the scene.

In the right-hand column of the table, which indicates what the nurse is doing whilst she is talking, we can observe that the nurse is literally and materially constructing and reconstructing the 'background' that allows her to make sense of the information provided by the patient. Whilst she is talking, the nurse rearranges the documents in front of her according to a precise geometry critical to obtain the desired effect. Before the call, for example, she arranges in front of her the distant and recent history of the patient. This information is contained in the large therapy sheet and the other tests (ECGs and laboratory tests) which she will handle during the call. She glances at these documents in quick succession. She gently leans forward to look at one of the faxes, then backwards to look at the sheet in front of her, then forward again to look at the other fax, then, importantly, she returns to glance at the therapy sheet, where the history of previous calls is registered in writing. By switching her attention between recent and not-so-recent pieces of information, she thus visibly reconstructs the trajectory of the state of the patient over time and establishes a set of expectations that allows her to interpret both the data sent in by the patient and what the patient is going to say. For example, this enables her not to be alarmed by the rise of weight in lines 15–17 (a significant variation that would have been looked at much more closely in another situation) and to foresee some defensiveness on the part of the patient, who also saw the tests before faxing them to the centre, and who is aware her mozzarella excesses have surfaced in her tests (hence the nurse's smile).

While at the beginning of the phone call the nurse concentrates on the documents which help her to establish a continuity between the past the present, during the call we can observe that, before the conversation segment they are needed in ends, she begins to move some of the tests. In this way she

		SAYINGS	SOME OF THE NURSE'S DOINGS
			The nurse moves away the ring binder and leans forward to look again at one of the faxes. She takes a look at the sheet with the tests which she had already looked at before. Then she puts down the sheet and smiles . . .
		[Phone ringing]	
1	N:	Good morning, how are you?	
2	P:	Not too bad, thank God . . . . however, you	
3		know . . . . my triglycerides.[19]	
4	N:	I know . . . . I've seen your tests	
5	P:	Yeah . . . . my triglycerides!	
6	N:	They are not exactly where they should be	
7	P:	(Mumble) . . . . well, you know, I cannot resist	
8	N:	I know . . . . some crisps here . . . . some cheese.	*While making this comment, the nurse pulls up the therapy sheet and takes a look at the data. She quickly glances at one of the faxes and then concentrates again on the therapy sheet.*
9		there . . . . and your triglycerides stay high.	
10		Can you tell me your pressure, please?	
11	P:	90 over 130.	
12	N:	Seems fine to me . . . Did you measure it in the	
13		morning?	
14	P:	Yes, yes.	
15	N:	How about your weight?	*The nurse turns slightly on the chair and smiles . . . she looks at the sheet and writes down the information.*
16	P:	Well . . . uh . . . . eighty . . . . eighty two kilos	
	N:	Eighty or eighty-two kilos?	
17	P:	Eighty-two (in a low voice) but it varies[20]	

[The rest of the call is omitted for reasons of space]

is, in practise, anticipating on a material level what she is about to do on a discursive level (see e.g. lines 8 and ff.). The layout of the sheets allows her to obtain an overview of the situation of the patient for the duration of the telephone call. This often allows the nurse to anticipate the patient's enquiries and questions (i.e. line 3), giving the nurse overall control of the interaction but also visibly producing a reassuring effect that is of great significance for the patients (who feel they are looked after).

Pollner and McDonald-Winkler (1985) use the terms 'framing' and 'post-scripting' to indicate those situations where the actors discursively build up a setting (before or after the call) within which to interpret what is said and done. On the basis of the information gathered, the nurse builds up a frame which she uses to formulate the questions as part of a self-sustaining process which progressively becomes clearer to the patient as well. This emerges clearly here: the nurse frames the call and the state of the patient in regards to over-eating. The nurse upholds this frame throughout the whole call, e.g. line 7 when she says 'But you have to be more strict with your diet...no crisps...' and again in the ending, omitted here for brevity, when she will say 'beware of what you eat.' The subsequent exchanges either reinforce or weaken the initial frame.[21] When saturation is reached, as in the call reproduced here, and the nurse initiates a *postscripting* process. In other words, she retrospect-ively reproduces the meaning of the event and 'puts in order what has just happened' (Pollner and McDonald-Wikler 1985, p. 245). Alternatively, the discussion can continue by following a new framing hypothesis, which some-times is suggested by the patient, until saturation occurs.

The close observation of the nurse's body choreography illustrates that framing and postscripting are obtained not only through talk but also though a visible bodily choreography and the active contribution of a variety of artefacts. Far from being engaged in some mysterious activity of sense-making that unfolds in her head or brain, the nurse's understanding depends on the use of a few simple discursive procedures and a variety of mundane artefacts. Among them, a central role is played by the therapy sheet. The therapy sheet allows a comparative reading of the data recorded from a number of calls, allowing the evolution of the patient's condition to be followed. It also gives operators an overview of all the patient's critical parameters that can be compared extremely effectively as in the call above. For this reason, as the nurse's movements show, the therapy sheet is the centre of attention repre-senting a sort of geographic core around which the other test results are arranged. The nurse always places the sheet directly in front of her, and only looks at another document when more information needs to be added to the sheet itself. The therapy sheet therefore acts as an active organizer of data and behaviour, a fully fledged trajectory-making device. The effect of 'creating a trajectory of the development of the patient's condition' is obtained by work sharing among human and non-human staff. As one of the nurses explicitly declared: *'the therapy sheet was used as a guide for a long time... it guided our calls... especially when we were still inexperienced... it was certainly the first thing we showed our colleagues'*.

▓ NOTES

1. The expression is taken from Psathas 1980, p. 15.
2. I find the following definition by George Psathas particularly illuminating: 'The topics of ethnomethological study thus become the methods contained within the ordinary activities of members which: (a) make practical actions and circumstances, commonsense knowledge of social structures, and practical sociological reasoning, analyzeable; and which (2) enable the discovery of the formal properties of practical actions themselves as ongoing accomplishments viewed "from within", i.e. from members' perspectives' (Psathas 1980, p. 4).
3. Reflexivity features prominently in what is commonly taken as the canonical, albeit somewhat arcane, definition of the EM programme by Garfinkel: 'Ethnomethodological studies analyse everyday activities as members' methods for making those same activities visibly-rational-and-reportable-for-all-practical-purposes, i.e., "accountable," as organisations of commonplace everyday activities. The reflexivity of that phenomenon is a singular feature of practical actions, of practical circumstances, of common sense knowledge of social structures, and of practical sociological reasoning. By permitting us to locate and examine their occurrence the reflexivity of that phenomenon establishes their study' (Garfinkel 1967, p. vii).
4. The full quotation is as follows: 'The notion of member is the heart of the matter. We do not use the term to refer to a person. It refers instead to mastery of natural language... We ask what it is about natural language that permits speakers and auditors to hear, and in other ways to witness, the objective production and objective display of common-sense knowledge, and of practical circumstances, practical actions, and practical sociological reasoning as well. What is it about natural language that makes these phenomena observable-reportable, that is account-able phenomena? For speakers and auditors the practices of natural language somehow exhibit these phenomena in the particulars of speaking and that these phenomena are exhibited is thereby itself made exhibitable in further description, remarks, questions, and in other ways for the telling' (Garfinkel and Sacks 1970, p. 342).
5. For a list of these works see Garfinkel and Wieder 1992.
6. See for example Garfinkel and Wieder 1992, p. 175.
7. The example was originally used by Llewellyn (2008). The author examines the work of some well-known ethnographers such as Casey, Burawoy, and Du Gay, noting their tendency to leave unexplained several of the central concepts and activities in their description which, on the contrary, constitute the central concern of EM investigation.
8. The felicitous expression is from Psathas 1980, p. 12.
9. '[...] the unique adequacy requirement of methods is identical with the requirement that for the analyst to recognise, or identify, or follow the development of, or describe phenomena of order in local production of coherent detail the analyst must be vulgarly competent in the local production and reflexively natural accountability of the phenomenon of order he is "studying."' (Garfinkel and Wieder 1992, p. 182).

10. One of the most famous cases is that of Sudnow (1978). Sudnow spent a decade first learning how to play piano, then how to play piano music that was recognized by other jazz musicians as jazz, and finally, how to instruct students in jazz piano. At the end of his inquiry, Sudnow fulfilled Garfinkel's recommendation by developing a commercially successful 'piano method' widely used in the USA and available for inspection at <http://www.sudnow.com>.

11. The attacks against ethno-methodology during meetings of the American Sociological Association, such as those by of Coleman in 1967 and Coser in 1975, are well-known and well-documented (see e.g. Mullins 1973; Dingwall 1981). What is less widely known is that the controversy surrounding EM determined the almost complete marginalization of its practitioners from the sociological community for almost two decades and, more significantly, their almost total exclusion from journals and the academic job market in US universities.

12. One could note that Garfinkel and Wieder's comments made in 1992 were, in fact, scarcely applicable to the European context. The attention to the lived work, the role of language, and processual and constructive nature of the organizing process, had already become a major concern in organization studies and had never disappeared from the agenda of labour process scholars in the UK and ergonomics in France.

13. The expression is taken from Heritage 1984, p. 243.

14. Empiricism is the philosophical position which emphasizes the primary role of experience, especially sensory perception, as the main source of ideas and knowledge. More specifically, empiricism is the epistemological theory that genuine information about the world must be acquired by *a posteriori* means, so that nothing can be thought without first being sensed. While overall the EM projects avoids the risk of overt naïve empiricism, it embraces a radical form of naturalism that espouses this type of criticism, especially when it affirms that the approach can actually access the hacceity of phenomena, and that its objects of work are 'raw data'. Accusations of erring on the side of empiricism have been directed towards certain varieties of EM such as conversational analysis. Consider, for example, the following statement by its founder and leading figure:

In naturalistic inquiry of the sort I am committed to, it happens that, while examining a naturally occurring event (or, rather, a record of it), one notices something [...] that presents itself as 'Oh, I've seen something like that before!' (Schegloff 1997, pp. 501–502).

While for the author this is only the first step in the articulation of conversational features which require further mediational work, he appears to endorse a strong and somewhat troublesome version of radical naturalism which is exposed to all the criticisms levelled, for example, at naturalistic ethnography (see e.g. Marcus and Fischer 1986; Clifford 1986). It is worth adding that Hilbert (1990) explicitly addressed the issue, suggesting that EM's commitment to empirical phenomena should not be taken to imply that ethnomethodology is a-theoretical or that it approaches human behavior 'from the point of view of pristine, crude, or neobehaviorist empiricism' (Hilbert 1990, p. 797). What the authors call 'ethno-methodological empiricism' does not remove the analyst as an interpreter of data 'nor do ethnomethodologists claim privileged exemption from the social practices they investigate' (ibid.). While ethno-methodologists, like all other scientists cannot engage in unmediated observation, says Hilbert, the sort of mediation embraced by EM is profoundly different from that of traditional social science where a theoretically constructed society replaces the 'concreteness of things'. For Hilbert (1990), then, it is to the 'concreteness of things' that ethno-methodologists return to, what he calls 'a form of empiricism similar, if social science ever is, to that of classical natural science' (ibid.).

As for realism, again it is particularly conversational analysis that comes under fire. For example, Weber (2003) notes that when Schegloff talks of 'objects in their own right', the possibility of 'a partial account of the object itself,' as well as of 'an internally grounded reality of its own', he does not leave much room for doubt in his realism. The issue of the philosophical status of EM is addressed, among others, by Lynch (1993).

15. I am borrowing the image from Levinson (2005), although I do not completely subscribe to his neo-Durkheimian view and language.

16. Some background information on the practice of telemedicine is provided at the end of Chapter 2.

17. Nurses always respond to all calls, even those which originate from patients who have a history of 'false' alarms. The nurses, however, approach these calls with much less apprehension than on other occasions. Very often, moreover, they exchange comments like 'uh ... this is Mr XY calling ... I was surprised he hadn't called already ...'.

18. See for example Anthony (1967).

19. Level of fat in the blood.

20. Patients with serious heart failure can retain water at an outstanding rate. For this reason diuretics constitute one of the main medications for this condition, and control of urination is crucial.

21. See, for example, in the call, line 14, ('eighty or eighty-two kilos?'): the nurse indicates she is expecting a patient who has let herself go (in relation to recommended behaviour) will have unhealthy test values.

7 Practice as the House of the Social: Contemporary Developments of the Heideggerian and Wittgensteinian Traditions

In previous chapters I have suggested that many of the contemporary theories of practice build in one way or another on the legacy of Heidegger, Wittgenstein, or a combination of the two. While authors such as Bourdieu and Giddens only make indirect mention of the work of these two great 'founders of discursivity',[1] others developed their practice-based theories building explicitly on the work of the two German masters. Authors such as Charles Taylor, Ernesto Laclau, and Chantal Mouffe, Joseph Rouse, Berry Barnes, Andrew Pickering, and Theodor Schatzki[2] elaborated and refined Heidegger and Wittgenstein's initial intuition that phenomena such as knowledge, meaning, identity, activity, power, language, social institutions, and transformation are 'housed in' and stem from the field of social practices. Although their views are often only partially aligned, so that there is no such thing as a unified Heideggerian and Wittgensteinian practice-based approach or school, these authors have all contributed to a common project according to which practices represent the basic component of social affairs, and as such they constitute the basic epistemic object of social theory. In other words, for all these authors the starting point for theorizing human affairs is social practices and their connections, and not well-formed individuals or overarching systems (in all the variants in which these theories manifest themselves). In a characteristic way, they thus suggest that social theory must start from the 'meso' level of practice.

As I shall show, what distinguishes this particular group of authors from other practice theorists discussed in this volume is the centrality granted to intelligibility in human affairs. The authors of the Heideggerian and Wittgensteinian tradition believe that at all times people mostly do (and say) whatever it makes sense for them to do (and say). Such sense, however, always manifests itself as part of an ongoing practical endeavour. It follows that practices, and neither sense nor the individuals that enact the sense-making, are the starting points for the investigation and understanding of human and social affairs. It is thus to the accomplishment of real-time practices that we need to turn if we want to understand human conduct and social order.

In my discussion I will focus particularly, albeit not exclusively, on the work of Theodore Schatzki. Over the last two decades, the author has developed one of the strongest versions of practice theories. Building on insights from Wittgenstein and Heidegger (hence the title of the chapter), the author has outlined a far-reaching theory that takes practice as the principal constitutive element of social life in all its manifestations—including work organizations. In the process, he has offered one of the more explicit and clear illustrations of the implications of a practice-based approach, not only for the understanding and studying of social phenomena, but also for the reconceptualization of issues such as agency, normativity, materiality, and organization.

7.1 **Why people do what they do**

Schatzki's theory of practice builds upon a specific view of human action derived more or less directly from the work of Wittgenstein and Heidegger. According to his view, in all circumstances, people do what it makes sense for them to do. Taylor, another prominent practice theorist who developed the legacy of Wittgenstein and Heidegger, suggests that this is a fundamental anthropological trait of humans that distinguishes them (us) from other primates: 'we have to think of man (sic) as a self-interpreting animal' (Taylor 1985, p. 26). Both for Wittgenstein and Heidegger, in fact, it is characteristic of human existence 'to experience one's situation in terms of certain meaning' (ibid., p. 27). This in turn can be thought of as a sort of 'proto-interpretation' that pervades every aspect of our life. Put differently, people respond to their conditions of life on the basis of how they make sense of what is going on, although such sense-making ought not to be explicit and too like decision-making. Humans are thus neither serial rational decision makers nor cultural/rule/habitus dupes. Schatzki calls this condition 'action intelligibility' (Schatzki 1996, p. 118; 2002, p. 75).

Action intelligibility is different from rationality. At any point in time, in fact, several things make sense to people (there are several things that seem rational). However, while people could do a number of things, they invariably 'carry out those [things] that are signified to them as the ones to perform' (Schatzki 1996, p.188). Rationality, in this sense, does not make people act or act one way or another.

Action intelligibility is also different from rule-like social normativity as intended in the traditional functionalist way. What makes sense for people to do is not the same as what is specified by a set of explicit rules or beliefs or even what the actors knows to be the appropriate or right thing to do (smokers being a good example). While action intelligibility is subject to constraints, these do not descend from the mysterious 'force' that norms and rules exercise, or from decisions that people take before action. This is because most of our conducts are unreflective reactions—they are not governed by conscious thoughts. This, however, does not imply that such conducts are either mindless or meaningless. Reactions (and actions) are indeed mindful and follow from what is signified by the existing conditions of life so that what a person does is structured by understanding and attunement. Understanding provides the logical component of the structuring of action while attunement articulates what matters and what people care about, and thus constitutes the 'locus of the affective component' of human conduct (Schatzki 1996, p. 122). Minding is heavily involved, but what counts as mind is different from traditional accounts that equate this to something that happens mainly between the ears.

As we will see below, practice is central to understanding human conduct because practices constitute horizons of intelligibility, and allow us to respond to different matters in different ways. In so doing, practices constitute conditions of life and worlds—and they do so 'inexorably' (Schatzki 1996, p. 115).

It is worth noting that the role of intelligibility is a watershed among the theories of practice examined in this book. According to Rouse (2006), for example, the importance accorded to active understanding at the point of action differentiates the group of authors discussed in this chapter from the likes of Bourdieu (who believes that people respond more or less blindly to the objective conditions carried by the habitus in the form of dispositions), Giddens (who gives space to rules and resources) and more traditional, non-practice-based views of culture and society.[3] The centrality of intelligibility is finally also responsible for what Schatzki calls his residual 'agential humanism'; that is, the idea to be discussed later in the chapter that practices are carried out by humans (although within a constellation of objects). First, however, we need to understand what practices are, and how they constitute the social world we inhabit.

7.2 **Practices and their organization**

Schatzki defines practices as 'open-ended spatial-temporal manifolds of actions' (Schatzki 2005, p. 471).[4] Examples of practices include marking essays, cooking, and trading online. The qualifier 'open' suggests that actions perpetuate and continually extend practices temporally, and that practices inevitably entail irregularities and unexpected elements. Hence, practices cannot be reduced to regularity and routine alone.

At the most basic level, practices are sets of doings and sayings. Schatzki is adamant that we should not grant priority to either one or the other when analysing practices.[5] According to most practice theorists,[6] in fact, the emphasis on bodily actions is one of the critical differences between practice theory and other traditions such as post-structuralism and hermeneutics which tend to privilege language over other types of activities.[7] From a practice perspective, moreover, language cannot always fully and exhaustively capture the understanding that underlies practice, and yet the two are inseparable. Practice is thus always linguistically under-determined yet language actively enters practice and makes it possible to transform what we do.

Similarly to cultural historical activity theory discussed in Chapter 5, doings and sayings are hierarchically organized, and are composed of increasingly complex wholes which Schatzki calls, respectively, tasks and projects. Sets of sayings and bodily doings make up a task, such as opening the fridge, turning on the water, or asking for help. Opening the fridge can, in turn, be part of the task of 'cooking a meal' or 'entertaining guests'. The same or similar sayings and doings can thus be mobilized within different tasks. In so doing, they come to mean different things. As several tasks in turn are usually involved in the accomplishment of a project (such as cooking a meal), the same term (e.g. writing) can therefore designate either a task (as in writing comments while marking) or a project (as in writing an article). In the first case, however, the practice is marking an essay, while the other is publishing an article which requires many more projects than just writing text.

Doings, sayings, tasks, and projects hang together according to a characteristic and meaningful organization. In so doing, they constitute integral and meaningful 'blocks', described here as practices. Accordingly, the term practice denotes a specific identifiable phenomenon and conceptual (and empirical) unit of analysis, not a generic field of human activity.[8]

The actions that comprise a practice (e.g. what goes into organizing a dinner party) are linked to each other through four main mechanisms: *practical understanding, rules, teleo-affective structure,* and *general understanding.*

In the accomplishment of a practice, actions are first linked together through *practical understanding*. Practical understanding refers to the knowing that derives from being a competent member of a practice. The concept derives from Wittgenstein's view that knowing manifests itself as being able to proceed unhampered in an activity. To say that two sets of doings and sayings are linked by the same practical understanding means that they express the same understanding of what is going on, so that the action of one person would be intelligible to another (as long as they are both competent in that practice). The actions of two people can also be considered as linked by practical understanding if the respective judgment of what is required to carry out that specific action is mutually intelligible. Put crudely, actions within a practice are linked by a practical understanding when most participants agree on what it makes sense to do—or at least participants tacitly understand that there is one particular way to go about it (which means that they can disagree, yet they still understand each other and what is going on). Because practical understanding only 'executes the actions that practical intelligibility singles out' (Schatzki 2002, p. 79), practice is never decided ahead of time, and action is never directly governed by habitus, norms, or systems of belief. Practising is a form of emergent coping guided by intelligibility. Intelligibility thus explains how particular, situated, and 'free' action is possible. In so doing, it carves a specific role for human actors as active carriers of practices. It is in this sense that Schatzki can claim that his version of practice is superior to that of Bourdieu and Giddens, whose notion of practice Schatzki accuses of being either over intellectualized (people need to decide at the point of action) or over-determined (people are causally governed by some structural principle).

Explicit *rules*, precepts, and instructions are a second way in which actions are kept together within a practice. Rules are programmes of action that specify what to do. In this sense they construct chains of actions and connect tasks and projects in complex arrangements. Although rules have to be interpreted against the background of the ongoing practice, there is nothing mysterious in their working. Rules connect actions because people take them into account when carrying out doings and sayings. In other words, they are elements of consideration when deciding what it makes sense to do; for example, when considering material consequences. They have the explicit purpose of orientating and determining the future course of activity, and it is for this purpose that they are introduced into social life by those with power or authority.

Thirdly, linking activities into a recognizable practice is its *teleo-affective structure*. The term refers to the fact that all practices unfold according to a specific direction and 'oughtness', or 'how they should be carried out'. Here Schatzki builds directly on the work of Heidegger, who saw purposiveness as one of the most basic conditions of being human. According to the author, life unfolds in term of endeavours of which we are only occasionally fully aware: we talk, we cook, we write, we go to work, and only realize what we are doing when something interrupts our train of thought. All practices thus entail 'a set of ends that participants should or may pursue' (Schatzki 2002, p. 80), and a complex combination of tasks and projects that are necessary to pursue those ends. Coordinated with this internalized set of 'where next' and 'how to get there' questions are a set of emotions and moods[9] that connote ends and project affectively (we feel happy when we win). This internal structure and affective colouring of a practice is learned by novices through instruction and corrections when they are socialized into a practice and taught how to see and make sense of things. It is then reinforced by repetition, sanctions, and peer pressure. It is in this way that it acquires a strong normative flavour that gives the impression that the structure of practice is what guides action. This is not the case, however, as activity is always governed by practical intelligibility—the teleo-affective structure only contributes by shaping what it makes sense to do.

It is important to note that the teleo-affective structure is a property of a practice that is expressed in the doings and sayings that comprise it.[10] It is not the property of the actors. The teleo-affective structure is upheld in a distributed manner by all participants; it is learnt and perpetuated through the socialization of novices. Novices embrace this structure when they learn a practice—in effect attuning to something that is already there to be understood and apprehended. The structure is also different from the explicit individual goals that people may seek to realize. In fact, the teleo-affective structure is subject to controversy because determining which ends, projects, and emotions are obligatory or mandatory is open-ended (Schatzki 2002, p. 83). Discussion, contestation, and a certain level of conflict are thus all compatible with practice. It is through such disputes that practices continually evolve in response to changes of circumstance. Conflict can continue until there is at least a basic agreement about what is acceptable or not in a practice. When such basic agreement falters, practices cease to exist, or the camps split, and the practice is divided into two or more distinct practices. Notably, all these processes need not to be mediated by discursivity. The teleo-affective dimension of practice may manifest itself in fact (and being treated), as a matter of fact, or as a matter of taste or feeling (we 'feel' that something is wrong).

Finally, the activities of a practice hang together through a set of *general understandings*. These are reflexive understandings of the overall project in which people are involved, and which contribute to practical intelligibility and hence action—as when a person on a walk remarks 'there is no need to rush as we are here to have fun' to his faster co-walkers. The general understanding of the project gives the practice its identity, both discursively and practically (and, in fact, faster walkers may slow down without the slower walker needing to speak aloud his/her comment).

In later writings, Schatzki added an interesting time-related dimension to this characterization of practice. In short, his suggestion is that practical understanding, rules, teleo-affective structure, and general understandings are perpetuated both by their repeated performance but also through what he calls collective or social memory (Schatzki 2006, p. 167). Social memories are unevenly distributed among participants, and they are inscribed in language, identity, and artefacts.[11] This state of affairs has far-reaching implications especially for those studying these phenomena empirically. To understand social life as it happens, it is not enough to grasp its real-time happening. One also has to grasp what is not happening. This means, firstly, that understanding a practice (or an organization) as it happens requires a considerable grasp of its past. Secondly, this means that to understand what is happening here and now requires understanding to some extent what else could have happened. According to the Heideggerian tradition, in fact, any action is a coming together of a projection towards a future, a 'coming from' some past, and 'coping with the present circumstances'. All these dimensions are always present in real-time actions, and this is what gives human conduct (and life) its inherent teleological character (death makes this teleological dimension tragically evident and present by prospecting the end of it). Accordingly, to understand the accomplishment of a practice one has to take notice not only of its 'sequence' (as in the ethno-methodological tradition) but also of the landscape of the ends, purposes, and motivations that made one happen while others remained mere possibilities. In Schatzki's words: 'Fully understanding the real time in which an organization occurs requires grasping this nexus of pasts and futures' (Schatzki 2006, p. 172).

In summary, practices are open-ended, temporally unfolding nexuses of actions linked by practical understanding, rules, teleo-affective structure, and general understandings. The organization of a practice defines its distinctiveness and its boundaries: an action or task belongs to a practice to the extent that it expresses an aspect of its organization. In this sense, practices can easily overlap and the same doing can be part of two practices (as in the above example of writing). Practices, moreover, are by definition social phenomena, first because they keep participants together, and second because their organization and accomplishment depend on the working together of many people. It is in this sense that authors operating within this tradition insist that practices are not just what people do, and that adopting a practice approach is distinctly different from simply providing more accurate, or more detailed or 'thicker' descriptions of people's conduct.

7.3 **Practices and materials**

I have noted above that the centrality of the human body and of bodily skills is a characterizing feature of practice theories stemming from the Heideggerian and Wittgensteinian traditions. The body is, in fact, the locus of agency and affective response, and also the target of power and normalization. By mobilizing its capacity to act intimately with the world, the body supports a view of intentional action that does not require the mediation of language, representations, or decisions (Rouse 2006, p. 513). This is critical, especially for understanding social interaction, as people can respond or attune to the expressive conduct of others without the need to 'infer their intentions or articulate their meanings' (ibid.).[12] As we have seen, this in turns makes practices inherently 'heterogeneous' in that they include both doings and sayings intertwined in complex ways. Practice theorists, however, also recognize that other material aspects enter the accomplishment of practices. Cooking, teaching, and hiking are always accomplished with, and amid, things. How objects and materiality participate in practices constitute, however, another major line of distinction between the practice theorists discussed in this chapter. While most of them would agree that the material world does not have an independent existence, and only becomes apparent insofar as it becomes an object of interpretation within meaning structures established by a specific practice, their views of how much work materials do, and how they do it, differ substantially.

At one extreme of the debate is the work of Bruno Latour. Although Latour is a reluctant practice theorist (he would not agree that practices are the basic unit of analysis of the social),[13] he is adamant that artefacts and things fully participate in social practices just as human beings do.[14] Social networks or practices consist both of inter-subjective relationships among human beings and heterogeneous interactions between human and non-human actors. To make clear what this means, Latour invites us to compare the sociality among humans with that of other primates. He notes that the fundamental difference is that for baboons, 'the social is always woven with the social: hence it lacks of durability' (Latour 1996, p. 234). In contrast, the stability of human social orders beyond particular contexts of action can only be explained when one allows for the active role played by objects—symbols alone do not resolve this puzzle. As the author writes: 'by dislocating interaction so as to associate ourselves with non-humans, we can endure beyond the present, in a matter other than our body, and we can interact at a distance...' (Latour 1996, p. 239). What makes human sociality distinctive, then, is that practices are not merely constellations of inter-subjectivity, they are also constellations of 'inter-objectivity'. In other words, things that are necessary and active elements of human practice must be given equal citizenship in our analysis and explanation of the social (without deciding a priori who is doing which part of the work).

At the other end of the extreme are 'agential humanists' such as Schatzki. In open disagreement with actor network theory, Schatzki affirms that only humans carry out practices. While he concedes that artefacts do have agential power, he suggests that we need to keep human actions and material performatance distinct at least for analytical purposes. Although human activity implicates a world amid which it proceeds, and albeit materials do exert a direct impact on human action (when something breaks or when a new tool is introduced), the two are set apart by the notion of intelligibility, and the fact that only human actions can attribute intentionality and affectivity. This is not to say that Schatzki endorses the idea that sociality is mainly derived from the interaction of humans alone. In fact, as I will clarify later, his view is that human co-existence and organized phenomena emerge from a mesh of people, things, and other entities (that he calls 'orders'). However, activities and objects are not equal: human practices are, in fact, carried out within a social order that they contribute to, so creating a perpetuate (more about this later) and, in the end, human action bears more responsibility for social existence than the context in which takes place (Schatzki 2002, pp. 105–122).

Several others authors have developed arguments that are positioned somewhere between these two extremes (authors who do not take into consideration the active role of bodies and materiality are not considered here as they cannot be considered practice theorists).

Pickering (1993) suggests that the agency of both humans and materials is not pre-given—it is not something that is inherent to objects or beings. Rather, both human and material agency emerges from the events they both contribute to determining. While human and non-human elements *are different*, in that intentional agency can be attributed to the former but not to the latter; such intentional agency does not emerge in a vacuum but within the temporally-emergent structure of real-time practices. The author here quotes a fragment of Deleuze and Parnet's *Dialogues* that is extremely enlightening:

> Desire only exists when assembled or machined. You cannot grasp or conceive a desire outside a determinate assemblage, on a plane which is not pre-existent but which must itself be constructed . . . In retrospect every assemblage expresses and creates a desire by constructing the plane which makes it possible and, by making it possible, brings it about . . . [desire] is constructivist, not at all spontaneist (Deleuze and Parnet, quoted in Pickering 1993, p. 559).

Pickering suggests that what holds for desire in Deleuze and Parnet's quotation can be extended to agency as well. Agency is the result of the mutual dialectic of resistance and accommodation between the performativity of materials and human intentionality. In this sense, material and human agencies are mutually and emergently productive of one another as they emerge together. Actions, intentions, and ends are thus unstable, open, and emergent, just as the way in which the material will respond to such actions, intentions, and ends. The two are continuously reconfigured as they are 'mangled' together while the practice proceeds, and none of them can be said to prevail in determining the future.[15]

Barad (2007) addressed the same issue in terms of intra-action and entanglement. The author uses the neologism 'intra-action' to emphasize that most of the time, the components of a phenomenon are originally and agentially inseparable, and we can operate an agential cut (that is to say, we can attribute causality to one bit or another) only within a specified material discursive practice. Barad's argument goes as follows: imagine that a new lamp that emits special UV light and which reveals the presence of infectious bacteria is purchased by a university lab. The lamp can be turned towards the surfaces of the lab to check whether there are risks of infections, or the light emitted by the lamp can be examined to understand its effect on the bacteria, how the light works, and to discover a cheaper way to produce the same effect. The first case essentially describes the process of inspecting surfaces with a UV lamp. In this case, the light is part of a diagnostic apparatus. In the latter case, the light itself is being measured and hence it is part of the object in question. Nothing about the interaction between the light and the bacteria alone fixes what property is defined by their intra-action, or where a cut occurs between the analysing and analysed components of the phenomenon. The 'agential cut' that establishes the different components of the original entangled phenomenon is part of a specific material and discursive practice (cleaning in the first case, engineering in the second). Such a cut is performed as part of a specific agential apparatus (to examine the light itself, you need an arrangement of concepts and instruments that is very different from those used in the other case). It is such a cut that establishes distinctions and defines what matters. The 'phenomenon', its components, what they mean, and why they matter are all the result of a specific way of configuring the world and resolving the original entanglement within a specific discursive *and* material practice. In other words, the phenomenon and its features are contextually made to be relevant, where 'made' is understood in a material, not metaphorical way.

What all these positions have in common is the notion that practices are inherently heterogeneous and sociomaterial.[16] When we examine the world in terms of a (multiplicity of) practice, we cannot avoid taking into consideration the central role of artefacts and the entanglement between human and non-human performativity. More than this, the practice approach warns us that the nature and identity of objects cannot be apprehended independently of the practice in which they are involved—just as we cannot make sense of our practices without taking into account the materials that enter it. Objects, materials, and technology need thus to be studied 'in practice' and with reference to the practices in which they are involved.

7.4 How practices constitute action, sociality, the world, and themselves

To summarize, the Heideggerian/Wittgensteinian tradition directs us to conceive human affairs in terms of open-ended organized temporal manifolds of actions that take place amid, and thanks to, the active contribution of a variety of materials. Practices are social (they help people combine as a group), are set in motion by processes of intelligibility, and are given some coherence and identity by their inherent teleological nature.

Many of these elements, however, are not exclusive characteristics of this genus of practice theory, and they have been used by a variety of non-functionalist or post-functionalist approaches in the study of human affairs.[17] What is distinctive to practice theory is the claim that practices are necessarily where the analysis must start (and end). Practices are thus the basic unit of any analysis of social science and the necessary keystone of any account of social phenomena, including work organizations. This is for the following reasons:

Practices institute the spaces of intelligibility in whose terms they themselves proceed

Heideggerian and Wittgensteinian[18] accounts of the human condition suggest that intelligibility, i.e. interpreting something as such and such, is only possible against the background of a prior understanding of the situation. We often refer (rather clumsily) to this in terms of context.[19] A typical example would be Bateson's intuition that defining a situation as a fight or as a game constitutes completely different sets of actions and reactions, and also mental states and identities. This, however, requires that we first understand the difference between what constitutes a fight and a game. Both Heidegger and Wittgenstein argue that this background understanding is provided as a matter of fact by the practices in which we are involved. In Heidegger's famous example of hammering, we can understand a hammer (both as a tool or something we can talk about) only against the background of a set of practices. These provide: first, the general understanding of the context of carpentry (the idea of building with timber; what a hammer can be used for; the relation between hammer, nail, and boards, and between boards, etc.); second, they give a sense of how to proceed (you hold the hammer by the handle and hit the nail with the head); and third, a general sense of what would bring hammering to a completion (when we can say that a nail is hammered down and when we can considered it done properly—if it's bent, it ain't!) Practices, usually more than one at a time, thus constitute fields of action intelligibility that, in turn, inform participants about what makes sense for them to do next. They do so simply, but inexorably, by making things appear just so. Practices thus create the intelligibility spaces within which they proceed. Actions presuppose practices and only become 'actions' as a moment of a practice.

Heidegger referred to such spaces of intelligibility as clearings (as in the clearing of a forest, or the spotlight via which things are suddenly illuminated and which allows us to perceive them). Foucault had probably something very similar in mind when he developed his notion of discursive space and discursive positions. Schatzki prefers to call these openings 'sites' to indicate that human action and other phenomena take form within, and transpire through, these horizons of possibilities.[20] All these formulations emphasize the central concept that horizons of intelligibility are inherently collective and historically determined: they are social and not individual phenomena. At the same time, these horizons are local and situated: they are constituted by practices within specific material and power conditions, and as such they are subject to change.

Finally, these horizons do not have causal powers as in the old structuralist tradition where culture, or collective representations, or ideology, were taken causally as the motors of conduct and the direct trigger of emotions. Practices only provide the site, and the 'work' of living still needs to be done. In Schatzki's words: 'practices such as those of politics, cooking, gardening, and educations [are] collective, social arenas of action that are pervaded by a space of meaning in whose terms people live, interact, and coexist intelligibly' (Schatzki 2005, p. 470).

Practices (together with materials) constitute social phenomena and 'house' them.

According to Schatzki and most other authors belonging to what I have called here (with some liberty) the Heideggerian/Wittgensteinian tradition, practices also constitute social phenomena and house them. Sociality (and organization) therefore take place amid and transpire through a nexus of interconnected practices and material arrangements.

Firstly, as I have indicated above, practices are collective phenomena and they make participants co-exist and come together within specific projects and horizons of intelligibility. Interaction is thus an effect of practices. As I suggested, harmony and sharing are not prerequisites for this to take place, and political controversy or even open conflict are forms of practice through which people are interconnected and some sort of relationship established.

Secondly, practices are largely responsible for the establishment of social orders, the arrangement of people, artefacts, organisms, and things in which we conduct our lives, and which make our life possible (think of the social orders of 'office' or 'factory').[21] According to Schatzki,[22] in any social arrangement such as a factory, hospital ward, or disco, humans co-exist and their actions are coordinated through three main social mechanisms—chains of actions (one action follows the other, as in the case when an action from a doctor leads to another by a nurse); commonalities in, and orchestration of, the ends, projects, and emotions (when people react together to the same thing without a need to agree); and prefiguration actions (through the establishment of how future things are channelled, in terms of constraints and possibilities). Human lives and conducts are also linked in a fourth way—through the material arrangements where they take place. Spaces, the position and layout of artefacts and objects, and also some of the properties of such materials (i.e. the capacity of phones to carry voices) are a further way in which lives of people hang together and co-existence takes place. In this sense, as I explained above, human co-existence is the effect of the joint work of human practices and the performativity of materials, and the existence of phenomena such as an office or a hospital ward would entail the presence (and tangle) of all these types of relations. What is critical for our discussion, however, is that all these relations are largely established in practice:

- Chains of actions descend very much from the fact that actions presuppose practice, as explained above.
- Commonality, orchestration, and prefiguration descend from the teleo-affective structure of the practices, and the rules and general understandings associated with them. The same also applies for the non-human elements.
- Material arrangements (artefacts, objects, symbols, and how they relate to each other and are positioned) are themselves organized according to the unfolding of the practice and its teleo-affective structure.

People doing things together and social order (Schatzki's socio-material arrangements) are thus the outcome and effect of order-establishing nexuses of practices. Offices, hospital wards, and organizations, but also conferences, parties, concerts, weddings, and funerals, are thus the result of the coming together of practices and material arrangements. They are sites where practices are conducted and intertwined, each of them organized by their structure—telos, and understanding etc.—and where these practices are made possible (to be a hospital nurse you need a functioning hospital). Because our life is largely conducted in such sites (also including classes, gyms, bars, and households) we can state that practice and orders make up the site of human co-existence: 'Human lives hang together through a mesh of interlocked practices and orders, as a constitutive part of which this hanging together occurs' (Schatzki 2002, p. 70). At the same time, because human practices are carried out amid, and transpire through, socio-material orders, we can argue that social orders are at the same time also the site or 'house' of practices. The relationship is, broadly speaking, one of recursion and mutual emergence: practices establish the orders through which they transpire and proceed, perpetuate, and change.[23] In any case, if you want to make sense of social order on a grand scale ('society') or more locally ('organization') the place to start is necessarily the ongoing practices and the material arrangements that compose them.

The world is a vast nexus of practices

The mechanisms which keep actions together within a practice or a specific form of social order also sustain relationships between practices. For example, the same tasks and project may enter more than one practice and the outcome of one practice may become the input for another. Chains of actions thus quickly become chains of practices. The practice of setting up and conducting a review meeting is part of a wider set of practices that, when joined together, make an office or a company. Similar considerations apply to prefiguration and spaces. Not only actions but also practices are joined through prefiguration, co-location, and positioning. Practices can be conducted in remote and dispersed places and times, and still compose arrangements. Finally, material arrangements and technologies also link practices both temporally and causally. The book you are reading establishes a relationship between me (the author), the publisher, the printer, the distributer, and you. As a 'reader', you are the result not only of your own reading practices, but also of the practices along the chain just described. The same applies to me as an author, the publisher, etc. We all depend on other's people practices.

The result is an immense, evolving, and irregular mesh of practices and orders. These 'bundles, nets, confederations, regions and dispersed and scattered practices are linked together as one gigantic, intricate, and evolving mesh of practices and orders. At its fullest, this web is co-extensive with sociohistorical space and time' (Schatzki 2002, p. 155). Within this mesh, practices do not live in harmony and instead they 'overlap, interweave, cohere, conflict, diverge, scatter and enable as well constrain each other' (ibid., p. 156). It is amid, and through, such a pulsating extended nexus of practices that modern life transpires and is made possible. It is for this reason that, for Schatzki and others, social theory should take a serious interest in practices.

7.5 **Some further theoretical implications**

To summarize from previous sections, according to Schatzki, who I take as representative of the Heideggerian and Wittgensteinian ways of understanding practices, sociality is established through practices and takes place within an immense array of interconnected practice-order bundles. Human lives hang together through a combination of 'intentional relations, chains of action, the interpersonal structuring of mentality and intelligibility, as well as through layouts of, events occurring in, and connections among the components of material settings' which are all effects of practices (Schatzki 2002, p. 149). For this reason, we are justified in giving primacy to practices as the basic building blocks of social theory, both theoretically and empirically.

At this point it should be clear why, at the outset, I claimed that Schatzki's project was 'far reaching'. In effect, what we are offered here is an extensive and detailed *micro foundationalist ontology* that amounts to a practice-based reconstruction of the social. As I have discussed above, this has relevant theoretical implications for a variety of issues—from how we conceive action, sociality, and order, to the relationship between doings and sayings, and between activity objects. However, this particular social ontology also has some considerable implication for the issues of normativity, meaning/identity, and agency. Let us examine briefly how these issues are reframed from a practice perspective.

As concerns normativity, many of the authors who uphold variants of the positions discussed in the present chapter argue that by rooting rules and norms in publicly accessible activity (instead of, for example, explicit rules or inner beliefs), we can readily explain their authority and force without incurring some well-known problems,[24] or presenting a weaker version of normativity. On the contrary, they argue, practice-based views of rules and norms are stronger, not weaker, than their alternatives. Rouse (2001, 2006) notes that practice theory has two advantages over competing explanations of normativity. First, and most well-known, practice-based approaches can solve the infinite regress identified by Wittgenstein (1953). The argument goes as follows. Because all rules (or instructions) need to be interpreted in order to be followed, to follow a rule (or an instruction) we need another rule (or instruction) that guides our interpretation, and so on. According to Wittgenstein (and Heidegger), in the real world we never encounter such a situation because when we run out of justifications, we say something like 'this is simply what I do' (Wittgenstein 1953, p. 217). Practice is thus the bedrock not only of meaning, but also of normativity, as rules are literally grounded in practices.

Secondly, practice theories help make such a position stronger thus preventing possible criticisms.[25] This is because contemporary Wittgensteinian practice theorists would slightly reformulate the above answer as follows: 'things are so and so because this is what *we* do'. In other words, according to Rouse (1999, 2001, 2006), practices are a source of normativity because they are social and always constituted in terms of mutual accountability. The performance of an action 'belongs to a practice only if it is appropriate to hold it accountable as a correct or incorrect performance of that practice' (Rouse 2006, p. 530). Practices are thus normative 'real life mechanisms' that operate in the real world and select appropriate conducts (and acceptable attributions of intelligibility) through mutual accountability. They are not just descriptive devices that capture the shared dispositions that supposedly make us all act in the same way (as, for example, in the ideas of paradigm, *Weltanshauung*, habit, and certain views of culture). Such active selection is sedimented as action intelligibility through socialization and sanctioning in the ways discussed above. As a result, what is intelligible, and what is right and wrong are apprehended together as something that makes it present to us in the performance of a practice. It is according to this sense that I said above that practices create worlds inexorably.

The fact that rules are usually about things that matter to people gives them further authority and weight. In the performance of practices, resolving conflict regarding what is appropriate and what is not makes a significant difference to peoples' lives. If you make a mistake in following the modern practice of being employed by failing to show up without providing a justification, you are likely to lose your livelihood. Thus, employment practices not only describe the recurrent pattern of activity of 'going to work', they also establish the right and wrong way to carry out such an activity, and they do so in a consequential, that is, 'real' way.

The authority of norms as constituted in practice, and through practice, is not affected by the fact that rules (just like practices) are contestable and often contested. Contestation does not affect the validity of rules, and when the conflict is resolved, this is perceived as a turning point in how things ought to be done. Because the normativity is implicit in what we do, we move from one regime of mutual accountability to another with no gaps or normative vacuums. In Rouse's terms, 'normativity is an interactive orientation towards the future encompassing present circumstances within its past' (Rouse 2006, p. 533). Practices carry and sustain normativity, and practice-based ontologies derived from the Heideggerian and Wittgensteinian traditions resolutely oppose the idea of relativism (meaning all is in the eye of the beholder, and 'anything goes'), just as they discount any form of crude realism. While meaning is practically established through empirically observable processes as part of practising, meaning attribution at an individual level (making sense of things here and now) is cogent and 'inexorable'. It can be contested, but only by proposing an equally strong alternative form of 'inexorability'.

Social ontologies based on the notion of practice discussed here also have a significant bearing on the notion of meaning and identity. Meaning (what something is) and identity (who someone is) necessarily emerge from practices, and through practices. As concerns the former, this descends from the fact that to mean something simply amounts to being intelligible as something. As we have seen above, what something means depends very much on the practice at hand and the intelligibility space constituted by it. A hammer can thus be understood as a tool, but also as a prize, or a symbol of people power.

Identity follows the same fate. Identity, understood as being intelligible as someone, is very much linked to the position(s) we occupy within the flow of activities we are involved in. You are an umpire within the practice of an organized game of baseball. If baseball is forgotten, outlawed, and not practised any more, there is no more umpiring to talk about. Umpiring thus comes before umpires, and the same holds for other phenomena such as gender and leadership. Put another way, from the perspective analysed here, both meaning and identity are relational (something is, or someone is, because of the relations they establish with other elements within the practice); they are multiple (the same thing may change meaning depending on the practice at hand, albeit some meanings may be more entrenched than others, and hence more durable); and they are provisional (meaning and identity can never be fixed, and they always subject to contestation and negotiation).

Finally, the views discussed here have profound effects on how we conceive of agency. I have partly addressed this issue above, so I will be brief. At the basic level, what unites all the scholars that I have loosely collected under the

Wittgensteinian and Heideggerian banner is the belief that a focus on practice helps resolve the traditional opposition between the views that either individuals or the system are ultimate sources of agency. This is achieved by accepting that both aspects are at work all the time, and that human action and interaction is where the two meet and can be altered.[26] Most of these scholars also agree that practice theory offers a promising way to reintroduce localized action and discretion into the picture (through intelligibility) without the need to resort to the traditional device of the well-formed individual who makes decisions. Practice theory is, in this sense, neither individualist nor anti-individualist, but rather post-individualist. This is achieved through the idea that practice carries the possibility for action and opens spaces for people to occupy such spaces and take action (or not). In this sense, practice and practitioners emerge together; we cannot grant ontological primacy to each of them. If in doubt, we should grant *temporal* primacy to the practice and not the practitioner—this as a provisional corrective to the possible excesses of individualism. The position is also achieved through the notion that agency is always shared with other entities, and as such, is largely a networked process. While how and how much entities participate in agency varies, as discussed above, there is no doubt among late followers of the Heideggerian and Wittgensteinian tradition in practice theory that agency is an attribute of heterogeneous arrangements. Just as in cultural historical activity theory discussed in Chapter 5, agency (and agents) are thus an instantaneous apprehension of multiplicity that finds its unity in practice and through practice (for example discursive practices). Like actors on stage, we are never alone but part of a larger apparatus (Latour 2005, p. 46). Agency is, thus, necessarily the result of the swarming together[27] of an array of entities and other practices that are manifested through doers (both human and non-human). In empirical terms, this translates into an injunction (contra traditional approaches) to start the investigation into social phenomena not via roles and individuals and their actions (entrepreneur, leader, managers), but via the material and discursive practices that allow them to occupy such subject positions. More than this, this view of agency warns us that humans will likely try to receive all the merit, probably claiming that other entities do not do any of the relevant work.

7.6 Empirical and methodological consequences: a 'site' still under construction?

Schatzki claims that his practice ontology also has relevant implications for empirical research. Although the author is a first and foremost a philosopher, he explicitly addressed this issue following his crossing into organizational research (Schatzki 2005, 2006). Paradoxically, however, this is where his project shows some of its limitations, demonstrating that in some ways Schatzki's site theory is still under construction.

According to Schatzki, studying organizations (and supposedly other social phenomena) implies three central tasks: identify the action that composes it; identify the practice-arrangement bundles of which these actions are part (using the local names as a starting point); and identify other nets of practices to which the practice-arrangements are tied. The suggestion is that to grasp the ties among nets, one has to focus especially on the 'commonalities and orchestrations in their actions, teleological orders, and rules; chains of action, including harmonious, competitive, and conflictual interactions; material connections among nets; and the desires, beliefs, and other attitudes that participants in one net have toward the other nets' (Schatzki 2005, p. 476). Most of this can only be achieved through participant observation, that is watching participants' activities, interacting with them (e.g. asking questions), and—at least ideally—attempting to learn (ibid.). Schatzki adds that investigators do not need to track and register the 'potentially labyrinthine complexity of bundles, nets of bundles, and so on', and that all that is needed is an overview of 'social phenomena and their workings that are couched in terms referring, not to the details of practice-arrangement bundles, but to entire formations and their relations' (ibid., p. 477).

The problem is that while Schatzki's methodological intimations are powerful tools to sensitize empirical observation and theorization (in the sense of helping social scientists direct their attention towards certain aspects of the phenomena instead of others), they are, at the same time, so prescriptive and imprecise that they risk hampering, instead of facilitating, the work of empirical social researchers.

On the one hand, Schatzki's theoretical outline, no matter how sophisticated, is still what it says on the tin: an outline. In this sense, Schatzki's attempt to exhaust, through theory, all the permutations of practice—for example when he explains that all practices are linked together by four basic mechanisms—is problematic. This is because exploring how practices are linked together is an empirical, not a theoretical, question. For example, Schatzki does not provide any mechanism to account for how practices can be connected at a distance (one of the central topics of Latour's sociology of translation). This is, of course, a central issue if one is to study social phenomena in a highly interconnected and 'globalized' world. At the same time, the suggestion to use participant observation, while agreeable, is still vague, as it tells us very little about where to go, what to look for, etc. The limits of Schatzki's 'complete' architecture can be appreciated against the comparative strengths and pragmatic appeal of less prescriptive approaches such as actor network theory. Faced with the question of how to investigate and provide accounts for a heterogeneous world that is constantly made and remade, Latour pursued,[28] in fact, a different strategy that is almost opposite to Schatzki's. Latour's solution was to develop and refine an open-ended infra-language that sets the scene for a performative material way of doing social science *without* however defining *ex-ante* the characters who will do it. By using 'open' concepts such as translation, stabilization, and actor network (all trademark concepts of actor network theory), Latour offered a grammar and toolkit for reconstructing the social in terms of a stabilized network of relations, without committing to specific mechanisms. Unlike Schatzki, Latour left the task of filling the blanks to social scientists and their empirical intelligence—a move that goes some way to explain the success of the approach. At the same time, Latour offered a powerful methodological principle ('follow the actor') that again addresses one of the issues left unresolved by Schatzki and many of his colleagues: that of how to view the bundle of practice and go about describing it. In short, the work conducted within what I call the Heideggerian and Wittgensteinian traditions often betrays their philosophical origin and actually highlights the limit of trying to study social phenomena from the vantage point of university offices or writing retreats. In this sense, as I elaborate in the final chapter, I see Latour's approach and Schatzki's sensitivity working together in spite of their differences—at least until practice theory develops something even remotely as powerful as actor network theory which is intended as an empirical orientation rather than a static body of theories.

While, on the one hand, Schatzki's approach is too prescriptive, at the same time it is also empirically contentious and ambiguous. One case in point is the idea that practices are identifiable phenomenon and conceptually (and empirically) bounded units of analysis.[29] While speaking of 'units' and arguing that practices have 'frontiers' to highlight what practices can, and should, adopt as the object of inquiry, the use of such spatial language has some far-reaching implications when the approach is put to work in social research. The idea of a 'unit' raises, in fact, the questions of 'where does a practice end', and 'what are the boundaries' of a practice'—questions that practice theorists have been asked,[30] and will increasingly be asked, as the approach becomes more successful. The problem, of course, is that these are the wrong questions from a practice perspective, in that they re-introduce structuralist and functionalist preoccupations that practice theory had tried to eliminate. Although practices can be differentiated and named, they do not have 'boundaries' as such. Thinking of the social in terms of well-bounded units and their relations is part of a theoretical discourse that is alien and, in many ways, opposite to that of practice theory. Practice theory starts, in fact, with process, and takes the emergence and creation of (provisionally) identifiable units (individuals, groups, organizations) as the thing to be explained. Practices are regimes of activity and processes. As such, they can be used as building blocks for theorizing and as objects of analysis, but they are not bounded 'units'. In other words, the attempt to bind the operational unit of analysis by drawing up lists of inclusion and exclusion criteria takes us outside practice theory and more towards a traditional functionalist and positivist paradigm. It also orients research towards questions such as 'how do individuals bridge the frontier between practices'. This is an inappropriate question with regards to a community of practice, as I discussed in Chapter 4.

While notions such as 'unit of analysis', 'frontier', 'role', and 'collective memory' are contentious as they expose this radical and innovative theory of practice to a potential reductionist reading—especially when the intuitions currently developed mainly at philosophical level are used in practice by social science researchers—others are simply ambiguous. The notion of teleo-affective structure, for example, while constituting a powerful concept that accounts for how practitioners experience participating in an ongoing practice, is difficult to grasp and describe in practice. To the extent that such a structure is indefinitively complex 'due to the indefinite variety of circumstances' (Scatzki, 2002, p. 83), and subject to contention and contestation, it is also empirically elusive.[31] Arguing that such a structure is there is one thing, representing it as part of empirical research is another.

In summary, my view is that contemporary developments of the Heideggerian and Wittgensteinian traditions constitute a promising, yet still open, 'construction site'. Several of them, including Schatzki's monumental effort, beg for further development in order for their radical message to make a difference in the practice of researching and theorizing social phenomena. The question that I will take up in the final chapter is whether, instead of trying to develop these approaches, it is more appropriate to use them as part of 'toolkit logic' with some of other approaches described in this book. First, however, I need to address a final important issue—that of the relationship between practice and discourse.

Rolling case study: Telemonitoring as a practice-order bundle[32]

Telemonitoring at Garibaldi is a practice-order bundle. The (human) practice involved in the type of telemonitoring carried out at Garibaldi embraces a range of ends and activities, and takes place amid a characteristic material order from which it derives its 'tele-' name. In turn, telemonitoring takes place within a wider nexus of practices and orders that is the hospital at Garibaldi. Telemedicine, by the same token, also takes place within the wider confederation of practices and orders that comprise regional and national healthcare services.

Several overall ends are pursued in carrying out telemonitoring at Garibaldi. One end is to give patients a better and longer life by preventing crises and reducing the time they spend at the hospital. This is achieved by monitoring their health over time and detecting early signs of deterioration. Another end is to reduce the costs for the hospital of Garibaldi, as admissions are extremely resource-consuming. Furthermore, telemedicine is also a way for Garibaldi to confirm its status as an international centre of excellence for the treatment of chronic heart failure (CHF).

In the pursuit of these ends, doctors and nurses implement a variety of acceptable and connected projects. These include: enrolling patients in the service; teaching them how to use the device to send an EGC over the phone; prescribing tests that the patients have to do; scheduling and carrying out regular phone calls; prescribing specific courses of action (such as an urgent visit to an emergency room) to patients; reporting and discussing the evolution of a patient's state of health; collecting data on the service; and sharing their experience with others through scientific publications and communications.

Each of these projects is composed of a variety of tasks and actions. For example, 'scheduling and carrying out regular phone calls' includes agreeing a frequency of contacts with a cardiologist; knowing when is the best time to speak with a particular patient (taking into account, for example, that older patients like to go out in the morning, while younger working patients prefer lunchtime or evening calls); keeping a diary; updating a patient's file and therapy sheet. These tasks, in turn, are constituted by specific normativised doings and sayings. For example, making calls requires knowing how to read a phone number and how to dial (in a hospital, one needs to get an external line). It also requires following the conventions of 'making a good phone call', including: how to articulate greetings; how to ask questions in a manner comprehensible to patients; how to move a discussion to the next section, and how to formulate correct salutations. These sayings and doings are normativised in the sense that at each point in time there is a general agreement about what is acceptable or not acceptable in practice. The scope of this agreement is, of course, continuously under scrutiny. For example, at Garibaldi patients have to be treated with respect at all times. This can be tricky, as patients also do not want to be treated 'coldly'. So it is up to nurses to balance the use of formal and informal speech, and to sense when it is appropriate to be kind and friendly, and when more detached and professional. In this sense, the agreement of what is right is continually shifting. However, the fact that patients need to feel respected is never put under discussion, and people come to hold this view as a matter of fact when learning to 'do' telemedicine at Garibaldi.

In Garibaldi's hospital, the practice of telemonitoring remote patients unfolds as a sequence of regular telephone contacts and check-ups. The activities follow one another according to a visible organization that reflects the teleo-affective structure of the practice. Such structure manifests itself through instituting conditions of appropriateness for action; that is, articulating to practitioners what it makes sense to do next. If queried about why they proceeded in a certain manner, the practitioners would probably tell you that, 'this was the right thing to do for making the patient feeling respected and well cared for', or 'this is the right way to make a phone call'. The teleo-affective structure links the actions of the nurses, patients, doctors, and others by making things meaningful in a certain way. It also injects into the practice a sense of urgency and concern, so that practitioners experience carrying out the practice in terms of things that ought to be done and matters that need to be attended to in order for the job to be (well) done. It also colours the chain of actions with a particular emotional tone ('respect').

It is worth noting that the way in which projects and tasks are organized into a specific teleo-affective structure characterizes the telemedicine of Garibaldi vis-à-vis both other ways of taking care of CHF patients but also other ways of doing telemedicine. For example, doctors and nurses in traditional hospitals also use the telephone, and often respond to queries from patients and their families. Yet they cannot be said to be 'doing' telemonitoring. At the same time, even within the same region in northern Italy, other institutions carry out different ways of 'doing telemedicine'. Some, for example, did not have a pool of dedicated nurses who proactively 'followed' each patient, and used instead fully automated answering machines that the patients had to call to leave vital health parameters (software would then flag up anomalies to a clinical person who would call back the patient to check what was happening). Thus, the teleo-affective structure of the practice not only organizes the saying and doings, it also distinguishes one practice from another.

The practical understanding of all participants in the practice is reflected in the activities described above. This understanding consists both in knowing how to carry out actions and knowing how to recognize and respond to them. This is true for both practitioners and clinical staff. For example, during monitoring calls patients often do not wait for the nurses to ask about their vital parameters and instead offer the information at the 'right' time in the conversation. They also display competence in other ways; for example, by telling nurses that 'of course they had carried out the tests they knew were needed'. This is because all members have become part of the pattern of ordering called telemonitoring, and during the calls and other activities they tune into the horizons of intelligibility performed by the practice. On these occasions, they are not 'deciding' how to act, in the traditional sense of deliberating in their mind or brain. They simply follow what the practice of telemonitoring made sense for them to do, or what it told them they ought to do next.

Several rules enter the practice of telemonitoring. Some were established by those in authority when the practice was initially assembled, while others were imposed by the Garibaldi institution. Indeed, other rules derive from regulations imposed by central health authorities. For example, one local rule is that all important decisions regarding monitored patients have to be shared with a doctor, even if such a decision has been made by one of the specialist nurses. The idea is that, in view of possible liability claims, it should always be possible to demonstrate that 'at the end of the day' a doctor was in charge. For this reason, following certain calls, the nurse has to go and look for a cardiologist— usually a really hard task—or alternatively describe and record her decisions and actions as provisional until the next review meeting. Such a rule was never formally written down, yet it was carefully followed and enforced. It was often mentioned during meetings and explained to novices as a way to orientate and determine their course of activity. Other rules had different origins. Some emanated from scientific bodies, others from administrative authorities. Doctors and nurses followed established clinical protocols that prescribed how, and when, to use particular medicines. Other rules prescribed what kind of patients the service could take on (this was a regional service, so inclusion and exclusion rules applied).

Amid what arrangements of entities are the ends of telemonitoring pursued, its rules observed or ignored, and its projects and tasks, rapid doings, and intermittent sayings carried out?[33] Telemonitoring takes place amid, and through, an arrangement of spaces, materials, and artefacts. The nurses sit in a dedicated room and make frequent use of the phone, fax, and other material tools such as the diary and the folders where they keep patient records. The artefacts they use are intimately involved in the practice and, in fact, they exert a clear causal impact on activities. For example, the nurses often mention the importance of the therapy sheet (now substituted by a computer programme), which was a large A3 sheet to record information collected during different calls. The sheet allowed the comparative reading of the data recorded from a number of calls, allowing the evolution of the patient's condition to be followed. Because nurses needed to complete all the sections of the therapy sheet, they often followed the order of the headings in the sheet during their calls. In their words, *'the therapy sheet... guided our calls... especially when we were still inexperienced... it was certainly the first thing we showed our colleague'*. Because the computer software replicates the order of the questions in the therapy sheet, it continues to organize the sequence of the call (as in many other call centres).

The practice of telemonitoring is made possible by—and transpires through—a wider social order of people, relations, and entities. Such order has been patiently assembled by the founders of the service[34] who endeavoured for several months to set in place the necessary arrangement so that telemonitoring could happen. For example, telemonitoring requires the ongoing orchestration of the Garibaldi centre and a call centre with the equipment to receive data from the portable ECG, decode it, and relay it to nurses. The alignment was achieved by establishing agreed chains of action, and by connecting the two sites through a dedicated fax line which is continually maintained through personal contacts. The order that makes telemonitoring possible also requires alignment with the practices of the other part of the hospital at Garibaldi. For example, enrolling patients requires that nurses go and speak to patients before they leave the hospital. This, in turn, necessitates that nurses are informed when a patient is ready to return home. Finally, existing rules and identities also need to be aligned for telemonitoring to happen. For example, nurses had to learn how to become more proactive when engaging with patients than they were used to, and they had to be trained in how to administer powerful drugs. In effect, telemonitoring required a shift in professional identities so that nurses' perception of themselves fitted into the new arrangement.

In summary, the human practice of telemonitoring takes place within, and amid, this intricate fabric of practices, objects, meaning, and identities. Taken in its entirety, such a particular social and material order constitutes the 'site' of telemedicine. The complex mesh of people, things, identities, rules, etc., is at the same time the stage where telemonitoring is performed and the result of the practice itself.

The material, technological, and social mechanisms that kept the practice order together connected the practice of telemonitoring with other practice-order bundles. As we have seen, some of the practices of telemonitoring overlapped with those of other sites; for example, those carried out in the call centre and other parts of the hospital. The rules and protocols were shared with several other sites and linked the practices at Garibaldi to those, for example, at the central offices of regional health authorities. Indeed, the practice carried out in those offices could, and sometimes did, enable and constrain telemonitoring practice (as on the occasion when funding was provided or withheld). Both the practice and the material order within which it is performed are highly interconnected. For example, use of a phone and other electronic instruments establish links with the phone and utility companies. Special links were established with the providers (based abroad) of the portable ECG. The very space where telemonitoring takes place connects its order with other aspects of hospital life (the nurses were still formally employed by the same organization; the room was cleaned by the same company). In summary, the mesh of practice and order of telemonitoring was connected in multiple and complex ways to other practice-order bundles and nets of them. We can imagine that such practices and the orders they create constitute bundles, nets, and a vast confederation (think, for example, of the immense nexus of practice that is a regional healthcare authority with all its offices, hospitals, and emanations). Linked together, they form a gigantic, intricate, and evolving mesh of practice orders. At its fullest reach, this web is co-extensive with socio-historical space-time.[35]

▓ NOTES

1. The expression is borrowed from Foucault who in one of his lectures explicitly used it in reference to Heidegger. See Foucault 1979, p. 147.
2. In organization studies this position has been developed especially by authors such as Chia and Holt (2006) and Tsoukas (2009).
3. See Schatzki (1997) for an extensive discussion and criticism of Bourdieu and Giddens.
4. Other formulations of the definition of practice include 'temporary unfolding and spatially dispersed sets (or nexuses) of doings and sayings' (Schatzki 1996, p. 89) or 'open, temporally unfolding nexuses of action' (Schatzki 2002, p. 72). An analysis of the evolution of Schatzki's thought as transpiring from these different definitions goes beyond the scope of the present work.
5. He calls this a 'unity in difference' (Schatzki 1996, p. 47). The approach thus makes room for meaningful doings and speech acts that are performed by expressive bodies and do not require the intervention of verbal or written discourse. Shaking the head or winking, for example, are meaningful actions that do not have a discursive nature.
6. See for example Schatzki 1996; Schatzki et al. 2001; Rouse 2006.
7. Although several of these approaches also build on the work of Wittgenstein and Heidegger, they are strongly rejected as based on a fundamental misunderstanding: Schatzki, for example, calls Lyotard's linguistic-only interpretation of Wittgenstein's idea of language game 'radically wrong' (Schatzki 1996, p. 126).
8. Similarly to activity theory, these sets of sayings and doings are composed of increasingly complex wholes that Schatzki calls tasks and projects. Accordingly, the same sayings and doings can occur in different tasks, and several tasks often enter into the accomplishment of a project. The same term (e.g. writing) can designate either a task (as in writing comments

while marking) or a project (as in writing an article), although in the first case the practice is marking an essay, while the other is publishing an article.

9. A classic example would be the state of flow (Csikszentmihalyi 1997). Flow is the mental state of operation in which a person in an activity is fully immersed in a feeling of energized focus, full involvement, and success in the process of the activity.

10. In this sense it is not tacit.

11. '...memories are secured via complexes of actions, thoughts, and readinesses that are differentially distributed among participants in the practice: actions that pursue acceptable or enjoined orderings or that manifest general understandings; thoughts, discussions, and negotiations about which orderings are acceptable or enjoined or about what general understandings entail; all the sorts of acts of admonishment and sanction and readinesses thereto that contribute to the memory of rules; and feelings of satisfaction at certain events and distress at others' (Schatzki 2006, p. 1869).

12. This is, of course, where practice theory encounters the tradition of symbolic interactionism.

13. Latour uses the concept of practice in different passages of his works (see e.g. 2005) but does not develop his theory of the social within the recognizable framework of practice theory. Indeed, Schatzki (2002) excludes actor network theory from the count of practice theories, and Latour probably did not shed tears about this. Latour's debt to Heidegger and, less prominently, to Wittgenstein's work is however not in doubt (see Latour 2005). Hence his inclusion here.

14. See Reckwitz (2002) for an extensive discussion.

15. 'Accommodation' and 'mangling' are constant traits of practices. We do not know in advance what a new artefact will do, as we cannot predict what other people, or even we ourselves will do. Therefore, pursuing a (scientific) practice always entail an important dimension of tinkering and tuning that, according to Pickering, works both ways, on human and non-human agency: 'My basic image of science is a performative one, in which the performance—the doings—of human and material agency come to the fore. Scientists are human agents in a field of material agency which they struggle to capture in their machines. Further, human and material agencies are reciprocally and emergently intertwined in this struggle. Their contours emerge in the temporality of practice and are definitional and sustain one another. Existing culture constitutes the surface of emergence for the intentional structure of scientific practice, and such practice consists in the reciprocal tuning of human and material agency, tuning that can itself reconfigure human intentions' (Pickering 1995, p. 21).

16. The neologism sociomateriality without the dash was introduced in organization studies by Orlikowski (2010).

17. See, in particular, Schatzki (2002) Ch. 1 for an in-depth discussion.

18. Wittgenstein famously developed this view in reference to the question of how to follow a rule.

19. Schatzki (2002) goes to some length to demonstrate that there are a variety of ways to conceive the notion of context, and that most of the current conceptions are faulty. Many authors tend, in fact, to equate context to a sort of static background against which events happen (not unlike the set in a play). Alternatively, context is used as a residual category: what we cannot explain we call context. Schatzki suggests that practice theory uses a particularly strong understanding of context which he calls a 'contextured' site. A contexture is a particular type of context where entities of different types co-exist. Contextured sites are contextures where entities are intrinsically part of their own context (p. 64). In simple terms, practices are both the cause of themselves and their outcome—so that practices perpetuate themselves, albeit imperfectly, in a quasi-recursive movement.

20. See Schatzki (2002).

21. The term 'arrangement' is used here to signal that sociality requires a minimal level of lives hanging together, and does not require the level of integration, coherence, and regularity usually associated with the term 'order'.

22. Schatzki provided different versions of this argument. My illustration builds largely on Schatzki (2002, pp. 38–47) and Schatzki (2005).

23. We can see here the roots of Schatzki's residual humanism in the discussion of the relation between people and objects above. While, ontologically, the world is a recursive mesh of practice and material arrangements, analytically we must start from the practices and not from the arrangements. This means that activities and objects are not equal—activities are more equal than their material counterparts (they carry more responsibility).

24. The issue of following rules and the foundation of normativity are, of course, two of the most debated issues in the history of human sciences. On the debate on the sources of normativity, see e.g. Korsgaard (1996).

25. Turner (1994, 2001) has raised a number of serious criticisms to this solution, arguing that no description of practice can exhaust all the variants of its performance, and therefore the 'regularity' of conduct among people cannot be explained terms of rules. People have different ideas of how to dress for the beach and to decide whether they are part of the same habitus or practice is impossible.

26. As we have seen in Chapter 2 Ortner (1984) calls this a theoretical triangle. Views diverge with regards to how durable such structures are. As discussed in Chapter 3, Bourdieu believed that habitus is very much constituted by existing objective conditions, or 'the system', while authors such as Pickering would strongly disagree.

27. The expression is from Latour 2005, p. 46. Latour uses the image of the actor on stage 'who is never alone but part of a larger apparatus'.

28. See in particular Latour 2005.

29. Schatzki uses the expression emphatically in most of his writing. See Schatzki (1996) and especially Schatzki (2002): 'It is important to emphasize that the organization of a practice describes the practice's frontiers: A doing or saying belongs to a given practice if it expresses components of that practice's organization. This delimitation of boundaries entails that practices can overlap' (p. 87).

30. See for example Turner (1994).

31. See Schatzki 2002, p. 83.

32. Background information on the practice of telemedicine is provided in the Introduction.

33. I am using the same words to be found in Schatzki 2002, p. 166.

34. I told the story of the emergence of telemonitoring in Nicolini (2010).

35. The two sentences are taken from Schatzki 2002, p. 155.

8 Discourse and Practice

In the context of an investigation into theories of practice, there are several good reasons to reserve special attention for discourse. Firstly, interest in these two issues stems from similar, if not identical, historical conditions. As I noted in the opening chapter, according to Hiley 'philosophy's interpretive [i.e., *linguistic* A/N] turn is ... a practical turn, one that insists on the philosophical centrality of practice ... ' (Hiley *et al.* 1991, p. 11). Secondly, understanding the relation between discursive and non-discursive practices is a critical aspect of our discussion. As we have seen in previous chapters, different theories of practice grant very different roles to language and discourse. For example, while Bourdieu almost ignores the role of linguistic matters (see my criticisms in Chapter 3), Schatzki describes practices as nexuses of 'sayings and doings', warning that no priority should be granted to either of the terms (see Chapter 7). Thirdly, and most importantly, the study of discourse can offer some fundamental insights into the general understanding of practice. This is because, over the last five decades, a number of research programmes have developed the idea that discourse is, first and foremost, a form of action, a way of making things happen in the world, and not a mere way of representing it. From this perspective, language is seen as a discursive practice, a form of social and situated action.[1] It follows that many of the theoretical and methodological insights of research programmes such as speech act theory (Austin 1962), interactional sociolinguistics (Davies and Harre 1990), functional grammar (Halliday 1978), ethnography of communication (Gumperz and Hymes 1972), conversational analysis (Sacks *et al.* 1974), and critical discourse analysis (Fairclough 1992, 1995) are directly applicable, or at least highly relevant, to the understanding of social practice. Accordingly, in the next section I will briefly examine three of these approaches, trying to identify their specific contribution to practice theory. My aim is not to survey existing theories of discourse, or discuss them in depth as this task goes well beyond the scope of the present work. More modestly, my goal here is to examine the explicit or implicit views of practice upheld by some contemporary theories of discourse, and discuss how their assumptions translate into particular research questions and methodological orientations regarding the nature of social practice.

It should be added that even this more limited task is not straightforward. Within the subset of approaches that understand discourse as a form of action there are, in fact, significantly divergent points of view. This is because, according to Gee (2011), the term 'discourse' is used to refer to (at least) two different spheres of phenomena. One the one hand, discourse is taken to mean the mundane use of language in social interaction. The interest here is in exploring and analysing the actual use of language to accomplish some activity in a specific scene of action; for example, making a call, or greeting someone. At the same time, 'discourse' is also used to refer to a quite different types of phenomena, that is, the ways in which humans integrate linguistic and non-linguistic features to 'enact and recognize different identities...give the material world certain meanings, distribute social goods in a certain way, make certain sorts of meaningful connections in our experience, and privilege certain symbols systems and ways of knowing over others' (Gee 2011, p. 13). Gee refers to this second use of the term as 'Discourse with a capital D' (ibid.).[2]

The recent debate can thus be roughly represented as a continuum delimited by two divergent versions of discourse: one that sees discourse mainly, if not exclusively, as a local achievement, and the other which conceives discourse as a broad system for the formation and the articulation of ways of thinking, behaving, and, eventually, being. The former focuses on the study of the nature of (discursive) action and on the internal dynamics of the interaction. The latter is interested in exploring how social structures shape discourse and the relationships between discourse, knowledge, and power. Most importantly, their different ways of connoting 'discourse' underpin dissimilar sets of interests and units of analysis, with the result that different approaches maintain divergent views of what constitutes a discursive *practice*.

In the next sections I consider, in particular, three approaches that sit at very different points of this continuum. I will start by a short discussion of conversation analysis (CA). As we shall see, CA historically maintains that discursivity (and practice) are local accomplishments that need to be studied in terms of their moment-by-moment production. The focus is, therefore, on the actual production of conversational interactions and the discursive resources that go into it. CA thus stands at the small 'd' end of the continuum. I will then briefly introduce the Foucauldian tradition and critical discourse analysis (CDA), an approach that explicitly attempts to link discursive action with larger societal undercurrents. Although CDA maintains an interest in the local production of discourse, its main interest is to link the 'here and now' of discursive production to larger discursive formations that extend well beyond the current scene of action. As such, CDA and cognate approaches stand at the opposite end of the continuum, and they examine Discourse with a capital 'D'. Finally, at the end of the chapter, I will briefly examine mediated discourse analysis (MDA), an interesting attempt to synthesize these two positions and generate a comprehensive theory of discourse in action. As we shall see, MDA sits somewhere in the middle of the continuum and constitutes an effort to combine and reconcile the other two approaches.

8.1 **Conversation analysis: discourse as talk in interaction**

Conversation analysis (CA) is a research tradition aimed at deepening the understanding of the social organization of linguistic conduct ('talk-in-interaction') by investigating the sequential structure of naturally occurring conversation. Historically, CA grew out of ethno-methodology, and although over the years it progressively broke away to become a robust, separate, and self-standing research tradition, it retains many of the original basic assumptions of ethno-methodology. These include, for example, an emphasis on the accomplishment of social order by intelligible and artful actors, a focus on how people involved in talk-in-interaction handle, deal with, and use indexical expressions and, in general, an interest in the intricacies of (linguistic) practical action. To these basic tenets, CA adds a few specific ones which are relevant both for the understanding of discourse as practice and, more generally, for the understanding of practice itself. Having discussed ethno-methodology at some length in a previous chapter, here I will limit myself to a few brief remarks.

8.1.1 THE BASIC ASSUMPTIONS OF CA AND THEIR IMPLICATIONS FOR THE UNDERSTANDING OF PRACTICE

According to Heritage (1984) and Richards (2001), CA operates on the basis of three main assumptions:

(a) *All interaction, including linguistic interaction, is structurally organized.* In other words, talk and other forms of social interaction display organized and recurrent patterns.

(b) *Contributions to interaction are contextually and sequentially oriented.* CA believes that to understand the patterning of linguistic interaction, it is necessary to examine the local, situated, and sequential activities by which speakers give meaning to their talk. CA pays particular attention to the temporal organization and contingencies that arise in the unfolding development of action and interaction. Sequence is a central concern for many CA researchers, a fact that is usually captured by the colourful expression according to which talk is factually always 'closed to the left and open to the right'. According to Atkinson and Heritage (1984) 'speakers understand an utterance by reference to its turn-within-sequence character that provides a central resource for both the participants and the overhearing analyst to make sense of the talk' (p. 7). Hence, all conversational practices are both context-dependent and context-renewing. This means that talk-in-interaction—for speakers, audience, and social scientists—can only be understood in view of the sequence from which it emerges.

(c) *The two aspects above can (only) be identified by taking interaction-as-it-happens as the main object of inquiry.* In order to attend to the details of the interaction, and in order to prevent being caught in premature theorization, CA practitioners see their main task to be an examination of audio or video recording in order to highlight the recurrent devices used by members to 'do' interaction. Audio and video data, usually transcribed according to techniques that are a trademark of this particular approach, are used to investigate the orderliness of interaction, which is hence conceived of as the product of the systematic deployment of specifiable methods by members who use them to solve specifiable problems and challenges which emerge from the course of interactions.

These assumptions delineate a recognizable methodological approach, which Harvey Sacks summarized as follows:

The gross aim of the work I am doing is to see how finely the details of actual, naturally occurring conversation can be subjected to analysis that will yield the technology of conversation. The idea is to take singular sequences of conversation and tear them apart in such a way as to find rules, techniques, procedures, methods, maxims (a collection of terms that more or less relate to each other and that I use somewhat interchangeably) that can be used to generate the orderly features we find in the conversations we examine. The point is, then, to come back to the singular things we observe in a singular sequence, with some rules that handle those singular features, and also, necessarily, handle lots of other events (Sacks 1984, p. 411).

CA has thus the historical merit of having focused scholars' attention on the sequential organization of discursive (and non-discursive) practice, insisting that to understand it we need to analyse in detail its moment-by-moment production. Participants in a practice display an orientation to the previous unfolding of the practice, and it is on this basis that future contributions are generated. In so doing, CA contributes in two critical ways to the understanding of social practice. First, it contributes to disposing of the idea of context as the background or container of practice. CA analysis of talk-in-interaction demonstrates the sense in which any practice is both context-dependent and context-renewing. At the same time, CA introduces an analytical mentality into the study of practice (Llewellyn 1998, p. 764). CA requires, in fact, that we do not gloss over practices and treat them as taken for granted, not least when we operate as social scientists. Stating that a person has engaged in the (discursive) practice of making a promise may be sufficient for a participant who decides to trust the speaker, and therefore orientates to the fact that a promise institutes a sequence that should, at some point, deliver what was promised. This is not sufficient, however, for the analyst of discursive practices. For the analyst, the questions are: how an utterance becomes a promise, how trust is practically obtained and displayed in the sequence of talk, and what the devices are through which this seemingly simple, yet critical, linguistic practice is accomplished. In this sense, CA's main focus is cumulatively to identify and describe the methods and devices, such as adjacency pairs and repair mechanisms, which people use to accomplish talk, interaction, and meaning—that is, everyday discursive practices.

In its quest, CA has pursued two specific strategies—the search for the 'turn-taking machine' and the endorsement of a strong bottom-up, data-based, and 'non-theoretical' stance—which are, in many ways, applicable to all practices, not only discursive practice.

First, CA scholars have embarked on the collective and cumulative search for the conversational structures that people use, albeit non-reflexively, in their talk-in-interaction. Sacks *et al.* (1974) described this quest as the search for the 'turn-taking machine', defined as 'a speech exchange system for allocating participant's rights and obligations to take turns at speaking' (p. 699). The turn-taking machine, when completely outlined, would consist of a set of components and rules describing a hierarchical ordered set of options for constructing turns at talk and selecting the next speaker in a conversation. Therefore, the turn-taking machine constitutes not only a methodological device to investigate talk-in-interaction (in terms of sequence, timing, turn-taking, etc.), but also a normative model of such conduct, that is, how such interaction works from the perspectives of participants.

As it appears from Sachs' above quote, the 'turn-taking machine' aspires to capture the normative rules which members use to produce orderly talk-in-interaction. In this way, according to Lynch (1993), the idea and research strategy of the 'turn-taking machine', which is still broadly endorsed by many CA practitioners, is effectively an implicit practice theory that pushes the ethno-methodological notion of instructable reproducibility to its limit. In fact, the inventory of conversational devices assembled in this way not only accounts for the methodical production of orderly patterns of interactions which emerge from the analysis of audio and video recording, it also aspires to describe the methods which participants contextually use to produce those orderly conversations. Unfortunately, says Lynch (1993), the quest to identify a set of context-free devices that members can use in context-dependent ways means pushing the limits of instructable reproducibility too far. Once the inventory of formalized devices that people use to make linguistic interaction happen becomes a positive and normative model of the generative mechanisms of interaction, it is transformed into normative 'grammar' with all the issues this implies. For example, says Lynch, rule-like devices such as those identified by CA are necessarily internal to the practice they instruct or regulate, and cannot exhaustively account for the methodical practices in which they are used. Accordingly, CA in its extreme forms runs against the Wittgensteinian and ethno-methodological way of understanding rules discussed in Chapters 2 and 7.

Besides the 'turn-taking machine', CA employs a second strategy which, like the former, is highly relevant in terms of the attempt to theorize practice. CA, in fact, programmatically uses what is defined as a restricted set of data, i.e. recordings of naturally occurring interactions, as the only point of departure for the investigation. Not only does CA refrain from producing a hypothesis, it also carefully tries not to inject the formal analysis of transcripts with (second order) categories and theoretical presuppositions derived from the professional vocabulary of the social scientist. Different from other strands of discourse analysis such as critical discourse analysis (to be discussed shortly), CA does not discuss the relations between certain linguistic or interactional practice and other social 'factors' such ideology, power, gender, race, status, and hierarchical position. On the contrary, the aim of CA is to investigate how certain relations (power, gender, ethnicity, and status) manifest themselves in the interaction through the categories used by participants. In fact, in order to prevent prejudices from surreptitiously entering the picture, some CA analysts omit from their transcript any reference to the status of the speakers, as it could introduce bias. If any power or domination relationship exists, argue CA practitioners, it must emerge in the analysis, as a product of the local practices of participants.

The refusal to take into consideration any kind of exogenous and determining aspect, and the choice to focus on the (formal) analysis of how social relations are accomplished in the interaction has, however, also attracted criticisms of the CA programme from two different perspectives. Firstly, authors argue that restricting the focus of analysis on to usually a very small segment of interaction constitutes a severe limitation to the validity of its findings. Cicourel (1981) contends that when the institutional context of the interaction is analytically neglected, researchers therefore lack important aspects of contextual knowledge that members use during interaction. In this sense, the small gains obtained by CA's extreme formal approach are superseded by the losses. Secondly, others maintain that CA's exclusive focus on the formal aspects of the interaction can become a major hindrance. In a now well-known exchange between Schegloff (1997, 1999) and Wetherell (1998), the latter accused CA of being incapable, among other things, of explaining 'why is this utterance here' (Wetherell 1998). The author argues that by focusing too narrowly on the interactive moment, CA runs the risk of forgetting that the positions drawn up in that moment are one of many variations or options for reflecting the larger patterns or threads of intelligibility that make that very interaction possible. Wetherell believes that an adequate analysis must not only look at the conversational details of talk-in-sequence, but also at the *trace* these detailed linguistic formulations leave through the larger argumentative threads that are displayed in the participants' orientations (Wetherell 1998). In his rejoinder, which I omit here for reasons of space, Schegloff (1999) argued that far too many works in other strands of analysis of conversation, such as critical conversation analysis (to be discussed below), side-step an explicit grounding of their analysis in linguistic detail. Instead, they too quickly invoke something like 'power differences' or 'hegemony' when it is not always clear how the participants are linguistically indexing (or orientating themselves) to something like 'power', or what 'power' even is for such analysts.

The exchange is of course critical for the understanding of practice. Schegloff's warning is valuable, even though CA's model of practice is severely limited. Schegloff is, in fact, suggesting that when discussing practice, 'assuming' and 'claiming' in theory is not enough. A consistent practice approach requires that the analyst demonstrates *in* practice what he or she is claiming *about* practice. As Schegloff (1999) puts it, those committed to understanding how inequality and oppression operate in practice and through practices should harness CA's tools as a resource for their work rather than complain about them as ideological distractions. Those who are convinced that social interactions are the marketplace for oppression and power relations should undertake to demonstrate this, rather than simply assume it first, and then 'find' what they assumed in the corpus of data. They should realize that CA's tools of analysis—as well as the general methodological toolbox of ethnomethodology—in no way preclude the empirical demonstration of such ideological convictions. In fact, they can make it more convincing.

8.2 **Practice as discourse: Foucault and the Foucauldian tradition**

A distinctly different way to approach discourse and discourse analysis stems from the work of Michael Foucault.

Discourse played a central role in the work of the French scholar, and his way of approaching the issue has been widely referred to as a model by several other social scientists. Although a major shift occurred in his approach during his career—the well-known shift of interest between archaeology and genealogy (Davidson 1986: the distinction is discussed below)—discourse remained a central concern throughout his career, especially the relationship between discourse and power, the discursive construction of social subjects and knowledge, and the role of discourse in social change.

The main object of inquiry in Foucault's work was not language and its mundane use as much as the conditions of possibility of discourse, that is, the rules of formation that give rise to a particular set of discursive practices and the domains of knowledge that are constituted in this way. His main interest was not in the formulation of a general theory of language as much as in the investigation of how material and discursive practices confer certain patterns and regularities on social life by framing it in terms of specific problems (Reed 1998).

Central to Foucault's analysis are 'discursive formations'[3] and their dynamic configurations into historical orders of discourse (Foucault 1970, 1972). A 'discursive formation' consists of a number of rules that bestow a certain order to the statements (*énoncès*) which belong to it. These rules of formation are obtained by assembling in a novel way existing discursive and non-discursive elements through the institutions of new social and discursive practices. In particular, these rules of formation and practice determine what can be spoken of, who is allowed to speak (or write) and how, and a field of possibilities with regards to the creation of theories and themes; that is, how the discursive formation is used in the wider institutional and societal arena. As Fairclough (1992) notes, discursive formations always constitute themselves in relation to each other within what Foucault terms the overall 'order of discourse'—the totality of discursive practices within an institution or a society at a given point in time (Foucault 1970). The study of the emergence of a new discursive formation cannot therefore be divorced from the consideration of its effects on the existing social order of discourse, and of the conflict and power struggle inherent in the process. For Foucault, moreover, the 'possibilities of discourse' are never fully realized. Which of the possibilities of discourse are developed and which are ignored or silenced depends on how discourse enters into the wider economic and political games of which it is part.

Foucault's view of discourse can be summarized under the following headings:

- *Discourse has a constitutive nature.* Far from being a way of signifying and representing the world, discourse is involved in the definition and structuring of the lived world.
- *Discourse is inherently material and heterogeneous.* For Foucault, discourse is never to be reduced only to language and its mundane use. In fact, discursive formations cannot be reduced to their linguistic and symbolic elements alone. Rather, they must be seen as configurations of statements, techniques, interventions, and norms held loosely together by a body of anonymous historical rules directed to the practical exercise of power and control in specific organizational sites. The governmental technologies that constitute power in modern society are always heterogeneous, thus combining seamlessly discursive and non-discursive practices. Heterogeneity refers also to the fact that the rules of formation of discourses are obtained by assembling, in a novel way, existing discursive and non-discursive

elements. Any discursive practice builds upon others and is defined in relation to them. Intertextuality[4] and interdiscursivity are therefore inherent in any discourse formation, and the relation between discursive practices, both historically and synchronically, is therefore complex and non-linear. Moreover, because of all the tensions and conflicts implicated in this complex process of assembling and aligning heterogeneous and, at times, contradicting elements, the order of discourses, discursive formations, and their fields of statements are in a state of constant flux; that is to say, discourse is not a static entity as much as a living and constantly shifting process.

- *Discourse ties the exercise of power and control to an organized array of socio-material discursive and non-discursive practices.* At least later in his career, Foucault tended to conceive of power in discursive ways, or at least to focus on the discursive ways in which power manifests itself: 'the practices that Foucault places so much weight upon—interview, counselling, and so forth—are to a substantial degree discursive practices' (Fairclough 1992, p. 50). This establishes at the same time an inherent relation between power and knowledge, insofar as knowledge and belief are embodied and ingrained in the power relations and practices that give rise to them. It also clarifies the discursive nature of power, insofar as many of the practices and techniques of modern control are of a discursive nature; it finally sets discourse as both a major locus of power struggle and an object for that struggle. Discursive practices are not, therefore, simply the traces of past struggles or the outcome of systems of domination. Instead, they become both the object and the media of power struggles, the 'very thing which is to be seized' (Foucault 1970, p. 107) and the arenas where such struggles take place.

- *Discourse and power are contingent and 'subject-less' overarching effects. The analysis of power and discourse should follow a 'bottom-up' or ascending, rather than descending, path.* This aspect is especially visible in Foucault's genealogic works. It descends from his notion of power as 'employed and exercised through a net-like organization' (Foucault 1980, in Reed 1998, p. 196) as opposed to the prevailing juridical or sovereign conceptions. Power/knowledge discourses should not be conceived of and/or studied as the result of intentional hegemony or domination strategies put in place by organized groups or classes. They must rather be considered as 'highly provisional, localized and contingent expressions of a multiplicity of forces, energies, materials, and interventions consistent with an overarching framework of ontological imperatives and methodological protocols' (Reed 1998, p. 197).

Foucault's view on discourse translates almost directly into a set of tools for understanding practice, as visible in the work of authors such as Laclau and

Mouffe (see Torfing 1999, for a discussion) and Schatzki (see Chapter 7 above). In fact, Foucault's view of discourse brings to the fore the material and heterogeneous nature of practices and orders, and alerts us to the centrality of discursive and power phenomena as critical aspects of practice matters. Foucault, moreover, has the merit of emphasizing that the appropriate units of inquiry for practice theories are not unique, coherent, and stable objects, as much as emergent nexuses of local diversities. For Foucault, in fact, the unity of discourse does not lie in the repetition of the same activity (be it the production of a textual form or the carrying out of a medical diagnosis) as much as in the delimitation of diversity. Discourse, in this sense, must be considered a dispersion of objects and concepts which exhibits, at the same time 'order in the appearances of their elements, correlations in their simultaneity, assignable positions in common spaces, reciprocal functioning, and/or linked and hierarchized transformations' (Foucault 1972, p. 37). In this sense, Foucault helps us see that the task of practice theories is not that of explaining social order on the basis of practice, as much as it is asking why and how practices come to exhibit overarching regularities across time and space, and how the apparent unity of (discursive) practices, from which discourse derives its power and influence, is achieved and maintained in practice.

8.3 Critical discourse analysis

A successful attempt at developing Foucault's perspective in a direction that combines an interest in the detailed mechanism of the production of discourse/practice and order with a broad concern for the relationship between discourse, power, and social change has been developed under the label of critical discourse analysis (Fairclough 1992, 1995; Fairclough and Wodak 1997; Van Dijk 1997; Iedema and Wodak 1999; Wodak and Weiss 2003).

Critical discourse analysis (CDA) is a particular variety of discourse analysis interested in exploring social interaction through its linguistic manifestation. CDA sees discourse as a form of activity, and argues that describing discourse as social practice implies 'a dialectical relationship between a particular discursive event and the situation(s), institution(s), and social structure(s) which frame it' (Fairclough and Wodak 1997, p. 258). Developing Foucault's intuitions briefly described above, CDA authors emphasize the constitutive and political nature of discourse, as well as its central role in the mechanisms of power and in social change. Bakhtin's influence is visible in their attention to discourse and texts as the 'arena for class struggle' and in the phenomenon of intertextuality. Finally, they follow the sociolinguistic tradition in focusing on both textual and social investigations.

Work conducted within this tradition often combines detailed textual analysis with some form of contextual social inquiry. The aim is to establish connections between the results of the detailed linguistic analysis, the inquiry into the interactional aspect of textual production, and the socio-cultural and historical conditions within which this takes place.

CDA is of a special interest in our discussion because of its particular way of understanding 'discourse' as a form of *social* practice. CDA takes, in fact, discourse as a way of acting in the world and assumes a dialectical relationship between local manifestations of discursive practices and the conditions that generate them. On the one hand, discourse is socially constitutive in that it contributes to the construction of social identities, relationships between people, and bodies of knowledge. This constitution is both conventional and creative, in that discourse contributes to the reproduction of society but also constitutes the locus of intertextual creativity, recomposition, and transformation. On the other hand, discourse, at all levels, is shaped and constrained by social structure. Counter to some extreme constructivist positions, CDA argues that the constitutive role of language should not lead to the idealist conclusion that the world emanates from people's heads and/or mouths. Discursive productions always take place within specific institutional settings, and their constitutive functions are always performed in conjunction with other practices. Thus 'the discursive constitution of society doesn't emanate from a free play of ideas in people's heads but from a social practice which is rooted in and oriented to real, material social structures' (Fairclough 1992, p. 66). These practices concur to define an intertextual field (what Foucault named 'order of discourses' and that critical discourse analysts call 'order of [discursive] practices'; see Fairclough 1992, p. 86) in which boundaries between (discursive) practices appear to be naturalized and institutionalized, but are, in fact, the result of past struggles and can then easily become potential lines of tension. That is to say, the constitution of society and the production of discourse do not define stable discursive communities connoted by a constant and univocal relationship of complementarity (Fish 1980). Boundaries between (discursive) practices are continually contested, they may be experienced as contradictory, and they can trigger struggles for the re-articulation of orders of discourse.

Accordingly, CDA scholars consider intertextuality and re-contextualization two central dimensions of the analysis of both discursive practices and social phenomena. Intertextuality—that is, the basic property of texts of 'being full of snatches of other texts, which may be explicitly demarcated or merged in, and which the text may assimilate, contradict, ironically echo, and so forth' (Fairclough 1992, p. 84)—stresses the historicity of texts and their capacity to constitute at the same time the instrument, the arena, the outcome, and the intermediary of power struggles. In fact, through intertextuality, texts and discursive practices carry ideology not only through their content and structure, but also through the material chains and stabilized networks which texts move, or do not move, along. At the same time, however, intertextuality and re-contextualization also constitute key resources for subjects who can reflexively establish innovative connections between practices and ideologies, therefore restructuring the existing field of positioning. The effort to control this inherent intertextuality, and how texts and discursive practices articulate prior texts and conventions, becomes (one of) the objects of hegemonic struggle understood as the effort to articulate or re-articulate existing elements so that they support a particular configuration of interests naturalized to a variable extent. Hegemony is therefore to be conceived as a generalized phenomenon associated with the effort of constructing alliances, established temporary and partial connections between material and discursive elements. Accordingly, any social order of discourses at the same time constitutes a facet of hegemony, understood as the provisional alignment of an array of elements as well as a tool for the maintenance of such a configuration (Fairclough 1992, 1995).[5]

CDA's dialectical approach is, therefore, extremely useful for respecifying the issue of the dispersion of local practices in terms of a clash of interests, political struggle, and hegemony. It does so by emphasizing that the inter-textual nature of (discursive) practices constitutes both a resource and a constraint which requires the intervention of some form of agency whose nature remains, however, tied to the conditions that generated it. CDA's approach is thus in many ways a potential corrective to an overdetermination of reality by discourse and of discourse by structures. According to Fairclough (1992), the fact that the word 'discourse' refers both to discursive practices and discursive events, as we have seen at the outset, constitutes a 'felicitous ambiguity' and implies that CDA's dialectical perspective sees 'practice and the event as contradictory and in struggle, with a complex and variable relationship to structures which themselves manifest only a temporary, partial and contradictory fixity' (ibid.).

The result is a view of discursive practice, but also of practice in general, which cuts across several levels of analysis and that, therefore, combines seemingly divergent research traditions into a unitary framework. Discourse is, in fact, understood (i) as a text, in the broad sense of spoken as well as written language; (ii) as the manifestation of a discursive practice; that is, as an instance of a particular process of text production, distribution, and consumption; and (iii) and as an instance of a social practice, a mode of action shaped by social structures. The framework is summarized in Figure 8.1.

In order to 'cut across' the levels described in Figure 8.1, CDA analyses 'context' in four related ways: (1) the immediate, co-textual, and linguistic context of texts (CDA often uses ethnographic methods); (2) the intertextual and inter-discursive relationships between utterances, texts, genres, and discourse; (3) the extra-linguistic social variables and local institutional frames; and (4) the broader sociopolitical and historical context within which

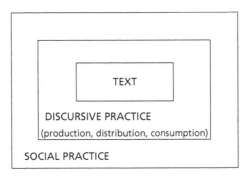

Figure 8.1 The interrelated levels of analysis identified by CDA. (from Fairclough, 1992, p. 73. Reprinted with permission)

discursive practices are embedded. This indication can be fruitfully used as a blueprint for the theorization of all practices. Although CDA, like other varieties of discourse analysis, understands discourse as a privileged modality of social conduct (for obvious disciplinary reasons) to the extent that all practices are partly discursive, several of the reflections developed by CDA can be extended to the understanding of all kind of practices. Inter-discursivity, re-contextualization, and embeddedness in a wider social and historical context should be considered as applicable to all practices. Moreover, CDA attracts attention to the fact that all practices are also discursively represented, not only locally, as the ethno-methodological principle of reflexivity had it, but also trans-locally. The representation of practices has an effect on the 'orders of practices', so to speak, in that it supports the creation of 'conjunctures' (cross-institutional assemblies of practices around specific projects: see Martin Rojo 2001), and can therefore be conceptualized as a form of hegemonic activity.

It must be added, however, that CDA also bears witness to the complexity and potential pitfalls of this broad project (Leitch and Palmer 2010). As some authors have noted, the dialectical relationship between the micro and the macro often boils down to an encounter 'in the middle' between the micro-analysis of how the social is represented in discourse and a macro analysis of how these representations relate to the broader sociopolitical context (see, e.g. Engeström 1999). In this way, as Engeström aptly put it, the analysis of how discourse is produced through the task performed by participants is often left unaccounted: 'between the artificially-isolated fragments of discourse and the ambiguously-global argumentative social fabric, there is the middle ground of the social situated activity' (Engeström 1999, p. 173). It is this middle ground that practice theory tries to occupy and that, according to its critics, CDA is only partially able to fill. While according to Martin Rojo (2001), this CDA shortcoming derives from the complexity of the task at hand,[6] Engeström's remarks bring to the surface some deeper shortcomings in the theory. The use by CDA authors of terms such as 'levels', 'structure', 'micro', and 'macro' suggests that, in spite of CDA's effort to take up a consistent 'dialectical perspective', its underlying sociology is still a sociology of assumed differences and discontinuities. These discontinuities, such as those between micro and macro, discursive and non-discursive, local and global, are assumed in the framework and are only later reconciled through dialectic movement, not unlike what Giddens tried to do. Although this tendency is distributed in an uneven way between the different CDA strands, texts, and authors, this is the reason why the approach is generally ill-equipped when it comes to explain the middle ground of social-situated activity.

8.4 **Mediated discourse analysis**

Mediated discourse analysis (MDA) is the name of an approach that tries to address some of the issues left unresolved by CDA. This is achieved by positing social practice at the core of the study of discourse, and by adopting a bottom-up approach to the explanation of practice and its relationship to broader orders of discourse. Thus, MDA is particularly relevant for this book as it constitutes 'a theory about social action with a specific focus on discourse *as a kind of social action* as well as upon discourse *as a component of social action,* (Scollon 2001, p. 6, emphasis added). In other words, MDA is first and foremost a discursive theory of practice that tries to understand discourse *in* action.[7] It argues that at any point in time, actors operate at the intersection of a number of discourses, social identities, and goals carried on the scene by discourse and other mediational tools (in the sense discussed in Chapter 5). Situated action is thus inherently hybrid, intertextual, and therefore 'open to the right' (as in the case of CA discussed above). Action, however, does not happen in a vacuum. All actions are in fact part of circuits of discourse that extend in space and time and that circulate in the moment of the action. In other words, all activities (drinking coffee, teaching a lesson, making a phone call) take place at the intersection of multiple discourses brought to the scene by speech, texts, tools, spatial arrangements, etc. The tension between the possibilities prefigured by the different discursive, cultural, and material forms of mediation is thus resolved in the immediate circumstances of the action. Each action can thus extend one or more circuits of discourse (what Gee calls 'Discourses'), or it can problematize them, interfere with their reproduction, and, in extreme cases, derail them. In this sense, MDA differs from CDA in that 'rather than approaching the question of how discourse is a matter of discourse through the discourse, [it] approaches it through the action' (Jones and Norris 2005, p. 10).

8.4.1 THE FIVE PILLARS OF MEDIATED DISCOURSE ANALYSIS

According to Scollon (2001, p. 3), MDA builds on five core concepts: mediated action, mediational means, practice, site of engagement, and nexus of practice. By Scollon's own admission (Scollon and Scollon 2001, 2004), several of the concepts employed by MDA are derived from other theories of practice surveyed in previous parts of this volume—a further reason to justify the discussion of MDA here.

Mediated action. Unlike CA and CDA, MDA takes mediated action, rather than discourse, text, or conversation as its focus of analysis and what needs to be understood and explained. The rationale is that even the most complex social phenomena and historical conditions are grounded in, and in a sense boil down to, mundane activities and micro-actions. For example, participating in consumer society implies, among many other things, using money to buy something in a shop or ordering goods online using a computer and credit card. At the same time, buying something or accessing an online store using a computer necessarily entails participating in, and perpetuating, the consumer society or the information society (or both). In short, we cannot understand phenomena such as the consumer society or the information society (or imperialism or democracy) without referring to specific mediated actions. The idea of mediation is derived from the Vygotskyian tradition discussed in Chapter 5, and implies that all action needs to be analysed in terms of an agent and a set of mediational means that make the action possible. In the example above, buying is necessarily mediated either by money or a credit service. There is no buying without such mediation. In other words 'action is materially grounded in persons and objects' (Scollon 2001, p. 3), and here is where the analysis should start and return. It should be added that, for MDA, the relationship between action and mediation, between actor and cultural and semiotic resources, is always problematic because tension always exists between the two aspects. Mediation is, in fact, a process: while sometimes the agent is of greater importance, at other times the opposite is true. The mediated nature of action—what is mediated and how, and how the situated action reflects historic and material conditions—is thus necessarily the object of empirical inquiry. Any form of discursive or social or material determinism is thus excluded.

Mediational means. All mediated action is carried out through material objects in the world. These include tools, texts, and other semiotic resources, and the habituated body (habitus is used in the sense proposed by Bourdieu and discussed in Chapter 3). As in the Vygotskyian tradition, mediational means operate as material and semiotic resources for action (see Chapter 5). For this reason they both expand the affordances of actors and bring to the scene biases, orientations, and ideologies which derive from the history of their formation. Mediational means thus both amplify and constrain certain aspects of action, realizing the possible futures that were inscribed in them. Unlike in the Vygotskyian tradition, however, MDA underscores that language is one of many mediational tools, and language does not always occupy a preferential position. This is because discursivity can be mediated ('carried') in a scene of action through a number of mediational means besides language and conversation. Think, for example, of the material expertise required to undertake a piece of DIY. You can obtain advice from a friend over the phone or get hold of a manual or download a video. Some of the expertise will even travel in the products that have been modified to simplify your task. Expertise is thus brought to the scene of action through all these mediational means and used as a basis for further discourse (especially if there is someone helping you and you need to agree what to do). The same applies for all other social phenomena. Accordingly, the analysis of discourse in practice requires a multimodal approach, as focusing only on talk in inter-action may mean missing much of the 'discursivity' that circulates in the scene of action. By the same token, the analyst needs to keep in mind that media-tional means are necessarily polysemic, and thus open to interpretation and change, which again requires that we examine mediation *in situ* (as it happens), instead of assuming that one particular semiotic resource will be always used in the same way and for the same purpose.

Practices. MDA shares with most other performative approaches to dis-course the notion that mediated action is only interpretable within practices (Scollon 2001, p. 4).[8] It also agrees with CDA that identity, power, and ideology are all produced and reproduced at the intersection between social practices and mediational means. Where it diverges from other approaches that focus on the analysis of Discourse with a capital 'D', is in the scale of the inquiry. While in the Foucauldian tradition, 'practice' is often used broadly to refer to generic activities such as cooking, farming, and teaching, MDA authors use 'practice' in a much narrower sense. For MDA scholars, in fact, practice is 'a single, recognizable, repeatable action such as the practice of handling an object, filling a form, switching on a computer, or answering a direct question in an interview' (Scollon and Scollon 2005, p. 13). Practices are thus countable nouns that refer to actions that are perceived and performed as recognizable wholes. The difference between mediated action and practice is thus fundamentally one of '*durée*'. Actions are events, while practices are actions with a history. The aim of such a narrow focus is programmatic. By reducing the scale of the unit of analysis MDA tries not to lose sight of the ethno-methods that go into performing even the most mundane of activities, a risk that, as we have seen, lurks behind any attempt at offering sociological explanations of discursive practices.

Sites of engagement are the moments when different practices come together to generate actions in real time. The practices inscribed in the body and mediated by semiotic resources come to life in specific places, times, and socio-historical conditions. Sites of engagement are thus space/time stations (Saint-Georges 2005), real-time windows opened at the intersection of diverse social practices and mediational means. The idea of 'sites of engagement' emphasizes the unique and irreversible nature of mediated action and practices. Practices always manifest themselves in such openings (see Chapter 7), and for this reason the study of practice and discourses cannot but start from here. Studying practice in practice thus entails observing sites of engagement, and examining what mediational means are at work, and how specific systems of relevance and rules of attention make certain practices relevant while putting others in the background.

Nexus of practice. 'When a site of engagement is repeated regularly, we refer to that as a nexus of practice' (Scollon and Scollon 2004, p. 12). MDA intentionally takes a narrow view of social practices in the attempt to build on the insights of micro approaches such as ethno-methodology and CA which show that minute variations in the performance of (discursive) practices can produce significantly different outcomes. MDA, however, recognizes that practices are usually linked to other practices, discursive and non-discursive. Only when working together do practices generate sites of engagement. Nexuses of practice are perpetuated in time through repetition and institutionalization. The idea of a nexus of practice thus captures a molar level of analysis analogous to the idea of a scene of action discussed in Chapter 6 and activity system discussed in Chapter 5. It suggests that the analysis of practice should focus on explaining why nexuses of practices occur, what type of discursivity they are entailed through, and what epiphenomena they produce or reproduce. For example, when we talk about 'teaching a class' we refer to a nexus of practices such as registering attendance, speaking, posing questions to students, and possibly using slides. Calling this a nexus of practice allows us to examine how a class is accomplished and to compare different ways to 'do a class'; for example, comparing a traditional teacher-led class with a nexus-class where there are no slides, the teacher is not the centre of attention, students come and go as they see fit, and discussion is mediated by some form of technology.[9] Only once we grasp how the class is accomplished can we examine what the implications are, in terms of the identity and power relations among participants. In short, if the task is to understand how different forms of discursivity orient towards the creation of specific sites of engagement, and the production or reproduction of specific social practices, we need to retain sensitivity for both the nexus and its components, lest we lose sight of discourse in the attempt to purse the understanding of Discourses.

8.4.2 NEXUS ANALYSIS

Building on the previous assumption, MDA conceives, as its main project, analysing which forms of discursivity circulate through specific sites of engagement and lead to the emergence of specific mediated actions and nexuses of practice. This is, in effect, an attempt to study social practice by mapping the discourses, semiotic cycles, and meditational means that go into it.[10] The analysis starts ethnographically by examining a specific site of engagement, with special attention to the social arrangement (interactional order), the historical body of the participants (the lived experience of the participants), and the discourses that are active in the particular scene; that is, the discourses towards which participants' attention appears to be directed. The ethnographic analysis of the site of engagement and the mediated actions allows identification of what are the crucial discourses operating on the scene. This is, however, only part of the task. The next step of the analysis consists of navigating these discourses 'as a way of seeing how those moments are constituted out of past practices and how in turn they lead to new forms of action...' (Scollon and Scollon 2004, p. 29). This is achieved by 'circumferen- cing'[11] the existing cycles of discourse, and examining their historical origin and the way they constitute local action through anticipating consequences and providing motives. Key to this task is the idea that discourses mutate in time through what Iedema calls 'resemiotization' (Iedema 2001, 2003). This term describes the process through which discourses are progressively materi- alized from situated and quite 'local' talk towards increasingly durable— because they are written, multiplied, and filed—forms of language use (Iedema 2003, p. 42). When introduced into a different scene of action, these durable manifestations of discourse perform locally the discourse in- scribed in them. For example, it may be decided (talk) that a focus group aimed at discussing some social policies may be organized by inviting heads of a family. The decision is then resemiotized in terms of an invitation letter (text) that is sent to male addressees. These accept the invitation and partici- pate in the focus group (talk). The site of engagement actively reproduces a gender bias that is brought to bear by a cycle of discourse. The discourse of gender bias is both manifested in, and perpetuated through, the nexus of practice (focus group). The situation is sealed by the fact that it is likely that male participants carry onto the scene historical bodies that predispose them to perceive themselves as the family spokesperson (even if they are not necessarily the actual breadwinner). The two cycles of discourse render par- ticipants doubly blind to the gendered nature of the practice. They do not see, and they do not see the discourse that makes them not see. Following in reverse the multiple socio-historical chains of resemiotization, it is thus critical to uncover 'how and why what we confront as "real" has come about through networks of transmission and assemblage of semiotic resources' (ibid., p. 48).

This necessarily short illustration of MDA should help explain why above I suggested that the approach is positioned somewhere between CA and CDA. By shifting the central focus of interest from discourse to practices, MDA tries to strike a balance between the analytical attention to the accomplishment of the scene of action and the connections that link one scene to many others in space and history. In many ways, however, MDA is both an ambitious and unfinished project. It is ambitious because it tries to offer nothing less than a practice-discursive ontology of the social. It is unfinished as many of the details of the project remained undeveloped, possibly because nexus analysis was the last salvo of Scollon's long and prolific career, and he did not have time to develop the theory further due to illness and his premature death in early 2009. Questions that remain include how discourses travel in space and time; how resemiotization happens; how the body is inscribed and interpreted; how interactional orders are created and perpetuated; and how practices and nexuses are brought together, and what keeps them going. Even the relation between mediated action and nexus of practice remains partly unexplored, with attention shifting between these two different levels of phenomena. Above all, it is unfortunate that MDA failed to enter into a productive conversation with other cognate projects such as the sociology of translation (also known as actor network theory: see Latour 2005; Law 2009). The sociology of translation (itself an application of Foucault's notion of discourse)[12] offers, in fact, a set of powerful conceptual tools for explaining the emergence of assemblages, conjunctures, and organized forms of social order, without reintroducing traditional dichotomies; e.g. that between local and global effects. In this sense, MDA and the sociology of translation respond to the same project and their failed encounter is both a missed opportunity and a fruitful possibility.

Rolling case study: Telemonitoring: a conversation analysis view[13]

Telephone contacts constitute a critical aspect of the type of telemedicine provided by the Garibaldi centre. Telephone encounters take up a substantial proportion of the nurses' time and a lot of work is accomplished through, and during, them. In order to understand the practice of telemedicine, it is therefore necessary to examine in detail how the interactional encounter between nurses and patients are accomplished, and to what effect.

Below, I present a transcript of part of a monitoring phone call recorded during routine contact between one of the nurses and a patient. The call is part of a corpus of twelve calls recorded and transcribed (several others were 'observed' but not recorded for legal reasons). The transcript was produced using the conventions of the Jefferson notation system that is widely used by CA authors and reproduced at the end of this section. The nurse's speech is identified in italics in the text.

From a CA perspective this is quite a long (33 seconds) and extremely rich interaction (many things are going on). For reasons of space, I will limit myself to drawing out only one aspect of the call. I will focus specifically on the issue of expertise. Telemedicine is often said to empower patients. Yet a clinical encounter is also traditionally marked by a display of unequal expertise that constitutes one of the speakers as the clinical practitioner and the other as the patient. Accordingly, in my analysis I will examine how this unequal distribution of expertise is accomplished in the talk in interaction during the call. As I shall show, this is skilfully achieved by a series of recognizable devices starting with the opening sequence of the call. (Please see end of case study for explanation of symbols used in the following transcription).

1 *Good morning how are you?*

2 Not too bad thank God (.)

3 however (.) you know (0.8)

4 (.) my triglycerides[14] =

5   = *I know (.) I've seen your tests*

6 (.) Yeah::my triglycerides =

7   = *They are not exactly where they should be (.)*

8 mm (0.3) well you::know:: I cannot resist =

9   = *I know (.) some crisps here some cheese there::*

10 *and your triglycerides stay high (.)*

11 <u>Can you tell</u> *me your pressure, please?*

12 90 over 130.

13 *Seems fine to me::*

14 *Did you measure it in the morning?*

15 [Yes: yes

We can start with some general observations. The overall exchange is structured through a turn-type pre-allocation typical of highly institutionalized medical encounters (ten Have 1999). While the nurse maintains a caring, informal, and slightly playful tone (the beginning of the exchange is heard by the patient as playful teasing), the formality and institutional nature of the interaction is performed by the recognizable patterns of talking in turns and the overall structural organization of the exchange. In general, the nurse always talks first. She sets the scene for the next turn, and orients the conversation towards the specific (institutional) topics and features while excluding other possibilities such as small talk (see line 11, which is heard as an invitation to the patient to get back to serious business).

The call starts with a short sequence, namely summons-answer, recognition, and greetings. According to Schegloff (1986) this is one of the recurrent and canonical phone call openings. The organization of the opening solves the problem of (re)establishing the interaction, identifying who is involved, and who they are in relation to each other, and determining the reason for the call. It is worth noting that a recurrent feature of call-opening organization is that callers typically position themselves to be the asker of the first 'how are you?' sequence. This allows them to assume the position of being the answerer of the second response customarily produced by the person responding, that in the US is customarily a second 'how are you?' (elsewhere, the turn may include a brief response and commentary such as 'not too good' as in the call under examination). This, in turn, allows the caller to move towards the first topic or reason for the call which, in medical encounters, opens the information-gathering/diagnostic section of the interaction. We can see here, however, that the sequence is intentionally subverted. The patient occupies the third turn (line 3) and presents an issue ('my triglycerides') that, according to the canonical organization of the talk, should have appeared much later (during the information-gathering phase that here occupies the section starting with line 11). That this is a deviation from the norm emerges clearly in line 11 when the nurse uses the same device (the occupation of a second turn) to bring this section of the interaction to an end and put the conversation 'back on track'. We can also notice that although there is no 'recognition talk', this is not heard as a deviance from the canon as the nurse and the patient have regular phone contact which is carefully scheduled at precise times. It follows that the summons produced by the ringing of the phone, and the greeting exchange functionally satisfy the identification/recognition phase.

The question is thus: what is the patient accomplishing by occupying this critical third turn in the phone call and initiating a sequence that last ten more turns (until line 11)? We can note first that the patient is pre-emptively defending herself from an infraction. By bringing the topic up front, she is both recognizing the infringement of the moral order established by her dietary regime (that, for this type of patient, is potentially life-threatening) and trying to elicit the indulgence of the nurse. She is, therefore, constructing herself as a well-intentioned but weak patient who is in need of support and comprehension rather than reproach. By anticipating the discussion of the results of the tests before the results have even been addressed the patient engages in what we could call 'guilt work'.

There is, however, another very interesting aspect to this unusual opening. By bringing forward the discussion of her infringement, the patient also publicly displays her competence, positioning herself as an expert participant in the interaction to follow. It is she who is telling the nurse that something is not right—and not vice versa, as in traditional medical encounters. For example, studying phone calls between qualified nurses and occasional patients in the context of a national healthcare public helpline,[15] Pooler (2009) found that turn taking was as follows: after the canonical opening the nurses collected information and then designed their turns to provide a candidate formulation of the problem, often audibly in lay (i.e. non-medical) language. The 'tentative' formulation acted as a prelude to the advice-giving sequence, and provided an interactional resource for design and delivery of advice. Only at this point was the diagnosis and advice further discussed (and often disputed) by the caller (Pooler 2009, p. 149 and ff.) This is not, however, what is going on in the telemedicine call. Here, in fact, the patient does not wait for the nurse to inform her that her level of blood fat is too high. On the contrary, she proceeds to single this fact out by anticipating it in the sequential order of the call. By reversing the turn-taking, the patient constitutes herself as a guilty but competent subject. The expertise is also recognizable in the content of the utterance, but the sequence alone constructs the patient as a competent member who wishes to be acknowledged as such.

It is also interesting to analyse how the nurse reacts to such display, and actively re-establishes a specific order of expertise within this interaction. We can observe that lines 2–10 in the transcript display the typical structural features of an instructional encounter (Mehan 1985). In these situations, the person in the teaching position withholds the response during his or her turn, so eliciting an extended dialogue by the 'learner'. In the call, this continues until the symmetry between initiation and reply is re-established (this happens in line 11). The patient pauses twice: in line 3 where the pause is 0.8 seconds (quite a long time in a phone exchange), and again in line 4. The pause would allow the nurse to regain control of the exchange. However, the nurse chooses to wait until the patient clearly identifies the problem and the cause, something she would not need as she has seen the results of the test before calling the patient. By managing the sequence of the turns after the non-canonical opening, the nurse obtains two results: she acknowledges the expertise of the patient and casts her in a learner's position. Without denying the patient's competence, she re-establishes her own authority as the expert by involving the patient in a type of interaction that is structurally hierarchical. By line 11 the positions have been fully re-established and the interaction continues along more traditional and recognizable institutional lines.

List of the standard Jefferson notation system symbols used in the transcript (Please note this is not a complete list of symbols. For a discussion of the notation system see ten Have (1999).)

(.)	Just noticeable pause
(.8)	Pause (duration in seconds)
wor -	A dash shows a sharp cut-off
wo::rd	Colons show that the speaker has stretched the preceding sound.
word =	The equals sign shows that there is no discernible pause between
= word	two speakers' turns
word	Underlined sounds are louder
A: word [word	Square brackets aligned across adjacent lines denote the start of
B: [word	overlapping talk.

NOTES

1. According to Martin Rojo (2001), the emergence of the concept of discourse as practice stems from two related development in Western thinking: the 'linguistic turn' mentioned above and the more recent 'reflexive turn' in social theory. Both these development have been touched upon in Chapter 2, but it is useful to rehearse them again here in the context of the study of language and discourse.

The 'linguistic turn' or, to be more precise, the turn towards language consists of two related developments: (1) the abandonment of the classic idea that speaking is uttering ideas and that language is a mirror of nature as, for example, in the Saussurian notion that language is a system and a structure of signs and that meaning depends on relations within such system. The main consequence of this development is the emergence of an interest in the interdependence between things and representations and hence between discourses and knowledge production. The result is an increased centrality being accorded to language within social phenomena and, starting with the late 1960s, a tendency to use language as a model to understand social phenomena. (2) The introduction of the notion of language and meaning-making as activity. Once signification was placed in the context of social practices the attention shifted towards what people do with language and how people 'do' language. This on the one hand stimulated the concern for the relation between 'languaging', power, and hegemony. On the other hand, interest was drawn towards talking as human labour and a cooperative behaviour. This entailed the study of how discourse is produced in interaction, focusing not only on the on the linguistic but also on the social aspect, and the relationship between the two.

2. The distinction has been also discussed by Alvesson and Karreman (2000).

3. These are often referred to simply as 'discourses'.

4. According to Kristeva (in Moi 1986) intertextuality refers to the fact that any text is a link in a chain or system of texts. Any text therefore reacts to, dwells upon, and transforms all other texts. The notion was originally introduced by Mikhail Bakhtin.

5. A similar position has been developed by Laclau and Mouffe (Torfing 1999). The work of the two authors is heavily inspired by the work of Foucault and it bears a number of similarities to CDA.

6. 'It is impossible to cover all aspects, and to show how they interact' (Martin Rojo 2001, p. 58).

7. 'As a theory of how discourse and identity are implicated in situated social actions, MDA is essentially a theory of social practices' (Jones and Norris 2005, p. 38).

8. This was the main message of the Wittgensteinian tradition examined in Chapter 7.

9. The example of doing class as a nexus of practice is discussed in depth in Scollon and Scollon (2004), possibly the most comprehensive exposition of the approach.

10. 'Our interest as ethnographers is in social action and so for us a nexus analysis is the mapping of semiotic cycles of people, discourses, places, and mediational means involved in the social actions we are studying. We will use the term "nexus of practice" to focus on the point at which historical trajectories of people, places, discourses, ideas, and objects come together to enable some action which in itself alters those historical trajectories in some way as those trajectories emanate from this moment of social action' (Scollon and Scollon 2004, viii).

11. 'In order to get a perspective on the simple observable action we need to expand the circumference of the analysis to ask about its origins in the past, its direction in the future, and the expanding circles of engagement with others near and far. We need to know on what time scales, from minute to millennial, the action depends, as well as in what layers of geopolitical discourses it is embedded. Circumferencing is the analytical act of opening up the angle of observation to take into consideration these broader discourses in which the action operates' (Scollon and Scollon 2004, p. 13).

12. For a genealogy of the sociology of translation, see for example Law (1992).

13. Some background information on the practice of telemedicine is provided at the end of the Introduction.

14. Level of fat in the blood.

15. NHS Direct. This was a national telephone health helpline in England operating on a 24/7 basis from 1998 until it was phased out in early 2010.

9 Bringing it all Together: A Toolkit to Study and Represent Practice at Work

In the earlier parts of this book I offered an overview of contemporary practice theories, and I illustrated how they can help us to make sense of work, organizations, and other social phenomena. In this final chapter I would like to bring this multiplicity together, and offer some ideas on how we can go about studying the complex phenomenon that is practice. However, unlike most of the authors discussed in this volume, I am not interested in proposing a new theory of practice. Instead, I will embrace a different strategy that can be described as a form of programmatic eclecticism or, more simply, a toolkit approach. My main tenet is that to study practice empirically we are better served by a strategy based on deliberately switching between theoretical sensitivities. As I will explain in more depth below, adopting a cautious and reflective pluralist stance is perfectly legitimate as most practice theories share at least some common elements that allow them to be used in conjunction. A pluralist approach is also coherent with most of the practice theories discussed in this volume, as an eclectic strategy allows us to provide a thicker account of the world we live in—an aspiration common to all the authors examined in previous chapters. Finally, this approach adds value and offers benefits, as it enables us to exploit the strengths of the different theories in order to get a better grasp of the nexus of practices we live in.

This final chapter is organized as follows. I will start by summarizing (some of) the common traits of the theories discussed in previous chapters and ask what style of theorization is appropriate to study practice if we wish remain authentic to their radical message. I will then suggest how to go about studying practice, including what to do, what to watch out for (and listen, smell, touch, etc.), and how to write about it. As we shall see, the core suggestion here is that understanding and representing practice requires a reiteration of two basic movements: zooming in on the accomplishments of practice, and zooming out of their relationships in space and time. The chapter concludes with reflections on what zooming in and out is not, and on where the practice bandwagon is heading.

9.1 **The need for a toolkit approach**

As I have shown in previous chapters, the contemporary interest in practice is fuelled by the search for a new breed of social theory based on the intuition that basic phenomena such as knowledge, meaning, human activity, science, power, language, social institutions, and historical transformations occur and are components of the field of practices. What should emerge from the previous chapters, however, is that practice theories hardly constitute a uniform and homogeneous theoretical corpus. The contemporary interest in practice and practices is, in fact, rooted in a number of diverse approaches and traditions. Accordingly, it is without hesitation that authors such as Theodor Schatzki proclaims that there is no such thing as a unified practice approach (Schatzki 2001).

Under closer scrutiny, however, it is also apparent that contemporary practice theories do exhibit a number of family resemblances.[1] The idea of family resemblance allows us to think of all these theories as being related, in some partial ways, through a complicated network of similarities and dissimilarities, without assuming that they share one inherent common feature. For example, some (or many) of the authors discussed above believe that:

- Practices constitute the horizon within which all discursive and material actions are made possible and acquire meaning (see especially Chapters 4, 5, 7, and 8).
- Practices are inherently contingent, materially mediated, and cannot be understood without reference to a specific place, time, and concrete historical context (see especially Chapters 6, 7, and 8).
- Practices are social accomplishments, even when they are attributed to individuals. Social actors (and actants, in radical theories such as actor-network theory) emerge as part of a web of relationships and mutual dependencies on which they depend and to which they contribute (see especially Chapters 5, 7, and 8).
- While practices depend on reflexive human carriers to be accomplished and perpetuated, human agent capability always results from taking part in one or more socio-material practices (see especially Chapters 3, 4, and 7).
- Practices are mutually connected and constitute a nexus, texture, field, or network. Social co-existence is in this sense situated in the field of practice, and is both established by it and establishes it. At the same time, practices and their association perform different and unequal social and material positions, so that to study practice is also to study power in the making (see especially Chapters 3, 5, 7, and 8).

While no single practice theory or author supports all these tenets, all practice theorists subscribe to at least some of them—hence the notion of a family resemblance. My argument is that because of this complex web of similarities, these theories can be mobilized *together* to enrich our understanding of practice, and to provide a practice-based understanding of everything social (and organizational). As we shall see, mobilizing them together does not mean trying to unify them. On the contrary, the idea here is to exploit both their similarities and differences, following what I call a toolkit approach.

There are both tactical and strategic reasons for mobilizing these different theories together.

The tactical reason is that each of the approaches discussed in previous chapters have both advantages and limitations when it comes to the empirical study of practice. For example, both ethno-methodology and the Wittgensteinian tradition have very little to say about the central role of objects, contradictions, and about the evolving nature of practice—all concerns that are central in the cultural and historical activity theory tradition. In a similar way, while ethno-methodology provides a rich and sophisticated toolkit for investigating practice 'as it happens', it only takes into consideration phenomena such as social structure, institutions, and power to the extent that they visibly manifest themselves in the actual social practices of members. In this sense, the approach is far from adequate to evoke a positive relational organizational ontology whereby trans-local phenomena, seen as the result of the interlacing of local instances of order production, acquire the capacity to retroact at the local level. This in turn requires an integration of the ethno-methodological sensitivity with the intuition of semiotic-oriented social ontologies such as those discussed in Chapters 7 and 8. Put another way, to the extent that practice is a multifaceted and multidimensional phenomenon, it can only be empirically approached through toolkit logic and a collage or heteroglossia, or even carnivalesque, approach.

There is also another more strategic reason to adopt a programmatic form of eclecticism. This has to do less with empirical work and more with the issue of what is good social science and what can social science do for us (and for practitioners). In short, the toolkit approach that I advocate here responds to the principle that the aim of social science is to provide a richer and more nuanced understanding of the world, and not to offer simplified answers to complex questions. More clearly, good social science makes the world more complex, not simpler. Thicker, not thinner, descriptions are the aim of good social science. And so it should be in the attempt to understand practices.

The point has been made by several authors, but possibly the strongest available version to date has been provided by Isabelle Stengers (1997; see also Latour 2004). The Belgian philosopher of science has suggested a normative way to distinguish between good and bad science that is an alternative to the traditional Popperian model. According to the author, 'scientific' is an adjective that defines whether some (provisional) propositions about the world make us more articulate; that is, more capable of appreciating differences that matter. Being articulate (as opposed to inarticulate) means that we can make new and enlightening connections between things of the world. This in turn opens new opportunities for acting (or not acting) in a more informed way. Good science, no matter from which discipline, enriches the ingredients that make up the multi-faceted universe in which we live and makes us more articulate and capable of perceiving differences (and thus meaning). On the contrary, science focused on propositions that are tautological (i.e. when theories simply make you see their own reflection in the so-called 'phenomena') tends to be irrelevant and hence 'bad science'. It follows that good science is generative not eliminativist: its goal is to increase our capacity to make connections among phenomena, not to eradicate interesting features in the name of generalization.[2] For example, a theory that trades abstraction in exchange for wide reach may run the risk of becoming empty: in the attempt to explain too much, it ends up not explaining anything (or at least nothing that matters).

My programmatic eclecticism is a modest attempt to adhere to these canons of good science against the risk of eliminativism that lurks also among some practice theorists (see my comments on Bourdieu in Chapter 3 and my warning against ethno-methodological reductionism in Chapter 6). Adding, not abstracting or deconstructing, is the crucial point here (Stengers 2008, p. 3).

9.2 A package of theories and methods

One of the most interesting implications of the idea that good science is an effort to increase our articulated-ness is that it makes all science necessarily performative and constructivist. This is for two main reasons. Firstly, by doing nothing we learn nothing. Applying an existing theory to a phenomenon, an old medieval trick much in vogue in modern organization studies and other branches of social science, is an exercise of style similar to the rolling case study presented in this volume—a useful but in some ways literally redundant exercise. The problem is that while exercises of style, such as the rolling case study, where a pre-existing approach is imposed on some recalcitrant empirical material, may be useful for illustrating a theory it does not help to progress science. As indicated by pragmatist authors, learning requires engaging with the world, embarking on an inquiry which entails intervening in the world and giving it a chance of biting back at us, our presuppositions, and our inquiry tools. Good science is thus a mix of courage and hard work; a very rare feat! Secondly, an articulated view suggests that the more 'artificial' things we can throw at a phenomenon—theories, laboratories, experiments, assumptions, and prejudices—the more chances we have to discover something authentically new, as long as (a) we do not forget that the things we throw at the phenomenon and the distinctions we generate are intimately entangled; (b) we accept that the phenomenon can bite back (the lab can explode; the model can be found untenable; the informants can tell us that our findings are rubbish); and (c) we are ready to put our machinations, our ideas, and ourselves at risk and accept defeat when (b) applies.

In this sense, all theorization is a performative endeavour of world-making and reality reconfiguration where distinguishing between theory and method is a futile exercise (or a political move). All theories are, in fact, attempts at (re)configuring the world through which local determinations of boundaries, properties, and meanings are differentially enacted (Barad 2003, p. 821). In the context of the present discussion, this means that to generate a (social) world made of practices having a set of theories is not enough. What is needed, in fact, is a coherent practical package of theory *and* method. The idea of a disembodied theory of practice would contradict the basic assumption and ontological project of the approach. To the extent that the world we live in is made of practices (or activities or scenes of actions) 'all the way down',[3] theory can only be conceived itself as a form of (discursive) practice, a meaning-making socio-material performative endeavour. Practice theory, in other words, cannot escape the destiny of all other things social, and must itself be conceived as a form of theoriza(c)tion which, if successful, will enrich the multiverse with further propositions that shed light on things that matter.[4]

There is, of course a further reason why we need to conceive practice theory as a performative endeavour. As many of the authors discussed in previous chapters have noted, adopting real-time practice as the starting point of social and organizational inquiry poses a specific challenge exactly because of what makes it interesting; that is, the fact that it constitutes the unsung background amid which we conduct our existence. Heidegger hinted at this in his famous hammer example: practice is perfectly happy to stay in the background, supporting our daily commerce with the world without the need to come under the spotlight. In this sense, practice always needs to be brought to the fore, to be made visible or, more precisely, it needs to be turned into an epistemic object in order to enter discourse. This, in turn, requires work and activity: another practice. When we study practice we thus always and necessarily scrutinize two practices at the same time: our epistemic practice, and what concerns us.

It is for this reason that I call my approach a 'package'. The idea of a package of theory and methods emphasizes that, for studying practices, one needs to employ an internally coherent approach where ontological assumptions (the basic assumption about how the world is) and methodological choices (how to study things so that a particular ontology materializes) work together. For example, studying practices through surveys or interviews alone is unacceptable. These methods are, in fact, as unsuitable for studying work practices as they are unfaithful to the processual ontology that underpins the ethnography of practice approach. Studying practice-building exclusively by *post-hoc* verbal accounts is, therefore, an oxymoron.

In summary, to study and represent practice, we need a coherent theory–method package that allows us to do three things. First it needs to help us in building or slicing the social world in terms of practices instead of, say, systems or classes or rational economic actors. As I suggested above, this has important implications for how we investigate practices in that it means we need to use proximal research methods which allow us to get close enough to the activity at hand, and which are sensitive to its material and embodied nature.

Second, the theory–method package must also help us to *re*-present practice in the text. Although practices are not difficult to find, as this is what we are and what we do all the time, they are famously recalcitrant when it comes to being transposed in a text. This is because practices are extremely capable of speaking for themselves, and they not need to be verbalized in order to exist. Czarniawska (1997) referred to this as the two-pronged problem of 'ergonography' (the study of work as it happens, Czarniawska's neologism for practice theory). Studying work, activity, and practice requires, in fact, both generating '*logos*' about the work (*ergon*) and translating such *logos* into a textual artefact (the '*graphos*' bit, to be found also in ethno-graphy, geo-graphy, etc.) This aspect is particularly important for social scientists. According to Latour (2005), in fact, when it comes to social science the proof of the pudding is not in the eating (like cooks), or in the experiment (like some of our luckier colleagues), but in the text: 'The text, in our discipline, is not a story, not a nice story. Rather, it's the functional equivalent of a laboratory. It is a place for trials, experiments and simulations. Depending on what happens in it, there is or there is not [a practice].[5] And that depends entirely on the precise ways in which it is written—and every new topic requires a new way to be handled by a text' (ibid., p. 159).

Third, as suggested above, the theory–method package needs to be articulative and not eliminativist. In this sense, it has to offer resources for building narratives and for plotting the world, not readymade plots to be stitched upon 'phenomena'. A theory–method package that remains authentic to the criteria endorsed above should therefore offer a discursive repertoire or infra-language (Latour 2005) open enough so that it can be used to construct specific local stories, explanations, and further theories. Practice theory should, therefore, set a stage and establish a set of specific characters without then prescribing *ex ante* how the story should, or would, unfold. I see a practice theory–method package as a dispositive to be used to investigate the world, not as a fully-formed theory of how the world is. This explains my critical remarks against Schatzki in Chapter 7 who is, at times, guilty of providing a story that is too closed and conclusive—a plot about the world rather than a method for emplotting it. Latour (2005) expresses the same idea, noting that a good social theory should be limited to providing an infra-language that does not 'designate what is being mapped, but how it is possible to map anything from such a territory' (p. 172).

9.2.1 THE THEORY–METHOD PACKAGE: AN OVERVIEW

The theory–method package that I would like to propose is composed of a set of sensitizing concepts/questions to be discussed below, and an invitation to reiterate three basic movements: zooming in on the accomplishments of practice; zooming out to discern their relationships in space and time; and using the above devices to produce diffracting machinations that enrich our understanding through thick textual renditions of mundane practices. The sensitizing concepts and questions (see Table 9.1 for a summary) are the elements of my infra-language—my invitation to see. The movements are my apparatus: a strategy to 'cut' the world in terms of a nexus of interconnected practices.

The package requires first that we zoom in on the details of the accomplishment of a practice in a specific place to make sense of the local accomplishment of the practice and the other more or less distant activities. This is followed by, and alternated with, a zooming out movement through which we expand the scope of the observation following the trails of connections between practices and their products. The iterative zooming in and out stops when we can provide a convincing and defensible account of both the practice and its effects on the dynamics of organizing, showing how that which is local (e.g. the doctors' and nurses' conduct on one site) contributes to the generation of broader effects (for example, sustaining or upsetting the historical hierarchical relationship between the medical and nursing professions). Because the zooming in and out is achieved by switching theoretical lenses, the result is both a representation of practice and an exercise of diffraction whereby understanding is enriched through reading the results of one form of theorization through another. In the next three sections I examine these movements in detail.

9.2.2 ZOOMING IN ON PRACTICE: IN THE BEGINNING WAS THE DEED

Like other authors referenced in this book, my starting assumption is that much is to be gained if we take practices as our central epistemic object and focus of attention. Although a detailed attempt at defining practices is not what I am after, when I speak of practices I refer to 'practising', real-time doing and saying something in a specific place and time. Practices, in other words, are not objects, they are not in the heads of people, and they are not stored in

Table 9.1 A palette for zooming in

Focus	Theoretical resources	Examples of sensitizing research questions
Sayings and doings	Chs. 5, 7, 8	What are people doing and saying? What are they trying to do when they speak? What is said and done? How do the patterns of doing and saying flow in time? What temporal sequences do they conjure? With what effects? Through which moves, strategies, methods, and discursive practical devices do practitioners accomplish their work?
Interactional order	Chs. 4, 5, 6	What sort of interactional order is performed by this specific practice? How does this differ from similar practices performed elsewhere? What positions does this specific practice make available? How are these positions negotiated or resisted? What type of collective interests are sustained and perpetuated by the specific practice? How are asymmetries and inequalities produced or reproduced in the process?
Timing and tempo	Chs. 4, 8	How are the sayings and actions temporally organized? How do the patterns of doing and saying flow in time? What temporal sequences do they conjure? With what effect? What temporality/rhythm is produced by the practice? What is the relationship between the different temporalities and rhythms brought to bear on the scene of action by different practices?
Bodily choreography	Chs. 3, 7	What is the material and symbolic landscape in which the practice is carried out? How is practice accomplished through the body? What sorts of things are made present in the scenes of action through the bodies? How are bodies configured by the practice?
Tools, artefacts, and mediation work	Chs. 4, 6	What artefacts are used in the practice? How are the artefacts used in practice? What visible and invisible work do they perform? In which way do they contribute to giving sense to the practice itself? What connections do they establish with other practices? What sort of things do they carry into and make present in the scenes of action? Which type of practical concerns or sense do artefacts convey to the actual practising? What is the intermediation work they perform?
Practical concerns	Chs. 5, 7	What are the mundane practical concerns which ostensibly orient the daily work of the practitioners? What matters to them? What do they care about? What do they worry about in practice? What do they see as their main object of activity? Where do they direct their efforts? What do they see as the thing to do next? When would they say the practice has been accomplished?
Tension between creativity and normativity	Chs. 2, 4, 6, 7	How are mundane breakdowns addressed? What are the main ways in which practitioners make themselves accountable in practice? What do they do? How do they talk about it? What discursive resources do they use to sustain the local regime of accountability? Where and how are the disputes between right and wrong played out? What are the contentious areas of the practice? Where are the main tensions? For example, are the tools and the practice actually aligned or are there conflicts and tensions between them? And what about the formal and informal rules? In which direction is the practice being stretched?
Processes of legitimation and stabilization	Chs. 3, 4, 8	How are novices socialized? What are they told? What stories are used in this process? Do the practitioners use the practice to identify themselves as a community? How is the difference between insiders and outsiders brought to bear? How are practices made durable? What doings, sayings, and artifacts are employed for the purpose?

routines or programmes. Practices only exist to the extent that they are enacted and re-enacted. Focusing on practices is thus taking the social and material doing (of something: doing is never objectless) as the main focus of the inquiry.

A critical consequence which stems from such a processual understanding of practices is that their study necessarily entails a preliminary focus on the mundane activities at hand. Thus, the study of practices always starts in the middle of action: 'In the beginning was the deed', as proclaimed by Goethe's Faustus. More clearly, I surmise that to study practice we need to start our investigation by zooming in on practices and approaching them as a know-ledgeable accomplishment. Attention should be towards issues such as: what are people doing and saying? What are they trying to do when they speak? What is said and done? How do the patterns of doing and saying flow in time? What temporal sequences do they conjure? With what effect? Through which moves, strategies, methods, and discursive practical devices do practitioners accomplish their work?

A first way to zoom in on the actual accomplishment of work practices is to draw on the wisdom, toolkit, and writing style of ethno-methodologically-inspired approaches. The tools and cumulative practical experience of organizational ethnography (Ybema *et al.* 2009), micro-ethnography (Streeck and Mehus 2004), and organizational ethno-methodology (Luff *et al.* 2000; Llewellyn 2008; Rawls 2008; Llewellyn and Hindmarsh 2009) are precious resources here. Their aim is not to penetrate or to expose the actors' value systems, relying instead mainly on the observation and description of conduct. In this way, focus shifts from individuals performing actions to the capacities or competencies necessary to perform membership in that practice, bringing activity centre stage. As we have seen in Chapters 6 and 8, the vast corpus of research stemming from the pioneering work of Harold Garfinkel and Harvey Sacks orients the zooming in distinct directions.

Ethno-methodology and ethno-methodologically-informed micro-ethnography helps us in particular to understand *and* describe practice as a publicly available accomplishment based on the situated assembling of a number of discursive and non-discursive practices. The underlying assumption here is that enumerating the resources that enter into this accomplishment, e.g. rules, formal descriptions, categories, narratives, technologies, and other artefacts, is not sufficient. Representing practice requires that we capture and convey the actual work that goes into any practice. Ethno-methodology and micro-ethnography directs us to reconstruct painfully the public and publicly accountable methods that practitioners use to assemble collaboratively and accomplish scenes of action.

Ethno-methodology and micro-ethnography also invite us to observe the interactional order that stems from, and supports, the accomplishment of a practice. The specific guiding themes for the researcher are, in this case: what sort of interactional order is performed by this specific practice? How do they differ from similar practices performed elsewhere? What positions does this specific practice make available? How are these positions negotiated or resisted? What type of collective interests are sustained and perpetuated by the specific practice? How are asymmetries and inequalities produced or reproduced in the process?

As we have seen in Chapter 4, in order to shed light on the sociality which revolves around practices, valuable insights can be especially reached if one manages to zoom in on the activity of novices, apprentices, and learners, by using, for instance, the ethnographic method of shadowing (Czarniawska 2008). By following practitioners, researchers can thus attain an insider's view of the patterns of relationship, the different perspectives among co-participants—who is who and who knows what—the interests at stake, and how these different perspectives, usually sustained by specific discourses, are worked together, aligned, or played against each other, so creating differential power positions in the field. By the same token, researchers can also identify who occupies the different positions made available by the activity, and appreciate the expectations and privileges that come with them.

A different focus for the zooming in is suggested by conversation analysis. This analytical tradition directs us, in fact, towards producing fine-grained sets of pragmatic propositions on the assumption that practice is mainly collabora-tively accomplished through discursive procedures. It also draws attention to sequence, and to the temporal dimension of the practising (see also the work of Bourdieu in Chapter 4). Knowing when and when not to do certain things, and knowing when to expect certain things and not others, are indeed defining characteristics that identify a competent member of the practice and the practice itself.

As I have discussed in Chapter 8, contemporary conversational analysis is both a resource for practice theorists (both in terms of analytical procedures and findings), and also a good example of how zooming in on practices can lead to what I have described above as an eliminativist position. The extreme level of granularity of the descriptions produced through the use of conversa-tion analytical methods comes, in fact, at a high cost. The use of coding and analytical procedures, such as those exemplified in the rolling case study of Chapter 8, while revealing increasing levels of detail, steer us away from the account of observable reportable practices. By following the literally exoteric procedures of conversational analysis, we end up in a realm where, for example, corrigibility by members becomes almost impossible because of the high technicality involved. This means that we are left with an account that is only 'logically empirical' (Lynch 1993). The extreme formalization prevents practitioners from understanding what is going on and from biting back. Hence, in some of the most extreme formulations, conversation analysis would fail Stengers' test.

It is for this reason that I am positing a toolkit approach. Rather than zooming in by magnifying, say, the (discursive) data in the attempt to make visible aspects that are not viewable from a distance, we can opt for a different strategy. For example, we can zoom in on *other* equally important aspects, such as the objects used in the practice and their performative role. Or we can switch theoretical lenses and focus on the fact that accomplishing a practice is never a detached process, and that practising is organized by a set of observable and reportable practical concerns. In both cases the zooming in is not obtained by putting the practice under an ideal microscope but rather by expanding the number of tools in our bag of tricks.

9.2.3 REPRESENTING PRACTICE THROUGH FOREGROUNDING THE ACTIVE ROLE OF TOOLS, MATERIALS, AND THE BODY

A different strategy for zooming in on and representing practice, in line with several of the theories discussed in Chapters 5 and 7, is thus to focus on the heterogeneous nature of practising. Representing practices without thematizing the landscape of tools, artefacts, and resources which enter their accomplishments, and asking what they do and how they make a difference would produce, in fact, an impoverished and lacking account. The accomplishment of a practice is, in fact, always attained thanks to both the mastery of skilled, human, embodied actors and the active contribution of a variety of tools, this even when we are alone

Zooming in on this critical aspect implies first taking note that practice is always involved with the lived-in body. As we have seen in Chapters 4, 5, and 7, practice often speaks through disciplined and habituated bodies. Zooming in should therefore be oriented towards observing and recording the bodily choreography that goes into accomplishing any practice. How is practice accomplished with the body, and through the body? How is the body shaped by the practice? How is the practice resisted or translated in the body? This way of zooming in is not in conflict with the one discussed above. The invitation here is to appreciate practice as a bodily *and* discursive choreography. Combining insights from Bourdieu (Chapter 3), Schatzki (Chapter 7), and those of ethno-methodology and micro-ethnography, makes us appreciate that practices have both a material and a discursive dimension, and that discursive and non-discursive aspects blend seamlessly: the saying is a way of doing as much as the doing is in what is said or not said. Listening, and not only watching, is thus a critical tool for practice scholars.

The body is, of course, only one of the ways in which materiality enters the accomplishment of a practice. Zooming in on practice therefore also requires investigating the active contribution of all other artefacts, as well as the ways in which these artefacts establish relationships between practices. For example, we can interrogate the scene of the practising by asking what active effects are produced by different artefacts. Attention is, in this case, on the material (a desk) and the symbolic (a document) tools used in accomplishing the practice. How do these artefacts contribute to the accomplishing? Are the tools and the practice actually aligned, or are there conflicts and tensions between them? How are the artefacts used in practice? In which way do they contribute to giving sense to the practice itself? What is the visible and invisible work that artefacts perform? What connection do they establish with other practices? Which type of practical concerns, or sense, do artefacts convey to the actual practising? What is the intermediation work they perform?

9.2.4 REPRESENTING PRACTICE THROUGH ZOOMING IN ON ITS ORIENTED AND CONCERNED NATURE

Zooming in on practice can also be pursued along further theoretical axes that do not adhere to the assumptions of micro-ethnography and ethno-methodology. For instance, we could put to work the intuition of the Heideggerian tradition examined in Chapter 7 that to practise means always to care, or to take care of, something. Practices are always oriented and they are performed in view of the accomplishment of the meaning and direction that they carry. For those who are involved in it, the accomplishment of a practice is experienced as being governed by a drive that is based on both the sense of what to do and what ought to be done. Zooming in would require, in this case, bringing forward and articulating the lived directionality and telos of the practice, and to appreciate the fact that such an orientation is perceived in both cognitive and moral terms, so that 'the force that governs [practices] is based on some conception of the good...the moral element is crucial...' (Thevenot 2001, p. 59). This can be achieved, for example, if we focus on the mundane practical concerns which ostensibly orient the daily work of the practitioners. What matters to them? What do they care about? What is their main practical concern when they go to work? What do they worry about in practice? What do they see as their main object of activity? Where do they direct their efforts?

Practical concerns are thus a way to describe the cogent way in which members experience the meaning and orientation performed by practices (something akin to Schatzki's teleo-affective structure in Chapter 7). My suggestion here comes close to one of the basic recommendations of CHAT discussed in Chapter 5, which suggests that to understand any form of social activity, we need to foreground the object of work around which it unfolds, given that it is the perceived object that bestows actions with continuity, coherence, and meaning. What the notion of practical concern adds to this idea is the need to describe how the object of work is experienced by participants in the practising. To articulate this aspect of practice we could make the most of the fact that practical concerns (and the object of work) are never held tacitly. On the contrary, they are customarily verbally addressed and discussed in the course of the practising, either through a vocabulary of motives and goals, or through a vocabulary of accounts, explanations, justifications, and prescriptions. By using the appropriate methods, we can thus capture and represent them in a reportable and corrigible way. For example, parts of the rolling case study in Chapter 7 were obtained by using a form of qualitative interview called 'the interview to the double'.[6] This is a technique that requires interviewees to imagine they have a double who will have to show up at their job the next day. The informant is then asked to provide the necessary detailed instructions that will insure that the plot is not unveiled and the double is not unmasked. Through this device, we can thus represent both the going concerns of the practitioners and the local lexicon of accountability that all members have to learn in order to produce conduct which is observable and reportable.

While the interview to the double is only one of many methods that could be used for this purpose, it is important to underscore that this zooming in does not try to access the values, beliefs, or presumed inner motives which supposedly guide the conduct of the practitioners. The aim of the zooming in is, on the contrary, to surface the practical concerns which govern and affect all participants, and a way to appreciate that from the perspective of the members, practice unfolds in terms of an often pre-verbally experienced, and yet collectively upheld, sense of 'what needs to be done'.

9.2.5 APPRECIATING PRACTICE AS BOUNDED CREATIVITY

A focus on the practical concerns that organize the accomplishment of practice also directs attention towards the dynamic between poiesis and the bounded-ness of practice—a further focus of the zooming in. While practices need to be achieved each time for the first time (Garfinkel 1967), so that practising is fundamentally a poietic and creative affair, not 'everything goes' in practice. Bounded-ness and poiesis co-exist in uneasy tension, as we have seen in Chapters 4 and 7.

The external boundaries of a practice, so to speak, are in fact dependent upon what people agree needs to be done and what can be rendered accountable. These boundaries are expressed and sustained discursively through a local repertoire (the content) and lexicon (the right way of asserting it) of accountability. The repertoire and lexicon of accountability, like other features, are learned by novices through their socialization. They establish discursively what is appropriate and what is not, what is admissible and what is not, what the correct style of practising is and what is not. What is not understood, or what is not acceptable, does not belong to the practice and therefore needs to be dropped.

A further focus for the zooming in is, therefore, the tension between repetition of the same and reproduction, what is indeterminate and what is bounded. Practice is indeterminate in that neither patients nor doctors behave in the same manner on any two occasions, and two telephone calls or meetings are never identical. Practising is therefore inherently and necessarily an act of poiesis, creation, invention, and improvisation, aimed at producing sameness with what is, by definition, different and changeable. Practices are literally re-produced on each novel occasion. At the same time, however, practising is also bounded. The sense established by the practice is a horizon which prevents us from seeing things differently. Analogously, the variety of ways in which we can creatively engage with the practical concerns set up by a practice is bounded by the limits imposed by the extant conditions and criteria of accountability.

The orientation, sense, and accountability of a practice are, of course, specific to each historically situated practice and are, thus, in continual evolution. This is because any assemblage of resources expresses and creates a set of practical concerns and, by making it possible, brings it about. However, even though these boundaries are continuously materially and discursively contested, debated, and moved, they are always there.

Accordingly, a further focus for the zooming in is the tension between the drive to fulfill a practice's perceived sense and the limits imposed by the extant conditions of accountability. We can focus on how orientation, accountability, and practical concerns conjure up the conditions of conduct by allowing practitioners to understand what is going on, what direction things ought to take, what is expected of them, and what is appropriate. Focus can also be directed towards the fact that these three aspects—orientation, accountability, and practical concerns—rarely co-exist in harmony, and tensions are common. In both cases, the goal is to represent practices as dynamic, contested, and provisional affairs.

9.2.6 REPRESENTING PRACTICE BY FOCUSING ON LEGITIMACY AND LEARNING

A final focus for the zooming in movement is provided by the consideration that a practice counts, as such, only for those who are capable of recognizing it. 'Recognizing' is intended here both in a cognitive and normative sense. I may fail to recognize a practice either because I have no idea about what is going on (a sensation we have all experienced as novices in a certain practice), or because I do not want it or cannot accept it (because 'we do things differently here'). In both cases, however, as suggested originally by Wittgenstein, the implication is that the notion of a private or arbitrary practice is a nonsense. Practices are, by definition, social because it is only at this level that morality, meaning, and normativity can be sustained. For this reason, I have omitted the qualification 'social' from the term 'practice' in this book. The term 'social practice' says the same thing twice.

From the above it follows that all practices imply some level of durability and, in this sense, they carry traces, no matter how weak, of institutionalization. Practices differ from events in that they constitute enduring regimes of activity. As I noted before, this does not imply that practices are necessarily only replicated. In fact, the contrary applies, and practice continuously changes, expands, and evolves. Therefore, the question for organizational scholars should not be 'do practices change?' Instead, the question is the opposite—'through which mechanisms does practice achieve durability in time?'

It is my contention that to understand the durability and perpetuation of practices we should zoom in on at least four main aspects: learning, mediation, other people, and other practices.

Firstly, one can observe that methods for accomplishing practice, its orientation, and normative force, need to be learned. The sense and meaning of a practice are acquired in the social process through which novices become progressively proficient practitioners. It follows that if we are to provide a convincing account of both how ingrained ways of doing and saying persist in time, and why people stick to them, we need to zoom in on learning. Without a coherent theory of learning, we are left with an obscure notion of practice as a hidden and metaphysical collective object that exerts some form of causal power over the behaviour of individuals.[7] As Jean Lave once put it,[8] without such an element, any account of practice is bound to collapse, 'like a table without a leg'. Shadowing novices is a particularly useful exercise in this sense. Senior members often feel a moral duty to explain, illustrate, and teach features of the current practice to novices. In so doing, they pry open the logic of the practice, something that a researcher can appreciate. At the same time, by observing the unfolding of the socialization process, investigators can learn the specific ways of seeing, talking, and feeling that make a person a member of that specific practice.

Secondly, practices are perpetuated and made durable by people who come to share similar skills, practical concerns, and ways of making themselves accountable. This concept could be expressed by the idea that all practices are sustained by a community (Lave and Wenger 1991), as long as we agree that it is the practice which generates the social relations which emerge around it and not vice versa. Practice always generates sociality, but whether it also gives rise to recognizable and self-aware communities is dependent on local historical conditions. What is more important, however, is that the nature of the practical concerns and the boundary of the legitimate practices are continuously tested and contested within the social circle created by the joint endeavour. Questions of what is appropriate, what is legitimate, and what can be done are continuously tested in action so that practice is necessarily provisional and tied to specific historical and material conditions.

Thirdly, we can focus on the fact that the durability of practices derives from the tools and instruments that mediate it (see above). Tools and artefacts carry the script their designers embodied into them, and for this reason they convey a particular culture of action. As a result, cultural artefacts constitute a means of transmission of social knowledge by carrying inscribed within them objectified norms of cognition, assumptions about how work should be carried out, and the purposes of their use. These all participate as formative elements in the practice itself (Miettinen 1999). Tools mediate a historical and social dimension into the accomplishment of any practices. This renders every practice, even the most apparently solitary, a highly social and historical matter.

Finally, we can focus on the fact that the durability of practices is partly an effect of one practice becoming a resource in the accomplishment of other practices. Once it becomes part of a larger configuration, a practice is expected to be reproduced as a matter of course in order to contribute to the whole of which it is part. I will return to this idea shortly, but it is clear that zooming in on practice is also a way to focus on connections and relationships between practices.

To sum up, representing and understanding practice requires, among other things, that we zoom in on the patterns of relationships among human individuals, and how such patterns are learned and made durable. If, on the one hand, this requires that we focus on the learned and mediated nature of practice, on the other, it points out that practice always occurs amid a texture of other interconnected practices that, while making possible the practice under scrutiny, also keep it in place. Attention is thus diverted from the practice itself to the texture of connection in which it is immersed. In turn, this type of attention requires that we widen our angle and zoom out to consider the field in which practices are carried out.

9.3 **Zooming out by trailing practices and their connections**

Examining in detail the local production of accountable and meaningful order through zooming in is only part of the job of studying, understanding, and representing practice.

Activities, in fact, never happen in isolation, and to a large extent they cannot be carried out independently of other practices. In the rolling case study, for example, it appears that the local accomplishment of telemedicine depends on the work and practices that take place outside, beyond, and before the scene of action immediately observable through the zooming. Making telemedicine happen cannot be fully understood if we limit our attention to the actions and relationships between nurses, patients, and their local ecology of artefacts and devices. Telemedicine in fact also builds upon the work and skilled practice of the makers of the electronic device for transmitting the ECG; the work of the manufacturers of the computer used by the nurses; the work of the people in the lab who conduct the tests patients have to carry out before telephoning the centre; the work of the managers running the institution where the nurses are based; the work of the regional health service that provides funding for the service to take place, all the way down to the work and practices of the local phone company and power station operatives. Of course, the converse is also true, and the practice of telemedicine contributes, in turn, to the activity of the hospital where employees of the phone company and power station go when they are ill. The practice also participates in the perpetuation of the discipline of cardiology that develops the protocols used by the nurses and, together with innumerable other practices, participates in making up what we call the Italian healthcare system.

In a sense, then, all practices are involved in a variety of relationships and associations that extend in both space and time, and form a gigantic, intricate, and evolving texture of dependencies and references. Paraphrasing Latour (2005, p. 44; see also Schatzki 2002), we can state that practice is always a node, a knot, and a conglomerate of many types of material and human agencies that have to be patiently untangled. For this reason, the study of practices cannot be limited to focusing on the details of their accomplishment, and requires instead that we also strive to appreciate how the local activity is affected by other practices; how other practices are affected or constrained or enabled by the practice under consideration; and what are the material consequences of such relationships. In other words, practices can only be studied *relationally*, and they can only be understood as part of a nexus of connections. In order to understand what happens here and now we also need to understand what happens somewhere else—next door, or much further afield. Accordingly, there is a need to integrate and alternate the zooming in movement described above with one which is horizon-widening and that, in accordance with the idea of zooming in, I would describe as zooming out of the texture of practice.[9] Zooming out of practice thus requires moving between practice in the making and the texture of practices which causally connect this particular instance to many others. This can be achieved if we develop sufficient conceptual lenses and methodological devices to describe the ways in which practices are associated, from living assemblages, and produce effects and phenomena—

from healthy patients to organized life, hierarchical and power inequalities, and institutions.

9.3.1 A PALETTE FOR ZOOMING OUT

The zooming out of the texture of practice requires patiently following the trails of connections between practices; observing how these connections come to form entrenched nexuses or nets; how such nets of action produce effects; how such overarching or global practice nets manifest themselves in the local practising; and how 'local' performances are in part constituted through distant flows and motilities.

This, in turn, can be achieved if we focus attention on the following:

- What are the connections between the 'here and now' of the practising and the 'then and there' of other practices? Which other practices affect, enable, constrain, conflict, and interfere, etc., with the practice under consideration? How are configurations, assemblages, bundles, and confederations of practices kept together?
- How does the practice under consideration contribute to the 'wider picture'? In which ways does the practice reproduce existing social arrangements or generate tension and conflict? How do different arrangements of practice establish the social world of interactions, scenes of action, organizations, and institutions in which we live? What worlds do they conjure for the practitioners?
- How did we get to where we are? What are the interests, projects, hopes, and manoeuvres, etc., that led us to the current state of affairs? How could the world be otherwise?

My suggested theoretical and methodological references for zooming out on practices are those of the sociology of translation and actor-network theory (Latour 2005; Czarniawska 2007; Law 2009). Although Latour and his followers cannot be considered practice theorists, they have collectively developed a sophisticated set of concepts and methodological recommendations that deal effectively with the spatiotemporal 'distributedness of ontological relations' and the consequent 'dislocation of action' (Oppenheim 2007, p. 477). These recommendations mostly centre around the injunction to follow the actors, tracing analytically the work that goes into making associations come about, and observing the effect produced by the ensuing socio-technical arrangement. The investigation can follow a compositional or decompositional strategy: following the actors can thus literally mean shadowing human or non-human actors, and observing their daily activity of weaving connections (Czarniawska 2007), or alternatively, it may mean retracing the steps, strategies, and events that led to the emergence, stabilization, or failure of specific assemblages using historical methods (Latour 2005). My tenet here, based on the principle that practice theory and actor-network theory also share a number of family resemblances, is that these concepts and methodological recommendations can be equally employed to investigate the connectedness of practices.

Following the associations between practices

Zooming out of practice to reveal and articulate its interconnected nature requires that we start with an empirical trailing of practices and their connections. Sensitizing questions here include, but are not limited to, how is the practice under consideration causally and materially connected with other practices? Which other practices affect, enable, constrain, conflict, interfere, etc., with the practice under consideration?

This initial zooming out, in turn, requires two basic moves. Firstly, we need to uncover the connections between practices by following them in space and time. Secondly, we need to study how these connections are kept in place. Only then we can start shedding light on their mutual effects, enablement, and interdependencies.

The first move (following the practice) can be accomplished using the methods and approaches of multi-site and focused ethnography (Marcus 1995; Hannerz 2003; Knoblauch 2005) or other techniques suitable to do field work on the move, such as shadowing, log studies, and diaries (Czarniawska 2007). Although these methods were originally developed to follow human and non-human actors, my experience is that they can be successfully extended to the study of practices. We can thus shadow the practice, extending our observation to the different places where it shows up. The basic move here is to follow its intermediaries (people, artefacts, and inscriptions) wherever they go. This implies, for instance, following telemedicine patients through their clinical trajectories (Strauss and Glaser 1975) from the moment they are enrolled into the service until they are discharged, or following the tele-nurses through their professional apprenticeship. It would also require, for example, attending conferences, meetings, and gatherings where the practice is debated; attending policy-making forums where the practice is taken into consideration and sanctioned; reading the scientific and clinical literature where the practice is legitimized; travelling to other hospitals where the practice is adopted; and so on.

The second move requires that we investigate how associations are kept in place. The infra-language of the sociology of translation is again very useful,[10] although other tricks in the practice bag can also come to the rescue here. The concept of translation describes, in fact, 'a relationship that does not transport causality but induces two mediators to co-exist' (Latour 2005, p. 108). The idea of translation invites us to appreciate that associations need to be 'knotted' and kept actively in place through the coordination of humans and non-human mediators such as forms, software, policy documents, plans, contracts, and spaces. Only when all these resources are aligned to form chains of translation in such a way that the results of an activity are stabilized and turned into a more or less solid black box, can effecting the activity of another practice be accomplished. The idea of translation also helps to shed light on how local and distant practices are connected in space and time, thus forming dynamic nexuses of connections. On many occasions, the mechanisms that keep distant practices together are the same that work locally. Discursive practices, plans, rules, contracts, and also ideologies and dreams all help in aligning dispersed practices into vast nexuses. Distant practices are also kept together through uninterrupted chains of translation whereby relationships of mutual interest and interdependencies are negotiated between practices. Finally, practices can also travel and be tentatively reproduced elsewhere in time and space without any sort of 'direct' contact. For this to happen, they must first be disembodied and materialized into mediators (objects such as texts, representations, or prototypes). Second, the mediators travel through time and space. Third, the practice is somewhat retranslated into a new locale in view of the new contextual conditions (Czarniawska 2000).[11]

Interestingly enough, while the sociology of translation is full of suggestions as to how to explain the durability of the connections between actions, it is silent or rather narrow-minded when it comes to explain the motives for knotting practices together in the first place. Most actor-network theory authors assume, in fact, that interests—which often translate as 'will to power'—is what cements practices and motivates practitioners. Contra this bleak, or simply restricted view, practice theories offer an alternative and wider range of mechanisms starting with the critical concept of the object of activity discussed in Chapter 5, and Schatzki's teleo-affective structure discussed in Chapter 7.[12] Accordingly, studying how practices are connected cannot be seperated from the understanding of what the object of work is, its practical concerns, and the underlying telos of the practice.[13]

Zooming out by studying the effects brought to bear by the associations between practices

A second and related way of zooming out is to focus on the local and trans-local effects produced by chains and assemblages of situated practices—what I call practice networks and Czarniawska (2004) described as 'action nets'. The interest here is on the types of opportunities for action that the association between practices conjures for those who live at their intersection. The guiding questions here are: where and how are the effects of the practice under consideration being felt? How are the results of the practice used in other contexts? How are the results of the practice used in other contexts? By whom?

In which conditions? What are the mutual dependencies? What are their implications? How does the practice under consideration contribute to other close or distant states of affairs? What types of actions and interactional pattern do the combined practices make available for the practitioners? What type of 'identity' do they conjure for the participants? In which ways does the practice reproduce existing social arrangements or generate tension and conflict?

The example of telemedicine used in the rolling case study is again a good case in point. The star-shaped practice of caring for patients at a distance through skilled phone contacts performs, or more precisely contributes to, the performance of a variety of effects that range from promoting the organizational legitimacy of its proponents (they had acted as institutional entrepreneurs and were now cashing in on their return in social capital), to modifying the relationships between nurses and doctors (nurses and patients became much more proactive and autonomous), to reconfiguring the provision of care (cardiology assistance could be now delivered from a distance to patients who were not physically present).

Trailing the effects of the practice also brought to light other, less obvious effects. Through shadowing the personnel of the telemedicine service and discussing with family doctors, it emerged that the nature of the tele-care process not only rendered the patients more active and autonomous; it also tended to marginalize family doctors and other community healthcare practitioners. Because telemedicine established a direct relationship between the patients and specialized providers which might be far away from their communities, there is a risk that the telemonitoring service becomes a 'closed environment' which cuts out the general practice from the loop, first in terms of decision-making and, later (possibly), in terms of the flow of resources. This in turn could generate all sorts of ripple effects for the broader arrangement of an Italian healthcare system which is currently clearly divided into primary and secondary care. Although no single local practice can trigger such radical changes, it is possible (at least in principle) to describe and understand large-scale changes in terms of a shift in the overall nexus of connected (healthcare) practices.

The examples help highlight why zooming out is fundamental for gaining an in-depth understanding of practice. From the vantage point of observing, say, a video recorded scene of action, a practitioner one can only appreciate the activity as it happens and its immediate horizon of concern. One cannot 'see' the many ways in which the practice produces effects in the world or the mutual dependencies and constraints that conjure the lived world of the practitioner at the point of action. As many of the authors surveyed in this volume often observe, in fact, practice manifests itself inexorably to the practitioner at the point of action, and the machinations that conjure one particular opportunity of action (or understanding or feeling) over others remains largely invisible. A perception of the 'wider picture' can only be achieved if we expand our 'hermeneutic circle'[14] in space and time by changing conceptual lenses and moving in the field. Such a 'wider picture' is not, however, a mysterious entity or a metaphysical being that acts in the world over and above the head of practitioners. What I call 'the wider picture' amounts to nothing more and nothing less than an understanding of the association between practices and how they are kept together through the mechanism described above. It is for this reason that I use here the expression 'wider picture' instead of, say, 'context'. Studying 'context' from a practice perspective implies, in fact, studying analytically and processually how different practices are associates, and what are the practical implications of their relationships for the practice at hand. I use the terms 'analytically' and 'processually' because the reference to context as an explanatory factor is often a sign of bad or lazy social science. Too often, in fact, the notion of context (just like the ideas of system, structure and the like) is used as a shortcut and substitute for a more detailed analysis of how the conditions for actions came about. In this sense, the notion of context plays an eliminativist role, and as such it should be avoided or used extremely cautiously by those interested in a practice-based approach. In the case of telemedicine, for example, as soon as we widen our analytical gaze, we start to appreciate that the practice at hand is implicated in a number of such things as the definition of the identity of what counts as a good patient and a skilled nurse, the health politics of the region where the telemedicine centre is based, and the conceptions of what a public health system may look like.

A useful methodological strategy to bring to the surface the effects produced by different nexuses of practice consists in identifying and comparing different sites where the same practice is carried out. Analyzing side by side the performance of the same practice in two or more locales and/or times provides important data, as it shows how very different meanings can be attributed to the same practice when the relationship with their practices change, thus producing different effects and consequences.

In the study behind the rolling case study, for instance, I identified two medical centres that were using variants of the same practice. By moving among these sites, I was able to document the capacity of different practices to perform quite different professional identities and power effects. For example, whereas at on one site, nurses managed medicines, made life-saving decisions, and were freely discussing clinical issues with doctors, the work which nurses carried out in the other site I observed was largely of a secretarial nature. The two practices produced 'nurses' who were significantly different, at least with respect to their level of competence and autonomy. Following and comparing different ways of carrying out the same activity helped to document that, far from being neutral, all practices, even minute ones, constitute identities and sustain hierarchical power relationships. The research illustrated how the unequal landscape of power that one can observe, e.g. in hospitals, can be conceived and described in terms of effects on the texture of the local practising that takes place daily in the specific site and in all the others connected with it.

9.3.2 HOW PRACTICE AND THEIR ASSOCIATIONS CAN ACT AT A DISTANCE

A further requirement of the zooming out is to explain how local practices can act at a distance and produce effects in different places and distant times, how they can contribute to an even 'wider picture' and, conversely, how events and phenomena that take place in distant places (and times) manifest through the actual local practice. This is, of course, a critical step in order to avoid the trap of localism (see Chapter 6 for a discussion) or its equally unpalatable alternative; that is, the need to invent mysterious metaphysical entities (collective conscience, culture, social representation, genes, and the traditional paraphernalia of realists at all times) to explain regularities and patterns in our daily commerce with the world. As before, in order to study empirically this dimension of the connectedness of practice, we can employ the theoretical and methodological toolkit of the sociology of translation. The theory provides, in fact, an interesting explanation for the ways in which effects are translated in time and space. It does so by noting that mediators, which include boundary objects, names, protocols, plans, forms of categorization, and rules do not only support the association between practices. They also move it around, acting as generalizers and localizers (Latour 2005, p. 181). As generalizers, mediators summarize and record the inherent multiplicity of practices, making them available as an object of work in another context. Human experts 'summarize' years of learning by doing, and artefacts record the work and knowledgeability of all those who designed and built it. Through generalizing mediators, large associations of practising can become objects of work of other, equally local and equally socio-material practices. It is through the mediatory work of these generalizers that local practices come to form what social scientists often describe as macro phenomena. Macro phenomena boil down to a complex texture of doings and sayings (meetings, conversations, debates, disputes), places (labs, offices), and objects (buildings, documents), which can all be observed proximally. Please note that this is also the crux of management. Managers are not omniscient and, of course, they cannot be everywhere at all times. They are finite people whose day job involves aligning black-boxed practices. From an articulative perspective, then, all social matters happen in a specific place and time, and macro or higher level phenomena are just another way of referring to the locales and the effects of people trading in generalizers. Chairing a large multinational corporation does not require supernatural powers. Managers simply trade in generalizers.

Mediators can also act as localizers. In this role mediators act as a gateway through which large and stabilized practice nets make themselves present in the local practising. Laws, rules, and recipes all work in this way. They translate in a specific local instance, the previous work, power, and legitimacy of existing practice nets. The notions of 'generalizer' and 'localizer' thus suggest that translation operates as two-way traffic. Just as the global can be explained as a nexus of locality, the local is itself fragmented and multiplied, a node in a complex nexus of actions that enter into it and that traverse it. Practice (including the practice of organizing) is the result of this complex interplay between local and global.

9.3.3 HOW DID WE GET HERE?

Until now, I described zooming out very much as an exercise of expanding our hermeneutical look in space following practices and their intermediaries. The real-time shadowing of the practice, however, should be integrated with a study of its emergence and evolution. As suggested by CHAT authors, an historical analysis allows us to build an appreciation of the unfolding material and political conditions that surrounded the birth of telemedicine and how these were inscribed in its current form (Engeström *et al.* 1999). The questions here are: how did we get to where we are? Why did things turn out the way they are and not differently? What were the interests, projects, hopes, manoeuvres, etc., that led us to the current state of affairs?

By shedding light on the power relations that determined the current state of affairs, a historical investigation provides vital clues to the type of power relations and interests that are inscribed in the current practice. This information is critical for those who are interested in changing (or perpetuating) the status quo. As I have shown elsewhere, for example, the particular way of practising telemonitoring used in my above examples emerged as the result of the incremental alignment of different interests over a period of several years, many of which left documentable traces (see Nicolini 2010 for an extensive discussion). By zooming out and combining real-time shadowing and historical reconstruction, we can thus start to build an appreciation of how local practices participate in larger configurations and how they enter as elements, ingredients, or resources in other activities.

In sum, by zooming out and trailing effects through their mediators (both generalizers and localizers), we can foreground and document how practices extend beyond the scope of the local set of practical concerns, so that locally accomplished practices become variably implicated in a variety of states of affairs which, in turn, may happen far from where the practising takes place. Local practices thus become a convenient starting point and a building block for explaining not only the local production of organized action and interaction, but also larger, more complex trans-local phenomena, such as the existence and functioning (the 'organization') of a ward, a hospital, or a health authority, without contradicting the fundamental notion that practice is an oriented and concerned matter. By using empirical methods such as shadowing and historical analysis, and by employing notions such as 'translation' and 'practice network', we can therefore extend our articulative and practice-based investigation well beyond the accomplishment of practice and into the realm of the translocal and durable. Practice becomes, in this way, a convenient and usable ontological unit for making sense of a variety of organizational phenomena, from the existence of local forms of coordination to complex organizational arrangements such as large corporations, multinational firms, and other highly-institutionalized forms such as markets (Knorr-Cetina 2004); all without having to forfeit the idea that it is practices all the way down.

9.3.4 WHEN TO STOP THE ZOOMING IN AND OUT?

Relevant questions at this point are how to start the processes of zooming in and out, and when to stop. As concerns the first issue, my discussion above suggests that for investigating practice one must always start by zooming in through immersion in the action. Only once the actual local accomplishment of a real-time practice is appreciated 'from within', so to speak, can one proceed to zoom out by making sense of the data collected, identifying connections, and trailing them. I would like to add that while the image of zooming in and out conjures up the image of an orderly and reiterative sequence, the reality of rhizomatic research is quite different. Very soon, in fact, instead of alternating between zooming in and out, the ethnographer finds herself handling multiple studies at the same time, each at different stages of the research (access, preliminary observation, in-depth observation), and each focusing on phenomena characterized by different temporalities (i.e. events, such as a phone call or the approval of new legislation, can take minutes or months to unfold). In the telemedicine research, for example, once I started to follow the practice I found myself carrying out observations in three different places (the telemedicine centre, the emergency room where all the nurses had worked before, and a second telemedicine centre), alternating more or less extensive periods of observation at each site. As these observations had different purposes, and were hence carried out with different intensity and duration, I soon found myself summarizing the results of one while continuing to work on others (observation in the telemedicine centre continued on and off for three years), and negotiating access to yet another one.

While the nature of the approach and the necessity of carrying out several parallel mini-projects makes each project unique and idiosyncratic, one aspect that stands out clearly is that the process is not linear. Contrary to descriptions of research which suggest an orderly progression from observation to interpretation of data and writing up, the rhizomatic character of the study design requires that the ethnographer goes through multiple cycles of observation, analysis, and reflection.

This leads us nicely to the second question. That is, when to stop the zooming out. The answer here is mainly practical, and requires striking a balance between two types of considerations. On the one hand, the aim of the zooming out is documenting and representing the texture of connections between practices. In this sense, the more we extend the zooming out in space and time, the better. On the other hand, the 'more is better' principle, which is often fed by the well-known anxiety of not having collected enough field data, is moderated by the constraints posed by the circumstances of the research, which can quickly spiral out of control in terms of number of sites and foci of attention. A sensible lower limit for the zooming out is the capacity for providing a convincing explanation of why the practising is the way it is, and not otherwise, and to document how the local practice connects with non-local effects. In my examples above, the connection is that which links the local practising of telemedicine with the policy-making process. The effects included the emergence of a new type of direct and protracted relationship between patients, and a secondary acute care establishment (which potentially subverts the very distinction between primary, secondary, and acute care), and the possible sidelining of the family doctor. My claim, then, is that the minimal unit of analysis and description for the ethnographic study of practice is not only the performance of a real-time activity in one specific time and place, nor the ethno-methods that are used to accomplish it. Studying practice also requires appreciating the texture of material relationships and other practices on which the practice depends and which it sustains. Alternatively put, the object of the package of method and theory to study work practices presented here is necessarily a practice net, a bundle of practices, and their causal and historical connections.

9.4 **The benefits and perils of the zooming metaphor**

To summarize the sections above, the practical and theoretical movement that I am suggesting to study practice is rhizomatic in nature. A rhizome is a form of 'bulb' that extends its roots in different directions. Every root extension forms a new small plant that, when matured, extends new roots and continues the spread. In a similar fashion, I propose that studying practices starts in one place with an in-depth study of that specific location and then spreads following emerging connections. These connections lead to other practices, which become in turn the target of a new round of zooming in. The study of practice thus starts with the zooming in movement to understand how the activity is accomplished in one site. It proceeds with a zooming out movement which exposes the relationships between practices, and continues with a new effort of zooming in on the new site, and so on. The goal of this recursive and alternating movement is to build an appreciation of why the practice is practised in the way it is, how it came to be this way, why it is not different, what are the consequences and effects that this state of affairs produces on the world at large, and what is different and who is empowered or disempowered in the process.

Implicit in the idea of zooming in and out, is that studying practice requires choosing different angles for observation and interpretation frameworks, without necessarily giving prominence to any one of these vistas. My effort is, therefore, one of sequential selective repositioning. It follows that both the strength and originality of my contribution stems largely from the attempt to combine existing insights, rather than introducing a totally new approach. I am in search of an eclectic set of sensitizing concepts that allow different features of practices and their associations to come to the fore while others are suspended. The zooming movement through which I propose to represent practice is achieved, in fact, by switching theoretical lenses and trailing connections according to a set of specific assumptions. The act of zooming in and out should be interpreted as foregrounding and backgrounding boundaries in the programmatic attempt to make more complex practice against all types of reductionism.

Like all other metaphors, the idea of zooming in and out is open to misunderstandings and betrayal. It is therefore also worth mentioning in passing some of the perils of the idea of zooming, and what the zooming is not. Firstly, as Latour (2005) aptly notes, the idea of zooming risks introducing the idea that the world is organized according to neatly arranged micro, meso, and macro levels that can be peeled like layers of an onion. This is, of course, contrary to what I am after here. In my view, the idea of zooming should be interpreted as an encouragement to appreciate and expose the connectedness of practices by patiently expanding the hermeneutic circle. Secondly, and strictly related, the visual idea of zooming risks introducing the idea that it is possible to provide a view of the social world from 'nowhere'. This is fundamentally contrary to my view. Zooming on practices can only be achieved by trailing connections on the ground, following people and artefacts as they move, chasing them wherever they go. Zooming is thus about moving around and amid practices, not hovering above them. Finally, zooming may well be the wrong metaphor altogether. As noted by Jim Taylor,[15] natural vision does not involve zooming: the eye spontaneously leaps from close-up to medium vision to long vision. For this reason, zooming is used rather sparingly by professionals. Zooming in, in fact, draws attention to the camera; in so doing, it distracts the viewer from treating the camera's presence as transparent and interferes with the attempt by the cameraman and director to create the illusion for the viewer of just seeing the scene. So 'zooming' may be the wrong word for what I am trying to do here, and its use may be just due to poor imagination and the lack of a better way to describe my praxaeological attempt to appreciate, investigate, and write talk about the connectedness, interdependence, and mutual imbrication of practices (Taylor and Van Every 2011).

9.5 **Where next**

In this chapter I have proposed a package of theory and method that connotes the study of practice in terms of patient, craft-like, and necessarily time-consuming articulative work of getting close to the practice and the practitioners, identifying connections and exploring relationships. The aim is to generate images of organizations, organizational life, and sociality as a contingent and ever-changing texture of human practices. The ambition and hope is to increase our understanding of the fragmented, distributed, and fast-moving reality of late-modern post-bureaucratic organizations, enabling us to come to grips with phenomena such as distant work, virtual organization, multiple memberships, and other fluid ways of organizing that other more traditional theoretical and methodological toolkits are increasingly incapable of capturing.

In spite of building on the shoulders of giants, practice theory is still in its infancy and whether it will ever become a powerful bandwagon[16] is yet to be determined. Most importantly, the practice approach is still largely untested. As suggested by Latour (see note 5), the proof of the approach will be in the capacity of future texts to represent practice in a rich and insightful way. Therefore, the way forward is, first and foremost, to develop the approach by using it. As suggested in the introduction, one of the features that practice theory shares with other strongly processual approaches is that it turns every phenomenon (both social and 'non-social') into a potential object of inquiry. The challenge is thus to put the toolkit to the test in different empirical settings, and taste what the pudding is like. At the same time, further enrolment and use is likely to modify the shape and composition of the toolkit. What I suggest here is, in fact, certainly open to further development and experimentation. The sensitizing concepts presented above here are, in fact, meant to be just that—suggestions. They are not cast in stone, and they are not meant to be applied formulaically. The second way forward is, therefore, to appropriate the toolkit, and adopt and adapt it, and possibly betray it, in an attempt to produce convincing, coherent representations of a world of practices. The exercise is, of course, not inconsequential as it is not true that in social science, everything goes. As Latour (2005, p. 159) reminds us, to the extent that our texts are the functional equivalent of a laboratory and the place for trials, experiments, and simulations, they are also the potential site for failures and delusion. Yet the subtle pleasure of constructing worlds, not unlike in mathematics, is part of what makes social theory such a exhilarating endeavour. So my last words are: give it a go and enjoy responsibly!

■ NOTES

1. The idea was introduced by Wittgenstein who suggested that things such as games do not share one essential common feature and are, in fact, connected by a series of overlapping similarities. It follows that there is no such thing as a feature common to all games, although we recognize games on the basis of their family resemblances which he defined as a 'complicated network of similarities, overlapping and criss-crossing' (Wittgenstein 1953, §66).
2. Here is where Stengers' criteria start to differ drastically from Popper's falsificationism.
3. I am paraphrasing Geertz's story about an Englishman who, having been told by an Indian man that the world rested on a platform, which rested on the back of an elephant, which in turn rested on the back of a turtle, was asked what the turtle rested on. 'Another turtle', was the response. 'And that turtle?' rebuked the Englishman 'Aha, Sahib', said the Indian, 'after that it is turtles all the way down' (Geertz 1973).
4. It follows that practice theorists are necessarily either empirically oriented philosophers or socially savvy philosophers. A quick review of the authors surveyed in the text will illustrate what I mean.
5. Latour's words here are, 'Depending on what happens in it, there is or there is not an actor and there is or there is not a network being traced'. I intentionally substituted the words 'actor' and 'network' with 'practice', as I believe that Latour's observation applies to any topic of social science.
6. See Gherardi (1995) and especially Nicolini (2009a) for an in-depth discussion.
7. See Turner (1984) for a discussion. Turner has the merit of raising this important issue, but then, by bundling all the practice theories together, he ends up 'throwing the baby out with the bath water'.
8. Jean Lave made this remark during a presentation in Manchester in 1999.
9. CHAT authors evoke a similar idea when they suggest that practices cannot be understood in isolation and that the appropriate primary unit of analysis to understand human affairs is, in fact, 'a historically evolving collective activity system, seen in its network relations to other activity systems' (Engeström 2000, p. 964).
10. According to Latour (2005), it constitutes an infra-language in that it sets the scene for a performative material way of doing social science without, however, defining *ex-ante* the characters who will play on it.
11. How the knotting and translation are actually performed is a matter of empirical study. Although it has become customary to refer to Callon's sequence of 'problematisation, interessement, enrollment and mobilization' (Callon 1986), there is a risk that the model itself becomes an eliminativist device. While undoubtedly useful, the 'problematisation, interessement, enrollment and mobilization' model is only a template and there is a real risk that it ends up hiding, instead of surfacing, interesting empirical phenomena.

12. While a comparison between these concepts goes well beyond the scope of the present work, it is apparent that we are better served by adding potential focuses for the inquiry—hence my call for an eclectic approach.
13. As we have seen in Chpater 5, the two often do not coincide.
14. The idea of hermeneutic circle refers to the movement back and forth between the parts and the whole that allows one to grasp the meaning of a text. For many hermeneutic scholars, the circle must go beyond the here and there of the text, and include the text's relationship to historical tradition and culture at large.
15. Personal communication.
16. Unlike Corradi *et al.* (2010), who have already declared the bandwagon of practice to be already well on its way, I still see only a very small carriage in need of more and bigger allies.

▨ BIBLIOGRAPHY

Ahrens, T. and Chapman, C. S. (2007). Management accounting as practice. *Accounting, Organizations and Society*, 32(1), 1–27.

Alvesson, M. and Karreman, D. (2000). Varieties of discourse: on the study of organizations through discourse analysis. *Human Relations*, 53, 1125–49.

Anderson, J. R. (1983). A Spreading Activation Theory of Memory. *Journal of Verbal Learning and Verbal Behavior*, 22(3), 261–95.

Andrew, E. (1975). A note on the unity of theory and practice in Marx and Nietzsche. *Political Theory*, 3(3), 305–16.

Anthony, R. N. (1967). *Planning and Control Systems: A Framework for Analysis*. Boston: Harvard Business School Press.

Aristotle (2004). *The Nicomachean ethics* (Rev. edn.). London: Penguin Books.

Atkinson, J. and Heritage, J. (1984). *Structures of Social Action (Studies in Conversation Analysis)*. Cambridge: Cambridge University Press.

Austin, J. L. (1962). *How to do things with words: the William James lectures delivered at Harvard University in 1955*. Oxford: Clarendon Press.

Avis, J. (2007). Engeström's version of Activity Theory: a conservative praxis? *Journal of Education and Work*, 20(3), 161–77.

Barad, K. (2003). Posthumanist performativity: Toward an understanding of how matter comes to matter. *Signs*, 28(3), 801–31.

Barad, K. (2007). *Meeting the Universe Halfway: Quantum Physics and the Entanglement of Matter and Meaning*. Durham: Duke University Press.

Barley, S. R. (1986). Technology as an occasion for structuring: evidence from observation of CT scanners and the social order of radiology departments. *Administrative Science Quarterly*, 31(1), 78–108.

Barley, S. R. and Kunda, G. (2001). Bringing work back in. *Organization Science*, 12(1), 76–95.

Barley, S. R. and Orr, J. E. (1997). *Between Craft and Science: Technical Settings in U.S. Settings*. London: ILR Press.

Barlow, J., Bayer, S., and Curry, R. (2006). Implementing complex innovations in fluid multi-stakeholder environments: experiences of 'telecare'. *Technovation*, 26(3), 396–406.

Barnes, B. (2001). Practice as collective action. In T. R. Schatzki, K. Knorr-Cetina and E. v. Savigny (eds.), *The practice turn in contemporary theory*. London: Routledge, 17–28.

Battilana, J. (2006). Agency and institutions: The enabling role of individuals' social position. *Organization*, 13(5), 653–76.

Bauman, Z. (1972). *Culture as praxis*. London: Routledge and Kegan Paul.

Bauman, Z. (1992). Legislators and Interpreters: Culture as the Ideology of Intellectuals. In Z. Bauman (ed.), *Intimations of Postmodernity*. London: Routledge, 1–25.

Becker, H. S. (1963). *Outsiders: studies in the sociology of deviance*. London: Free Press of Glencoe.

Berard, T. J. (2005). Rethinking practices and structures. *Philosophy of the Social Sciences*, 35(2), 196–230.

Bernstein, B. (1975). Class and Pedagogies: Visible and Invisible. In B. Bernstein (ed.), *Studies in the Learning Science*. Paris: O.E.C.D.

Bittner, E. (1967). The police on skid row: A study of peace keeping. *American Sociological Review*, 32(5), 699–715.

Blackler, F. (1993). Knowledge and the Theory of Organizations: Organizations as Activity Systems and the Reframing of Management. *Journal of Management Studies*, 30(6), 864–84.

Blackler, F. (1995). Knowledge, knowledge work and organizations: An overview and interpretation. *Organization Studies*, 16(6), 1021–46.

Blackler, F., Crump, N., and McDonald, S. (2000). Organizing processes in complex activity networks. *Organization*, 7(2), 277–300.

Blackler, F. H. and Regan, S. (2006). Institutional reform and the reorganisation of family support services. *Organization Studies*, 27(12), 1843–61.

Blackler, F. and Regan, S. (2009). Intentionality, agency, change: practice theory and management. *Management Learning*, 40(2), 161–76.

Blattner, W. (2000). The Primacy of Practice and Assertoric Truth. In M. A. Wrathall and J. Malpas (eds.), *Heidegger, Authenticity, and Modernity. Essays in Honour of Hubert L. Dreyfus*. Cambridge, Mass.: MIT Press, 231–49.

Blomquist, T., Hällgren, M., Nilsson, A., and Söderholm, A. (2010). Project as practice: In search of project management research that matters. *Project Management Journal*, 41(1), 5–16.

Bloor, D. (1976). *Knowledge and social imagery*. London; Boston: Routledge and Kegan Paul.

Boden, D. and Zimmerman, D. H. (1991). *Talk and social structure: studies in ethnomethodology and conversation analysis*. Cambridge: Polity Press.

Bourdieu, P. (1980). *Le Sens Pratique*. Paris: Minuit.

Bourdieu, P. (1977). *Outline of a theory of practice*. Cambridge: Cambridge University Press.

Bourdieu, P. (1984). *Distinction: A Social Critique of the Judgement of Taste*. Cambridge, Harvard University Press.

Bourdieu, P. (1990). *The Logic of Practice*. Cambridge: Polity.

Bourdieu, P. (1996). *The state nobility: elite schools in the field of power*. Oxford: Polity.

Bourdieu, P. (1998). *Practical reason: on the theory of action*. Cambridge: Polity Press.

Bourdieu, P. and Passeron, J. C. (1990). *Reproduction in education, society and culture*. London: Sage.

Bourdieu, P. and Wacquant, L. J. D. (1992). *An invitation to reflexive sociology*. Cambridge: Polity Press.

Brown, J. S. and Duguid, P. (1991). Organizational learning and communities-of-practice: Towards a unified view of working, learning and innovation. *Organization Science*, 2, 40–57.

Button, G. (1992). *Technology in working order: studies of work, interaction, and technology*. London; New York: Routledge.

Cabantous, L. and Gond, J. P. (2011). Rational Decision Making as Performative Praxis: Explaining Rationality's Éternel Retour. *Organization Science*, 22(3), 573–86.

Cabantous, L., Gond, J. P., and Johnson-Cramer, M. (2010). Decision theory as practice: Crafting rationality in organizations. *Organization Studies*, 31(11), 1531–66.

Callinicos, A. (1985). Anthony Giddens: A Contemporary Critique. *Theory and Society* 14(2), 133–66.

Callon, M. (1986). Some Elements of a Sociology of Translation: Domestication of the Scallops and the Fishermen of St Brieuc Bay. In J. Law (ed.), *Power, Action and Belief: A New Sociology of Knowledge*. London: Routledge and Kegan Paul, 196–233.

Certeau, M. de (1984). *The practice of everyday life*. Berkeley: University of California Press.

Chaiklin, S. and Lave, J. (1993). *Understanding practice: perspectives on activity and context*. Cambridge: Cambridge University Press.

Chia, R. and Holt, R. (2006). Strategy as practical coping: A Heideggerian perspective. *Organization Studies*, 27(5), 635–55.

Chia, R. and Holt, R. (2008). On managerial knowledge. *Management Learning*, 39(2), 141–58.

Chia, R. and MacKay, B. (2007). Post-processual challenges for the emerging strategy-as-practice perspective: Discovering strategy in the logic of practice. *Human Relations*, 60(1), 217–42.

Cicourel, A. V. (1981). The role of cognitive-linguistic concepts in understanding everyday social interactions. *Annual Review of Sociology*, 7, 87–106.

Cicourel, A. V. (1968). *The social organization of juvenile justice*. New York: Wiley.

Clegg, S. R., Hardy, C., and Nord, W. R. (eds.) (1996). Preface. In S. R. Clegg, C. Hardy, and W. R. Nord (eds.), *Handbook of organization studies Handbook of organization studies*. London: Sage, xxi–xix.

Clifford, J. (1986). Partial Truths. In: J. Clifford and G. E. Marcus (eds.) *Writing Culture: The Poetics and Politics of Ethnography*. Berkeley: University of California Press, 1–26.

Cohen, I. J. (1996). Theories of Action and Praxis. In B. S. Turner (ed.), *The Blackwell Companion to Social Theory*, 2, 73–111.

Cole, M. (1998). *Cultural psychology: A once and future discipline*. Cambridge: Harvard University Press.

Cole, M. and Wertsch, J. (1996). Beyond the individual-social antinomy in discussions of Piaget and Vygotsky. *Human Development*. 39 (5), 250–6.

Collins, R. (1981). On the microfoundations of macrosociology. *American Journal of Sociology*, 86(5), 984–1014.

Contu, A. and Willmott, H. (2000). Comment on Wenger and Yanow. Knowing in Practice: A Delicate Flower in the Organizational Learning Field. *Organization*, 7(2), 269–76.

Contu, A. and Willmott, H. (2003). Re-embedding situatedness: the importance of power relations in learning theory. *Organization Science*, 14(3), 283–97.

Cook, S. D. N. and Yanow, D. (1993). Culture and organizational learning. *Journal of Management Inquiry*, 2(4), 373–90.

Corlett, W. (1989). *Community without unity: a politics of Derridian extravagance*. Durham, N.C.: Duke University Press.

Corradi, G., Gherardi, S., and Verzelloni, L. (2010). Through the practice lens: Where is the bandwagon of practice-based studies heading? *Management Learning*, 41(3), 265–83.

Crabtree, A., O'Brien, J., Nichols, D., Rouncefield, M., and Twidale, M. (2000). Ethnomethodologically informed ethnography and information systems design. *Journal of the American Society for Information Science and Technology*, 51(7), 666–82.

Craig, I. (1992). *Anthony Giddens*. New York: Routledge.

Crossley, N. (2001). The Phenomenological habitus and its construction. *Theory and Society*, 30(1), 81–120(140).

Csikszentmihalyi, M. (1997). *Finding flow: the psychology of engagement with everyday life* (1st edn.). New York: BasicBooks.

Cunliffe, A. and Easterby-Smith, M. (1998). Reflexive Learning: A Critique of Experience-based Theories in Management Education. *Paper presented at the Learning and Critique Conference, Leeds,* 15–17 July.

Czarniawska, B. (1997). *Narrating the organization: dramas of institutional identity.* Chicago: University of Chicago Press.

Czarniawska, B. (2004). On time, space, and action nets. *Organization,* 11(6), 773–91.

Czarniawska, B. (2007). *Shadowing and other techniques for doing fieldwork in modern societies,* Malmo: Liber and Copenhagen Business School Press.

Czarniawska, B. (2008). *Shadowing: And Other Techniques for Doing Fieldwork in Modern Societies.* Malmö: Liber and Copenhagen Business School Press.

Czarniawska, B. and Joerges, B. (1996). Travels of ideas. In B. Czarniawska-Joerges and G. Sevón (eds.), *Translating organizational change.* Berlin: de Gruyter, 13–48.

Czarniawska, B. and Sevón, G. (1996). *Translating Organizational Change.* Berlin: Walter de Gruyter.

Czarniawska, B. and Sevón, G. (2005). *Global Ideas. How ideas, objects and practices travel in the global economy.* Malmö: Liber and Copenhagen Business School Press.

Daniels, H. (2001). *Vygotsky and pedagogy.* London: Routledge/Falmer.

Davidson, A. I. (1986). Archaeology, genealogy, ethics. In D. Hoy (ed.), *Foucault: A Critical Reader.* Oxford:Wiley-Blackwell.

Davies, B. and Harre, R. (1990). Positioning—The Discursive Production of Selves. *Journal for the Theory of Social Behaviour,* 20(1), 43–63.

de Saint-Georges, I. (2005). From anticipation to performance: sites of engagements as process. In R. Jones and S. E. Norris (eds.), *Discourse in Action: introduction to mediated discourse analysis.* London: Routledge, 155–65.

DeSanctis, G. and Poole, S. M. (1994). Capturing the Complexity in Advanced Technology Use: Adaptative Structuration Theory. *Organization Science,* 5(2), 121–47.

Detienne, M. and Vernant, J. (1974). *Les ruses de l'intelligence: la métis des Grecs.* Paris: Flammarion.

Dewey, J. (1929). *Experience and Nature.* New York: Dover.

Di Maggio, P. (1979). Review Essay: On Pierre Bourdieu. *American Journal of Sociology,* 84, 1460–74.

Dingwall, R. W. J. (1981). The ethnomethodological movement. In G. Payne, R. Dingwall, J. Payne and M. Carter (eds.), *Sociology and Social Reasearch.* London: Routledge and Kegan Paul, 124–38.

Dourish, P. and Button, G. (1998). On 'Technomethodology': Foundational Relationships Between Ethnomethodology and System Design. *Human-Computer Interaction,* 13(4), 395–432.

Drew, P. and Heritage, J. (1992). *Talk at work: interaction in institutional settings.* Cambridge Cambridge University Press.

Dreyfus, H. (1991). *Being-in-the-World: A Commentary on Heidegger's Being and Time Division.* Cambridge, MA: MIT Press.

Dreyfus, H. and Rabinow, P. (1993). Can there be a science of existential structure and social meaning? In C. Calhoun, E. LiPuma, and M. Postone (eds). *Bourdieu: Critical Perspectives.* Cambridge, UK: Polity Press, 35–44.

Echeverri, P. and Skålén, P. (2011). Co-creation and co-destruction: A practice-theory based study of interactive value formation. *Marketing Theory*, 11(3), 351–73.

Eikeland, O. (2008). *The Ways of Aristotle: Aristotelian Phronesis, Aristotelean Philosophy of Aiabgue, and Action Research*. Berlin: Peter Lang.

Eisenstadt, S. N. (1973). Intellectuals and Tradition. In S. N. Eisenstadt and S. R. Graubard (eds.), *Intellectuals and Tradition*. New York: Humanities Press.

Engels, F. (1998). F. Engels: Supplement to Capital, Volume Three. In K. Marx and F. Engels (eds.), *Karl Marx, Frederick Engels: Collected Works*, vol. 37. New York: International Publishers, 873–97.

Engeström, Y. (1987). *Learning by expanding: An activity-theoretical approach to developmental research*: Helsinki: Orienta-Konsultit.

Engeström, Y. (1990). *Learning, working, imagining: twelve studies in activity theory*. Helsinki: Orienta-Konsultit.

Engeström, Y. (1993). Developmental Studies of Work as a test bench of activity theory: the case of primary care medical practice. In S. Chaiklin and J. Lave (eds.), *Understanding Practice*: Cambridge: Cambridge University Press.

Engeström, Y. (1995). Objects, contradictions and collaboration in medical cognition: An activity theoretical perspective. *Artificial Intelligence in Medicine*, 7, 395–412.

Engeström, Y. (1999a). Expansive visibilization of work: An activity-theoretical perspective. *Computer-Supported Cooperative Work*, 8, 63–93.

Engeström, Y. (1999b). When the Centre Does Not Hold: The Importance of Knot working. In M. Chaiklin, U. Hedegaard and J. Juul (eds.), *Activity Theory and Social Practice: Cultural-Historical Approaches*. Aarhus: Aarhus University Press.

Engeström, Y. (2000). *Activity theory as a framework for analysing and redesigning work* Ergonomics 43(7), 960–74.

Engeström, Y. (2001). Expansive Learning at Work: Toward an Activity Theoretical Conceptualization. *Journal of Education and Work*, 14(1), 133–56.

Engeström, Y. (2005). *Developmental work research: expanding activity theory into practice*. Berlin: Lehmanns Media.

Engeström, Y. (2008). *From teams to knots: activity-theoretical studies of collaboration and learning at work*. Cambridge: Cambridge University Press.

Engeström, Y. and Blackler, F. (2005). On the life of the object. *Organization*, 12(3), 307–30.

Engeström, Y. and Escalante, V. (1995). Mundane tool or object of affection? The rise and fall of postal buddy. In B. Nardi (ed.), *Activity theory and human-computer interaction*. Cambridge, MA: MIT Press, 325–73.

Engeström, Y. and Miettinen, R. (1999). Introduction. In Y. Engeström, R. Miettinen and P. R. (eds.), *Perspectives on Activity Theory*. Cambridge: Cambridge University Press.

Engeström, Y., Miettinen, R., and Punumäki, R. (1999). *Perspective on Activity Theory*. Cambridge: Cambridge University Press.

Engeström, Y., Virrkkunen, J., Helle, M., Pihlaja, J., and Poikela, R. (1996). The Change laboratory as a tool for transforming work. *Lifelong Learning in Europe*, 1(2), 10–17.

Erlingsdottír, G. and Lindberg, K. (2005). Isomorphism, Isopraxism and Isonymism. In B. Czarniawska and G. Sevón (eds.), *Global Ideas. How ideas, objects and Practices Travel in the Global economy* (pp. 47–70). Malmo: Liber and Copenhagen Business School Press.

Fairclough, N. (1992). *Discourse and social change*. Oxford: Polity Press.

Fairclough, N. (1995). *Critical Discourse Analysis: Papers in the Critical Study of Language*. London: Longman.

Fairclough, N. and Wodak, R. (1997). Critical discourse analysis. In: T. Van Dijk (ed.): *Discourse Studies: A Multidisciplinary Introduction*. Vol. 2. London: Sage, 258–84.

Farr, R. M. and Moscovici, S. (1984). *Social representations*. Cambridge: Cambridge University Press.

Feldman, M. S. and Orlikowski, W. J. (2011). Theorizing Practice and Practicing Theory. *Organization Science*, 22(5), 1240–53.

Feldman, M. S. and Pentland, B. T. (2003). Reconceptualizing organizational routines as a source of flexibility and change. *Administrative Science Quarterly*, 48(1), 94–118.

Fele, G. (2002). *Etnometodologia*: Roma: Carocci.

Fish, S. E. (1980). *Is there a text in this class?: the authority of interpretive communities*. Cambridge, Mass: Harvard University Press.

Flynn, P. J. (1991). *The Ethnomethodological Movement: Sociosemiotic Interpretations*. New York: Mouton de Gruyter.

Flyvbjerg, B. (2001). *Making social science matter: why social inquiry fails and how it can count again*. New York: Cambridge University Press.

Foucault, M. (1966). *The order of things: an archaeology of the human sciences*. London: Tavistock.

Foucault, M. (1972). *The archaeology of knowledge*. London: Tavistock Publications.

Foucault, M. (1979). What is an author? In *Textual Strategies: Perspectives in Post-structuralist Criticism*. New York: Cornell University Press, 141–61.

Foucault, M. (1980). *Power/Knowledge: Selected Interviews and Other Writings 1972–1977*. Colin Gordon (ed.). New York: Pantheon.

Fox, S. (2000). Communities of practice, Foucault and actor-network theory. *Journal of Management Studies*, 37(6), 853–67.

Garfinkel, H. (1967). *Studies in ethnomethodology*. Englewood Cliffs, New Jersey: Prentice-Hall.

Garfinkel, H. (1996). Ethnomethodology's program. *Social Psychology Quarterly*, 59(1), 5–21.

Garfinkel, H., Lynch, M., and Livingston, E. (1981). The work of discovering science construed with materials from the optically discovered pulsar. *Philosophy of the Social Sciences*, 11(2), 131–58.

Garfinkel, H. and Sacks, H. (1970). On formal structures of practical action. In J. C. McKinney and E. A. Tiryakian (eds.), *Theoretical sociology: perspectives and developments*. New York: Appleton-Century-Crofts, 338–66.

Garfinkel, H. and Wieder, D. L. (1992). Two incommensurable, asymmetrically alternate technologies of social analysis. In W. G. and S. M. (eds.), *Text in Context: Studies in Ethnomethodology*. Newbury Park: Sage, 175–206.

Gee, J. P. (2011). *An introduction to discourse analysis: theory and method* (3rd edn.). New York: Routledge.

Geertz, C. (1973). *The Interpretation of Cultures*. New York: Basic Books.

Geiger, D. (2009). Revisiting the concept of practice: Toward an argumentative understanding of practicing. *Management Learning*, 40(2), 129–44.

Gherardi, S. (1995). 'When Will He Say: "Today the Plates Are Soft"? The Management of Ambiguity and Situated Decision-Making', *Studies in Cultures, Organizations and Societies*, 1(1), 9–27.

Gherardi, S. (2000). Practice-based theorizing on learning and knowing in organizations. *Organization*, 7(2), 211–23.

Gherardi, S. (2006). *Organizational knowledge: the texture of workplace learning.* Oxford: Blackwell.

Gherardi, S. and Nicolini, D. (2002). Learning the Trade. A Culture of Safety in Practice. *Organization*, 9(2), 191–223.

Gherardi, S., Nicolini, D., and Odella, F. (1998). Toward a Social Understanding of How People Learn in Organizations: The Notion of Situated Curriculum. *Management Learning*, 29(3), 273–97.

Giddens, A. (1976). *New rules of sociological method: a positive critique of interpretative sociologies.* London: Hutchinson.

Giddens, A. (1979). *Central problems in social theory: action, structure and contradiction in social analysis.* London: Macmillan.

Giddens, A. (1983). Comments on the theory of structuration. *Journal for the Theory of Social Behavior*, 13(1), 75–80.

Giddens, A. (1984). *The constitution of society: outline of the theory of structuration.* Cambridge: Polity Press.

Giddens, A. (1991). *Modernity and Self-Identity. Self and Society in the Late Modern Age.* Cambridge: Polity Press.

Giddens, A. and Pierson, C. (1998). *Conversations with Anthony Giddens: making sense of modernity.* Cambridge: Polity Press.

Golsorkhi, D. and Huault, I. (2006). Pierre Bourdieu: critique et réflexivité comme attitude analytique. *Revue Française de Gestion*, 32, 15–34.

Golsorkhi, D., Rouleau, L., and Seidl, D. (2010). *Cambridge handbook of strategy as practice.* Cambridge: Cambridge University Press.

Gomez, M. L. and Drucker-Godard, C. (2003). Developing knowing in practice: behind the scenes of a haute cuisine. In D. Nicolini, S. Gherardi and D. E. Yanow (eds.), *Knowing in organizations: a Practice-based Approach.* Armonk, NY: ME Sharpe, Inc.

Goode, W. J. (1957). Community within a Community—The Professions. *American Sociological Review*, 22(2), 194–200.

Gregson, N. (1989). The (ir)relevance of structuration theory. In H. David and J. B. Thompson (eds.), *Social theory of modern societies: Anthony Giddens and his Critics.* Cambridge: Cambridge University Press, 235–48.

Guignon, C. B. (1983). *Heidegger and the Problem of Knowledge.* Indianapolis: Hackett.

Gumperz, J. J. and Hymes, D. H. (1972). *Directions in sociolinguistics: the ethnography of communication.* London: Holt, Rinehart and Winston.

Gustavsen, B. (1996). Action research, democratic dialogue, and the issue of 'critical mass' in change. *Qualitative Inquiry*, 90–103.

Hall, S. (1996). Who needs identity? In S. Hall and P. DuGay (eds.), *Questions of Cultural Identity.* London: Sage, 1–17.

Hällgren, M. and Söderholm, A. (2011). Projects-as-Practice. New Approach, New Insights. In J. Söderlund, J. K. Pinto and P. W. G. Morris (eds.), *The Oxford Handbook of Project Management.* Oxford: Oxford University Press, 500–18.

Halliday, M. A. K. (1978). *Language as social semiotic: the social interpretation of language and meaning.* London: University Park Press.

Handley, K., Sturdy, A., Fincham, R., and Clark, T. (2006). Within and beyond communities of practice: Making sense of learning through participation, identity and practice. *Journal of Management Studies*, 43(3), 641–53.

Hannerz, U. (2003). Being There ... And There ... And There! Reflections on Multi-Site Ethnography. *Ethnography*, 4(2), 201–16.

Harker, R., Mahar, C., and Wilkes, C. (1990). *An introduction to the work of Pierre Bourdieu: the practice and theory*. London: Macmillan.

Have, P. T. (1999). *Doing conversation analysis: a practical guide*. Thousand Oaks, Calif.: Sage.

Have, P. T. (2002). Ontology or methodology? Comments on Speer's 'natural' and 'contrived' data: a sustainable distinction? *Discourse Studies*, 4, 527–30.

Heath, C. and Button, G. (2002). Special Issue on Workplace Studies. *British Journal of Sociology*, 53(2), 157–317.

Heath, C., Knoblauch, H., and Luff, P. (2000). Technology and social interaction: the emergence of 'workplace studies'. *The British Journal of Sociology*, 51(2), 299–320.

Heath, C. and Luff, P. K. (1996). Convergent activities: collaborative work and multimedia technology in London Underground Line Control Rooms. In D. Middleton and Y. Engeström (eds.), *Cognition and communication at work: Distributed cognition in the workplace*. 96–130.

Heath, C. and Luff, P. (2000). *Technology in Action*. Cambridge: Cambridge University Press.

Heath, C., Svensson, M. S., Hindmarsh, J., Luff, P., and Vom Lehn, D. (2002). Configuring Awareness. *Computer Supported Cooperative Work*, 11, 317–47.

Hedegaard, M. (2001). *Learning in classrooms: a cultural-historical approach*. Aarhus: Aarhus University Press.

Heidegger, M. (1929/1996). *Being and Time*. Albany: SUNY Press.

Heràn, F. (1987). La Seconde Nature de l'Habitus: Tradition Philosophique et Sens Commun dans le Langage Sociologique. *Revue Francaise de Sociologie, XXVIII*, 385–416.

Heritage, J. (1984). *Garfinkel and ethnomethodology*. Cambridge: Polity Press.

Heritage, J. (2009). Conversation Analysis as Social Theory. In B. S. Turner (ed.), *The New Blackwell Companion to Social Theory*. Oxford: Wiley-Blackwell, 300–20.

Hilbert, R. A. (1990). Ethno-methodology and the micro-macro order. *American Sociological Review*, 55(6), 794–808.

Hiley, D. R., Bohman, J., and Shusterman, R. (1991). *The Interpretive turn: philosophy, science, culture*. Ithaca; London: Cornell University Press.

Hillery, G. (1955). Definitions of Community. *Rural Sociology*, 20, 111–23.

Hindmarsh, J. and Pilnick, A. (2002). The tacit order of teamwork: Collaboration and embodied conduct in anaesthesia. *Sociological Quarterly* 43(2), 139–64.

Holt, R. and Morris, A. (1993). Activity theory and the analysis of organisations. *Human Organizations*, 52(1), 97–109.

Hutchins, E. (1995). *Cognition in the Wild*. Cambridge, MA: MIT Press.

Iedema, A. and Wodak, R. (1999). Introduction: Organizational Discourses and Practices. *Discourse and Society*, 10(1), 5–20.

Iedema, R. (2001). Resemiotization. *Semiotica*, 37(1/4), 23–40.

Iedema, R. (2003). *Discourses of post-bureaucratic organization*. Philadelphia, PA: John Benjamins.

Jarzabkowski, P. (2003). Strategic practices: An activity theory perspective on continuity and change. *Journal of Management Studies*, 40(1), 23–55.

Johannessen, K. S. (1981). The concept of practice in Wittgenstein's Later Philosophy. *Inquiry*, 31(3), 357–69.

Johannessen, K. (1996). Action Research and Epistemology. Some remarks concerning the Activity-relatedness and contextuality of Human Language. *Concepts and Transformation*, 1, (2/3), 281–97.

Johnson, G., Langley, A., Melin, l., and Whittington, R. (2007). *Strategy as practice: research directions and resources*. New York: Cambridge University Press.

Jones, M. and Karsten, H. (2003). 'Review: Gidden's Structuration Theory and Information Systems Research. *MIS Quarterly*, 32(1), 127—57.

Jones, R. and Norris, S. (2005). *Discourse In Action: Introducing Mediated Discourse Analysis*. Abingdon: Routledge.

Kaptelinin, V. and Nardi, B. (2006). *Acting with Technology: Activity Theory and Interaction Design*. Cambridge, Mass.: MIT Press.

Kitching, G. N. (1988). *Karl Marx and the philosophy of Praxis: an introduction and critique*. London: Methuen.

Knoblauch, H. (2005). Focused Ethnography, *Forum Qualitative Sozialforschung/Forum: Qualitative Social Research, North America, 6, Sep. 2005*. Available at: http://www.qualitativeresearch.net/index.php/fqs/article/view/20. Date accessed: 2 May 2009.

Knorr-Cetina, K. (1999). *Epistemic cultures: how the sciences make knowledge*. Cambridge, Mass.; London: Harvard University Press.

Korsgaard, C. (1996). *The Sources of Normativity*. Cambridge: Cambridge University Press.

Kristeva, J. and Moi, T. (1986). *The Kristeva reader*. Oxford: Blackwell.

Kunda, G. (1992). *Engineering culture: control and commitment in a high-tech corporation*. Philadelphia: Temple University Press.

Kuutti, K. (1996). Activity Theory as a potential framework for human-computer interaction research. In B. Nardi (ed.), *Context and Consciousness: Activity Theory and Human Computer Interaction*. Cambridge, Mass: MIT Press, 17–44.

Lash, S. (1993). Pierre Bourdieu: Cultural Economy and Social Change. In C. Calhoun, E. LiPuma, and M. Postone (eds), *Bourdieu: Critical Perspectives*. Cambridge, Polity Press, 193–211.

Latour, B. (1996). *Aramis, or, the love of technology*. Cambridge, Mass.: Harvard University Press.

Latour, B. (2005). *Reassembling the social: an introduction to actor-network-theory*. Oxford: Oxford University Press.

Lau, R. W. K. (2004). Habitus and the practical logic of practice: An interpretation. *Sociology*, 38(2), 369–86.

Lave, J. (1988). *Cognition in practice: mind, mathematics and culture in everyday life*. Cambridge: Cambridge University Press.

Lave, J. and Wenger, E. (1991). *Situated learning: legitimate peripheral participation*. Cambridge: Cambridge University Press.

Law, J. (1992). Notes on the theory of the actor-network: ordering, strategy and heterogeneity. *Systems Practice* 5(4), 379–393.

Law, J. (2009). Actor Network Theory and Material Semiotic. In B. S. Turner (ed.), *The New Blackwell Companion to Social Theory*. Oxford: Wiley-Blackwell, 141–58.

Lawrence, T. and Suddaby, R. (2006). Institutions and institutional work. In S. R. Clegg, C. Hardy, T. B. Lawrence and W. R. Nord (eds.), *Handbook of organization studies* (2nd edn.). London: Sage, 215–54.

Lawrence, T. B., Suddaby, R., and Leca, B. (2009). *Institutional work: actors and agency in institutional studies of organizations.* Cambridge, Cambridge University Press.

Leitch, S. and Palmer, I. (2010). Analysing texts in context: current practices and new protocols for critical discourse analysis in organization studies. *Journal of Management Studies*, 47(6), 1194–212.

Leont'ev, A. N. (1978). *Activity, Consciousness, Personality.* Englewood Cliffs, NJ: Prentice Hall.

Leont'ev, A. N. (1981). The problem of activity in psychology. In J. Wertsch (ed.), *The concept of activity in Soviet psychology.* Armonk, NY Sharpe.

Lesser, E. and Everest, K. (2001). Using communities of practice to manage intellectual capital. *Ivey Business Journal*, 65, 37–41.

Lesser, E. and Prusak, L. (1999). Communities of practice, social capital, and organizational knowledge. *Information Systems Review*, 1(1), 3–10.

Lévi-Strauss, C. (1950). *Introduction to the work of Marcel Mauss.* London: Routledge and Kegan Paul.

Levinson, S. C. (2005). Living with Manny's dangerous idea. *Discourse Studies*, 7(4–5), 431–53.

Lindberg, K. and Czarniawska, B. (2006). Knotting the action net, or organizing between organizations. *Scandinavian Journal of Management*, 22(4), 292–306.

Llewellyn, N. (2004). In Search of Modernisation: The Negotiation of Social identity in Organisational Reform. *Organization Studies*, 25(6), 947–68.

Llewellyn, N. (2008). Organization in actual episodes of work: Harvey Sacks and organization studies. *Organization Studies*, 29(5), 763–91.

Llewellyn, N. and Hindmarsh, J. (2009). *Organization, interaction and practice: Studies of real time work and organizing.* Cambridge: Cambridge University Press.

Llewellyn, N. and Hindmarsh, J. (2010). *Organisation, interaction and practice: studies in ethnomethodology and conversation analysis.* Cambridge: Cambridge University Press.

Lobkowicz, N. (1967). *Theory and practice: history of a concept from Aristotle to Marx.* Notre-Dame (Ind.); London: University of Notre Dame Press.

Lounsbury, M. (2008). Institutional rationality and practice variation: New directions in the institutional analysis of practice. *Accounting, Organizations and Society*, 33(4), 349–61.

Lounsbury, M. D. (2003). The Problem of Order Revisited: Power, Culture and Institutional Analysis. In R. Westwood and S. R. Clegg (eds.), *Point/Counterpoint: Central Debates in Organisation Theory.* Oxford: Blackwell, 210–20.

Lounsbury, M. and Crumley, E. T. (2007). New practice creation: An institutional perspective on innovation. *Organization Studies*, 28(7), 993–1012.

Lounsbury, M. and Ventresca, M. (2003). The new structuralism in organizational theory. *Organization*, 10(3), 457–80.

Luff, P., Hindmarsh, J., and Heath, C. (2000). *Workplace studies: recovering work practice and informing system design.* Cambridge: Cambridge University Press.

Luntley, M. (1992). Practice Makes Knowledge? *Inquiry*, 35 (3 and 4), 447–61.

Lynch, M. (1993). *Scientific practice and ordinary action: ethnomethodology and social studies of science.* Cambridge: Cambridge University Press.

Lynch, M. (2001). Ethnomethodology and the logic of practice. In K. D. Knorr-Cetina, E. v. Savigny and T. R. Schatzki (eds.), *The practice turn in Contemporary Theory*. London: Routledge.

Macbeth, D. (2001). On 'reflexivity' in qualitative research: Two readings, and a third. *Qualitative Inquiry*, 7, 35–68.

MacIntyre, A. C. (1981). *After virtue: a study in moral theory*. London: Duckworth.

Macquarrie, J. (1972). *Existentialism*. London: Hutchinson and Co.

Marcus, G. E. (1995). Ethnography in/of the world-system—The emergence of multi-sited ethnography. *Annual Review of Anthropology*, 24, 95–117.

Marcus, G. E. and Fischer, M. M. J. (1986). *Anthropology as Cultural Critique. An Experimental Moment in the Human Sciences*. Chicago: University of Chicago Press.

Martin, P. Y. (2003). 'Said and Done' Versus 'Saying and Doing'. *Gender and Society*, 17(3), 342–66.

Martin Rojo, L. (2001). New developments in discourse analysis: Discourse as social practice. *Folia Linguistica*, 35(1–2), 41–78.

Marx, K. (1845/1977). German Ideology. Economic and Philosophical Manuscripts. In D. M. L. (ed), *Karl Marx Selected Writings*. Oxford: University Press.

Marx, K. and Engels, F. (1867). *Das Kapital: Kritik der politischen Ökonomie*. Hamburg: Meissner.

Maynard, D. W. and Clayman, S. E. (1991). The Diversity of Ethnomethodology. *Annual Review of Sociology*, 17, 385–418.

McDonough, P. (2006). Habitus and the practice of public service. *Work Employment and Society*, 20(4), 629–47.

McMurray, J. and Steward, S. (2003). The burden of heart failure. *European Heart Journal*, 5 (Suppl), 3–13.

Mehan, H. (1985). The Structure of Classroom Discourse. In T. van Dijk (ed.), *Handbook of Discourse Analysis* (Vol. 3). London: Academic.

Mehan, H. and Wood, H. (1975). *The reality of ethnomethodology*. New York; London: Wiley-Interscience.

Merleau-Ponty, M. (1962). *The Phenomenology of Perception*. London: Routledge.

Meštrovic, S. G. (1998). *Anthony Giddens: the last modernist*. New York: Routledge.

Middleton, D. and Engeström, Y. (eds.) (1998) *Cognition and communication at work*. Cambridge: Cambridge University Press.

Miettinen, R. (1999). The riddle of things. Activity theory and Actor Network Theory as approaches of studying innovations. *Mind, Culture, and Activity*, 6(3), 170–95.

Miettinen, R. (2006). Epistemology of transformative material activity: John Dewey's pragmatism and cultural-historical activity theory. *Journal for the Theory of Social Behaviour*, 36(4), 389–408.

Miettinen, R., Samra-Fredericks, D., and Yanow, D. (2009). Re-turn to practice: An introductory essay. *Organization Studies*, 30(12), 1309–27.

Miettinen, R. and Virkkunen, J. (2005). Epistemic objects, artefacts and organizational change. *Organization*, 12(3), 437–56.

Mintzberg, H. (1973). *The Nature of Managerial Work*. New York: Harper and Row.

Moscovici, S. (1969). Preface. In C. Herzlich (ed.), *Santé et maladie: analyse d'une représentation sociale*. Paris: Mouton.

Mullins, N. C. (1973). The Development of Specialities in Social Sciences. The Case of Ethno-methodology. *Science Studies*, 3, 245–73.

Mutch, A. (2003). Communities of practice and habitus: A critique. *Organization Studies*, 24(3), 383–401.

Nardi, B. A. (1996). *Context and consciousness: activity theory and human-computer interaction.* Cambridge, Mass.: MIT Press.

Nicolini, D. (2006). The work to make telemedicine work: A social and articulative view. *Social Science and Medicine*, 62(11), 2754–67.

Nicolini, D. (2007). Stretching out and expanding work practices in time and space: The case of telemedicine. *Human Relations*, 60(6), 889–920.

Nicolini, D. (2009a). Articulating Practice through the Interview to the Double. *Management Learning*, 40(2), 195–212.

Nicolini, D. (2009b). Zooming In and Out: Studying Practices by Switching Theoretical Lenses and Trailing Connections. *Organization Studies*, 30(12), 1391–418.

Nicolini, D. (2010). Medical Innovation as a Process of Translation: a Case from the Field of Telemedicine. *British Journal of Management*, 21(4), 1011–26.

Nicolini, D. (2011). Practice as the Site of Knowing: Insights from the Field of Telemedicine. *Organization Science*, 22(3), 602–20.

Nicolini, D., Gherardi, S., and Yanow, D. (2003). *Knowing in organizations: A practice-based approach.* Armonk NY: ME Sharpe Inc.

Nicolini, D., Mengis, J., and Swan, J. (2012). Understanding the role of objects in multidisciplinary collaboration. *Organization Science*, 23(3), 612–29.

Nussbaum, M. C. (1986). *The fragility of goodness: luck and ethics in Greek tragedy and philosophy.* Cambridge: Cambridge University Press.

Nyiri, J. C. (1988). Tradition and practical knowledge. In J. C. Nyiri and B. E. Smith (eds.), *Practical Knowledge: Outlines of a Theory of Traditions and Skills.* Croon Helm: Beckenham, 17–52.

Okrent, M. (1988). *Heidegger's pragmatism: understanding, being, and the critique of metaphysics.* Ithaca, N.Y.; London: Cornell University Press.

Oppenheim, R. (2007). Actor-network theory and anthropology after science, technology, and society. *Anthropological Theory*, 7(4), 471–93.

Orbuch, T. L. (1997). People's Accounts Count: The Sociology of Accounts. *Annual Review of Sociology*, 23, 455–78.

Orlikowski, W. J. (1992). The duality of technology: rethinking the concept of technology in organizations. *Organization Science*, 3(3), 398–427.

Orlikowski, W. J. (2000). Using technology and constituting structures: A practice lens for studying technology in organizations. *Organization Science*, 11(4), 404–28.

Orlikowski, W. J. (2002). Knowing in practice: Enacting a collective capability in distributed organizing. *Organization Science*, 13(3), 249–73.

Orlikowski, W. J. 2010. The sociomateriality of organizational life: Considering technology in management research. *Cambridge Journal of Economics* 34(1): 125–41.

Orr, J. E. (1996). *Talking about machines: an ethnography of a modern job.* Ithaca, NY: ILR Press.

Ortner, S. (1984). Theory in anthropology since the 60s'. *Comparative Studies in Society and History*, 26/1, 126–66.

Özbilgin, M. and Tatli, A. (2005). Book review essay: Understanding Bourdieu's contribution to organization and management studies. *Academy of Management Review*, 30(4), 855–69.

Pantzar, M. and Shove, E. (2010). Understanding innovation in practice: a discussion of the production and re-production of Nordic Walking. *Technology Analysis and Strategic Management*, 22(4), 447–61.

Pentland, B. T. and Feldman, M. S. (2005). Organizational routines as a unit of analysis. *Industrial and Corporate Change*, 14(5), 793–815.

Pettigrew, A., Thomas, H., and Whittington, R. (2002). Strategic management: the strengths and limitations of a field. In A. Pettigrew, H. Thomas and R. Whittington (eds.), *Handbook of strategy and management*. London: Sage, 3–30.

Pickering, A. (1992). *Science as practice and culture*. Chicago: University of Chicago Press.

Pickering, A. (1993). The Mangle of Practice: Agency and Emergence in the Sociology of Science. *American Journal of Sociology*, 99(3), 559–89.

Pickering, A. (1995). *The mangle of practice: time, agency, and science*. Chicago: University of Chicago Press.

Polanyi, M. (1962). *Personal knowledge: towards a post-critical philosophy*. London: Routledge and Kegan Paul.

Pollner, M. and McDonald-Wikler, L. (1985). The Social Construction of Unreality: A Case Study of a Family's Attribution of Competence to a Severely Retarded Child. *Family Process*, 24(2), 241–54.

Pooler, J. (2009). Managing the diagnostic space in calls for help. In M. Büscher, D. Goodwin and J. Mesman (eds.), *Ethnographies of diagnostic work: Dimensions of transformative practice*. Basingstoke: Palgrave Macmillan, 149–70.

Pozzebon, M. (2004). The influence of a structurationist view on strategic management research. *Journal of Management Studies*, 41(2), 247–72.

Pozzebon, M. and Pinsonneault, A. (2005). Challenges in conducting empirical work using structuration theory: Learning from IT research. *Organization Studies*, 26(9), 1353–76.

Psathas, G. (1980). Approaches to the study of the World of Everyday Life. *Human Studies*, 3(1), 3–17.

Quattrone, P. (2009). Books to be practiced: Memory, the power of the visual, and the success of accounting. *Accounting, Organizations and Society*, 34(1), 85–118.

Queneau, R. and Wright, B. (1981). *Exercises in style* (Vol. 513). New Directions Publishing.

Raelin, J. (1997). A Model of Work Based Learning. *Organization Science*, 8(6), 563–78.

Rawls, A. W. (2008). Harold Garfinkel, ethnomethodology and workplace studies. *Organization Studies*, 29(5), 701–32.

Reckwitz, A. (2002). Toward a theory of social practices. *European journal of social theory*, 5(2), 243–63.

Reed, M. (1998). Organizational Analysis as Discourse Analysis: A critique. In D. Grant, T. Keenoy and C. E. Oswick (eds.), *Discourse and Organization*. London: Sage, 193–213.

Richards, D. S. (2001). Talking sense: Ethnomethodology, Postmodernism and Practical Action. In R. Westwood and S. E. Linstead (eds.), *The Language of Organization*. London: Sage, 20–45.

Røpke, I. (2009). Theories of practice—New inspiration for ecological economic studies on consumption. *Ecological Economics*, 68(10), 2490–97.

Rorty, R. (1989). *Contingency, Irony, and Solidarity*. Cambridge: Cambridge University Press.

Rossi-Landi, F. (1975). *Linguistics and economics.* The Hague: Mouton.

Roth, W.-M. and Lee, Y. J. (2007). Vygotsky's neglected legacy: cultural-historical activity theory. *Review of Educational Research*, 77(2), 186–232.

Rouse, J. (1999). 'Understanding scientific practices: cultural studies of science as a philosophical program'. In M. Biagioli (ed.), *The Science Studies Reader*. New York: Routledge, 442–56.

Rouse, J. (2001). Two concepts of Practice. In T. Schatzki, K. Cetina and E. E. Von Savigny (eds.), *The practice turn in Contemporary Theory*. London: Routledge.

Rouse, J. (2006). Practice Theories. In *Handbook of Philosophy of Science*. Vol. 15, 500–40.

Rouse, J. (2007). Social practices and normativity. *Philosophy of the social sciences*, 37(1), 46–56.

Rubin, I. (1983). Function and structure of community: Conceptual and theoretical analysis. In R. L. Warren and L. E. Lyon (eds.), *New perspectives on the American community*. Chicago: Dorsey Press.

Sacks, H. (1984). On doing being ordinary. In J. M. Atkinson and J. E. Heritage (eds.), *Structures of Social Action: Studies in Conversation Analysis*. Cambridge: Cambridge University Press, 413–29.

Sacks, H., Schegloff, E. A., and Jefferson, G. (1974). A Simplest Systematics for the Organization of Turn-Taking for Conversation *Language*, 50, 696–735.

Samra-Fredericks, D. (2003). Strategizing as lived experience and strategists' everyday efforts to shape strategic direction. *Journal of Management Studies*, 40(1), 141–74.

Samra-Fredericks, D. (2005). Strategic Practice, 'Discourse' and the Everyday Interactional Constitution of Power Effects. *Organization*, 12, 803–41.

Sandberg, J. and Tsoukas, H. (2011). Grasping the logic of practice: Theorizing through practical rationality. *The Academy of Management Review (AMR)*, 36(2), 338–60.

Schatzki, T. R. (1996). *Social practices: a Wittgensteinian approach to human activity and the social*. Cambridge: Cambridge University Press.

Schatzki, T. R. (1997). Practices and action: A Wittgenstenian Critique of Bourdieu and Giddens. *Philosophy and the Social Science*, 27(3), 283–308.

Schatzki, T. R. (2001). Practice Mind-ed Orders. In T. R. Schatzki, K. Knorr Cetina and E. E. Von Savigny (eds.), *The practice turn in Contemporary Theory*. London: Routledge.

Schatzki, T. R. (2002). *The site of the social: A philosophical exploration of the constitution of social life and change*. University Park, PA: Pennsylvania State University Press.

Schatzki, T. R. (2005). The Sites of Organizations. *Organization Studies*, 26, 465–84.

Schatzki, T. R. (2006). The time of activity. *Continental Philosophy Review*, 39(2), 155–82.

Schatzki, T. R., Knorr-Cetina, K., and Savigny, E. Von (2001). *The practice turn in contemporary theory*. London; New York: Routledge.

Schegloff, E. A. (1986). The routine as achievement. *Human studies*, 9(2), 111–51.

Schegloff, E. A. (1997). Whose Text? Whose Context? *Discourse and Society*, 8, 165–87.

Schegloff, E. A. (1999). Schegloff's texts' as Billig's data: A critical reply. *Discourse and Society*, 10, 558–72.

Scollon, R. (2001). *Mediated Discourse: The nexus of practice*. London/New York: Routledge.

Scollon, R. and Scollon, S. W. (2001). *Intercultural Communication: A Discourse Approach*. Oxford: Blackwell Publishers.

Scollon, R. and Scollon, S. W. (2004). *Nexus Analysis: Discourse and the Emerging Internet*. Abingdon: Routledge.

Scollon, R. and Scollon, S. W. (2005). Lighting the stove: Why habitus isn't enough for critical discourse analysis. In R. Wodak and P. E. Chilton (eds.), *A new agenda in (critical) discourse analysis*. Amsterdam: John Benjamins, 101–17.

Shotter, J. (1997). Wittgenstein in practice: from 'the way of theory' to a 'social poetics. In C. W. Tolman, F. Cherry, R. van Hezewijk and I. Lubek (eds.), *Problems of Theoretical Psychology* York, Ontario: Captus Press.

Shotter, J. and Katz, A. (1996). Articulating Practices: Methods and experience. *Concepts and Transformation*, 1:2/3, 213–37.

Shove, E. and Pantzar, M. (2005). Consumers, producers and practices. *Journal of consumer culture*, 5(1), 43–64.

Skålén, P. and Hackley, C. (2011). Marketing-as-practice. Introduction to the special issue. *Scandinavian Journal of Management*, 27(2), 189–95.

Smolka, A. L., De Goes, M. C., and Pino, A. (1995). The construction of the subject. A persistent question. In J. Wertsch, P. del Rio and A. Alvarez (eds.), *Sociocultural Studies of Mind*. Cambridge: Cambridge University Press, 1–46.

Star, S. L. (1989). The structure of ill-structured solutions: Boundary objects and heterogeneous distributed problem solving. In M. Huhns and L. E. Gasser (eds.), *Readings in Distributed Artificial Intelligence*. Menlo Park, CA: Morgan Kaufman.

Stengers, I. (1997). *Power and invention: situating science*. Minneapolis: University of Minnesota Press.

Stengers, I. (2008). A constructivist reading of Process and Reality. *Theory, Culture and Society*, 25(4), 91–110.

Steward, T. A. (1996). The invisible key to success. *Fortune*, 134(3), 173–6.

Stewart, T. and Ruckdeschel, C. (1998). Intellectual capital: The new wealth of organizations. *Performance Improvement*, 37(7), 56–9.

Storper, M. (1985). The Spatial and Temporal Constitution of Social Action: A Critical Reading of Giddens. *Environment and Planning*, 3, 407–24.

Strauss, A. L. and Glaser, B. (1975). *Chronic illness and the quality of life*. London: Mosby.

Streeck, J. and Mehus, S. (2005). Microethnography: The Study of Practices. In K. Fitch and R. Sanders (eds.), *Handbook of Language and Social Interaction*. Mahwa, NJ: Lawrence Erlbaum, 381–404.

Suchman, L. A. (1987). *Plans and situated actions: the problem of human-machine communication*. Cambridge: Cambridge University Press.

Suchman, L. (2003). *Organising alignment*. In D. Nicolini, S. Gherardi and D. E. Yanow (eds.), *Knowing in organizations: a Practice-based Approach* (pp. 187-203). Armonk, NY: ME Sharpe, Inc.

Suchman, L., Blomberg, J., Orr, J. E., and Trigg, R. (1999). Reconstructing technologies as social practice. *American Behavioral Scientist*, 43(3), 392–408.

Sudnow, D. (1967). *Passing on: the social organization of dying*. Englewood Cliffs, N.J.: Prentice-Hall.

Sudnow, D. (1981). *Ways of the hand: the organization of improvised conduct*. London: Routledge.

Swan, J., Scarbrough, H., and Robertson, M. (2002). The construction of 'communities of practice' in the management of innovation. *Management Learning*, 33(4), 477–96.

Taylor, C. (1985). *Philosophy and the human sciences*. Cambridge; New York: Cambridge University Press.

Taylor, C. (1995). *Philosophical Arguments*. Cambridge, Mass.: Harvard University Press.

Taylor, J. R. and Van Every, E. J. (2011). *The situated organization: Studies in the pragmatics of communication*. London: Routledge.

Thévenot, L. (2001). Pragmatic Regimes Governing the Engagement with the World. In T. Schatzki, K. Knorr-Cetina and E. E. Von Savigny (eds.), *The practice turn in Contemporary Theory*: London: Routledge.

Thompson, E. (2004). Life and mind: From autopoiesis to neurophenomenology. Une tribute to Francisco Varela. *Phenomenology and the Cognitive Sciences*, 3, 381–98.

Tönnies, F. (1887/2001). *Community and civil society*. New York: Cambridge University Press.

Torfing, J. (1999). *New theories of discourse: Laclau, Mouffe, and Zizek*. Oxford: Blackwell Publishers.

Tsoukas, H. (1996). The Firm as a Distributed Knowledge System: A constructionist approach. *Strategic management journal*, 17, 11–25.

Tsoukas, H. (2009). Craving for generality and small-N studies: a Wittgensteinian approach towards the epistemology of the particular in organization and management studies. In D. A. Buchanan and A. Bryman (eds.), *The sage handbook of organizational research methods*. London: Sage, 285–301.

Turner, B. S. (1984). *The body and society: explorations in social theory*. Oxford: Blackwell.

Turner, S. (1994). *The social theory of practices: tradition, tacit knowledge and presuppositions*. Cambridge: Polity Press.

Turner, S. (2001). Throwing away the tacit rule book. Learning and practices. In T. Schatzki, K. Knorr Cetina and E. E. Von Savigny (eds.), *The Practice turn in Contemporary Theory*. London: Routledge.

Van Dijk, A. T. E. (1997). *Discourse as Social Interaction*. London: Sage.

Van Maaden, J. and Barley, S. (1984). Occupational Communities: Culture and control in organizations. Research in Organizational Behaviour, 6: 287–365.

Vattimo, G. (1971). *Heidegger*. Bari: Laterza.

Virkkunen, J. and Ahonen, H. (2011). Supporting expansive learning through theoretical-genetic reflection in the Change Laboratory. *Journal of Organizational Change Management*, 24(2), 229–43.

Von Mises, L. (1949). *Human action: a treatise on economics*. New Haven: Yale University Press.

Vygotski, L. S. (1978). *Mind in society: the development of higher psychological processes*. Cambridge: Harvard University Press.

Wacquant, L. J. D. (1992). Toward a social praxeology: the structure and logic of Bourdieu's sociology. In P. Bourdieu and L. D. Wacquant (eds.), *An Invitation to Reflexive Sociology*. Oxford: Blackwell.

Wainwright, S. P., Williams, C., and Turner, B. S. (2007). Globalization, Habitus, and the Balletic Body. *Cultural Studies/Critical Methodologies*, 189–95.

Warde, A. (2005). Consumption and theories of practice. *Journal of consumer culture*, 5(2), 131–53.

Weber, T. (2003). There is no Objective Subjectivity in the Study of Social Interaction [53 paragraphs]. Forum Qualitative Sozialforschung/Forum: *Qualitative Social Research*, 4(2), Art. 43, <http://nbn-resolving.de/urn:nbn:de:0114-fqs0302432>.

Weick, K. E. (1979). *The social psychology of organizing* (2nd edn.). Reading, MA: McGraw Hill

Wenger, E. (1998). *Communities of practice: learning, meaning, and identity*. Cambridge: Cambridge University Press.

Wenger, E. C. and Snyder, W. M. (2000). Communities of practice: The organizational frontier. *Harvard Business Review*, 78(1), 139–45.

Wertsch, J. (1998). *Mind As Action*. Oxford: Oxford University Press.

Westwood, R. and Linstead, S. (2001). *The Language of Organizations*: London, Sage.

Whetherell, M. (1998). Positioning and interpretative repertoires: Conversation analysis and post-structuralism in dialogue. *Discourse and Society*, 9, 387–412.

Whittington, R. (1992). Putting Giddens into Action—Social-Systems and Managerial Agency. *Journal of Management Studies*, 29(6), 693–712.

Whittington, R. (1996). Strategy as practice. *Long Range Planning*, 29(5), 731–5.

Whittington, R. (2003). The Work of Strategizing and Organizing: For a Practice Perspective. *Strategic Organization*, 1(1), 117–25.

Whittington, R. (2006). Completing the practice turn in strategy research. *Organization Studies*, 27(5), 613–34.

Wieder, D. L. (1974). *Language and social reality: the case of telling the convict code*. The Hague: Mouton.

Willmott, R. (1999). Structure, agency and the sociology of education: rescuing analytical dualism. *British Journal of Sociology of Education*, 20(1), 5–21.

Wittgenstein, L. (1953). *Philosophical investigations*. Oxford: Blackwell.

Wittgenstein, L. (1969). *On certainty*. Oxford: Blackwell.

Wittgenstein, L. (1981). *Zettel* (2nd edn.). Oxford: Blackwell.

Wittgenstein, L. (1980). *Culture and value* (Amended 2nd edn.). Oxford: Blackwell.

Wodak, R. and Weiss, G. (2003). *Critical Discourse Analysis. Theory and Interdisciplinarity*. New York: Palgrave Macmillan.

Ybema, S., Keenoy, T., Oswick, C., Beverungen, A., Ellis, N., and Sabelis, I. (2009). Articulating identities. *Human Relations*, 62(3), 299–322.

Zietsma, C. and Lawrence, T. (2010). Institutional Work in the Transformation of an Organizational Field: The Interplay of Boundary Work and Practice Work. *Administrative Science Quarterly*, 55(2), 189–221.

■ INDEX

symbolic interactionism 8, 41, 42, 58, 90,
187 n.12
system theory 50, 121

tacit knowledge 47, 57, 58
central role in generating everyday
practices 56
Giddens gives a prominent role to 48
journal articles using the concept 66, 76 n.31
taken-for-grantedness 3, 39, 58–9, 69, 192
actions that are saturated with 48
talk-in-interaction 140, 142, 204, 208
discourse as 191–5
Tatli, A. 11, 76 n.33
Taylor, C. 39, 162, 163
Taylor, J. 239, 240
techne 26, 27
technology use 12
tele-assistance 19
telemedicine 15, 16, 17–18, 19, 22 n.9, 182,
210, 234, 237
as an activity system 123–33
background information on the
practice 161 n.16, 188 n.32,
212 n.13
becoming part of the practice 96–102
birth of 236
critical aspect of the type provided by
Garibaldi Centre 20
following patients through clinical
trajectories 231
local accomplishment of 229
nursing habitus 70–6
other ways of doing 183
policy-making process links with local
practising of 238
shadowing the personnel of 233
site of 185
telemonitoring 17–18, 18–19, 96, 100, 125,
130–2, 236
accomplishing 153–61
close analysis of calls during 155
conversation analysis view 208–12
helping patients follow practical
procedures correctly 98
most difficult calls 71
nature of 73
practice-order bundle 182–6
risk that the service becomes a closed
environment 233
textualism 6, 9
theory of action 54
Thévenot, L. 84, 224

Thomas (Aquinas), St 55
Thomas, W. I. 41
timing 62–3
Tönnies, Ferdinand 88
Torfing, J. 198, 212 n.5
Trento 20
Tsoukas, H. 21, 186 n.2
turn-taking procedure 140, 193–4, 210
Turner, B. S. 76 n.32, 100 nn.1, 3,
188 nn.25, 30
Turner, S. 78, 83

United Kingdom 160 n.11
unique adequacy principle 145, 150,
159 n.9

Van Dijk, A. T. 198
Van Every, E. J. 240
Van Maanen, J. 101 n.11
Ventresca, M. 76 n.33
Virkkunen, J. 112, 132 n.1
vita activa 28
Vygotsky, L. S. 103, 106, 108, 109, 126,
203, 204

Wacquant, L. J. D. 65, 74 n.1,
76 n.29
Wainwright, S. P. 76 n.32
Warde, A. 12
Weber, Max 46, 77
Weber, T. 161 n.14
Weiss, G. 198
Wenger, E. 9–10, 11, 79, 80, 81, 82, 83,
85–6, 87, 88, 90, 91, 92, 94, 100 n.6,
101 n.14, 102 n.15, 227
Wertsch, J. 103, 107, 132 n.1
Westwood, R. 149
Wetherell, M. 194–5
Whittington, R. 11, 21 n.7, 75 n.15
Wieder, D. L. 141, 142, 143, 146, 150,
159 nn.5–6 and 9, 160 n.12
Williams, C. 76 n.32
Willmott, H. 86, 91, 92
Willmott, R. 75 n.10
Winsor, B. 20
wisdom 25, 221
see also practical wisdom
Wittgenstein, Ludwig 15, 16, 23,
37–41, 46, 54, 61, 83, 85, 94, 136,
138, 162, 163, 165, 168, 171, 172,
173, 176, 177, 178, 180, 181,
186 n.7, 187 nn.13, 18, 194,
212 n.8, 215, 227, 241 n.1